CHINESE
FOREIGN POLICY
IN AN AGE OF
TRANSITION

CHINESE
FOREIGN POLICY
IN AN AGE OF
TRANSITION:
*THE DIPLOMACY
OF CULTURAL
DESPAIR*

By ISHWER C. OJHA

Beacon Press
Boston

SECOND EDITION

For Ellen

Contents

Preface

Studies of Communist China's foreign policy often lean heavily on a particular discipline or framework of analysis. One interpretation stresses historical continuity, viewing the Maoist phase as a mere ripple on the surface of China's vast space and timeless past. Traditional tribute relationships, reinforced by an ethnocentric concept of world order, are said to constitute the mainsprings of contemporary foreign policy. Preoccupied with historical parallels, proponents of the "eternal China" hypothesis even regard the infrequency of Mao's public appearances as simply the latest manifestation of a reincarnated emperor in seclusion.

At an opposite extreme are those who stress ideology. Some analysts, starting from the worldwide claims of Marx's vision, attribute to China an insatiable expansionism. Others postulate that a ravenous ideological hunger for struggle inhibits China from living in peace with the international community. A few reverse this argument while continuing to rely heavily on the ideological factor. According to them, ideology will become less and less relevant. Inability to maintain a permanent state of crisis, combined with economic development, will slowly emasculate ideology, thus permitting China to "settle down" and behave more normally.

A thoughtful and sophisticated analysis by Benjamin Schwartz has avoided the pitfall of treating ideology as an independent influence. Instead, he has shown how the development of Maoist thought became inextricably entangled with

both historical influences and modern nationalism. He finds
that while a traditional Chinese concept of world order proved
remarkably durable over the centuries, it has been largely discarded today.[1]

A final set of opinions focus on China's psychocultural attributes and even on Mao's own psychological make-up. Contributions range from the concept of a national identity crisis
to the reminder that Mao, like many revolutionary leaders,
began by rebelling against his father.

All of these views are helpful in one way or another. Yet
most of them lead to a static analysis. They tend to explain
the present in such a way as to make different behavior impossible by definition. The moment is now ripe for another
question. How do we explain change?

This book tries to put contemporary China in the context
of change, beginning with the failure of syncretism to meet
the nineteenth-century challenge of the West. In contrast to
the overall policy pursued by the Meiji emperors in Japan,
China experimented unsuccessfully with *ad hoc* measures.
Recognition of the need to borrow Western technology gave
way in turn to an intellectual demand for Western institutions. When the effort to transplant institutions failed to produce the "wealth and power" which Chinese leaders envied
in the West, the search for new values was born.

In broad terms, culturism, defined as loyalty to Chinese
culture and refusal to look elsewhere for models, could not
withstand the combination of foreign pressure and domestic
rebellion. Its successor was cultural nationalism, defined as
predominant concern for China as a nation rather than for

1. See Benjamin Schwartz, "Communism and China: Ideology in
Flux," in Benjamin Schwartz, *Communism and China: Ideology in
Flux* (Cambridge, Mass.: Harvard University Press, 1968), pp. 1–46.
See further, Benjamin Schwartz, "The Chinese Perception of World
Order, Past and Present," in John K. Fairbank, ed., *The Chinese
World Order: Traditional China's Foreign Relations* (Cambridge,
Mass.: Harvard University Press, 1968), pp. 276–288.

China as a culture. Yet this new outlook still justified borrowing from the West in terms of Chinese tradition. The aim was to preserve as much of the Chinese *t'i* or base as possible while minimizing Western imports.

It is in this context that the rise of Chinese Communism was most significant. Like their intellectual contemporaries, Chinese Communists of the 1920's shared the conviction that modern institutions could not be grafted onto the surface of a traditional substructure. Instead, the industrialization and even the survival of the Chinese state depended on transforming the behavior of the ordinary Chinese citizen. Like the *narodniki* in Russia, the Communists believed that the driving impetus for this change lay in the masses themselves.

This conviction justified a fundamental reinterpretation of Chinese history. Attributing revolutionary dynamism to the masses, the Communists relegated stagnant and outmoded Confucian patterns to the gentry. In so doing they freed themselves from the humiliation which had plagued their reformist predecessors. For if the new ideal was change and growth rather than a permanent and unchanging culture, the wholesale importation of modern values conformed to China's historical essence.

The new mood of pride and determination rather than humiliation and resignation also sprang from the critical nature of Marxism itself. Marx's love-hate relationship with the Western capitalist system has been discussed before, but it is important to understand that to the Chinese Communists, Marxism provided a criticism of the West from a Western point of view. Together with Lenin's views on imperialism, it provided both an outlet for resentment and an avenue for construction. Striving to overtake the West was perfectly compatible with pride in being Chinese.

Yet all these changes were painful. Although borrowing in the name of the nation is easier than admitting the failure of a supposedly self-sufficient culture, recognition of China's weakness and cultural irrelevance was agonizing. Significantly,

Mao has not glorified Chinese culture, although he draws on peasant proverbs and folklore whenever possible. Instead, he stresses China's poverty and "blankness." It is this negative aspect of intellectual change which is referred to here as "cultural despair" and which has left a profound mark on China's foreign policy.

This analysis places great weight on domestic developments unleashed by the Western challenge. Yet international circumstances also place obvious limits on contemporary foreign policy. China is an aspiring great power in a world already saturated with the military might of the United States and the Soviet Union. Her leaders demand international recognition of her economic progress and her growing military arsenal. The structured nature of Cold War politics, epitomized by America's containment policy, thwart this search for prestige. Hostilities with both India and the Soviet Union exacerbate the claustrophobia engendered by China's geopolitical position and by her status as a challenger of the status quo.

Peking's diplomats seek to transform these obstacles into advantages by identifying the Chinese masses with the oppressed and the exploited. Diplomatic tactics vary in sincerity but the undercurrent of hostility toward both superpowers is very real. The chapters on Sino-Soviet and Sino-American relations explore the sources of this resentment. The section on international law and organizations focuses on China's search for a new world order based on consent and mutual benefit. Her ambivalence toward present structures is compared to the West's own dualism toward the ideal of law and the fact of power.

In the discussion on China's boundaries, concern for territory is shown to be a part of the transition from culturism to full-blown nationalism. The contrasting examples of Burma and India are used to refute the view that China is inherently expansionist. Finally, the chapter on China and the Third World notes Peking's ambivalence toward revolutionary leaders and examines the ideological controversy surrounding the national liberation movement. The very contrast between China's self-proclaimed weakness and her great-power ambitions limits her success in this area.

This book thus attempts to put Chinese foreign policy in a comparative framework without losing sight of China's concrete experience in both domestic and international politics. While placing heaviest emphasis on the domestic repercussions of cultural despair, it analyzes the full weight of international pressures. It simultaneously takes note of the language of psychology and sociology on the one hand and international systems on the other. It allows for both the personal eccentricities of a man like Mao and the universal dictates of modern nationalism.

This framework, however complex, at least allows for change. Significant shifts in Chinese foreign policy could spring from either internal or external sources. Even without a leadership change, the eventual achievement of economic prosperity could dim the memory of past grievances. Alternatively, a major change in American policy toward Asia could erase the claustrophobia and resentment that cloud Sino-American relations. Any comprehensive analysis must allow for both types of change and for many types of questions. This book attempts to set up coherent categories without destroying this overall goal.

The following pages also try to bridge several useful but arbitrary gaps. Specifically, they attempt to relate China's modern history to Western and non-Western parallels, the breakdown of the Chinese empire to the fate of other imperial governments, and the uniqueness of domestic developments to the international rules of power politics. Even if only partially successful, this approach may strip the cloak of mysticism from the analysis of Chinese behavior and subject it to the scrutiny of comparative politics.

It is a pleasure to thank those persons and institutions who contributed to the creation of this book. I am grateful to the Graduate School of Boston University for travel support to

Hong Kong in the summer of 1967 and to the Universities Service Center in Kowloon for the research facilities which were provided during my stay. My research also drew heavily on the libraries of the East Asian Research Center of Harvard University and the Fletcher School of Law and Diplomacy.

In countless ways my work was aided by the generosity and concern of my friend Daniel Tretiak. I owe a long-standing debt of gratitude to two of my colleagues, Howard Zinn and Robert J. McShea, for their good-humored patience and helpful criticism. Exhaustive reference work and dedicated typing assistance came from Miss Elena Stein, whose cheerfulness and enthusiasm throughout long hours of typing and reference work were inspirational. I wish to thank Mrs. Joan Agri for her care, patience, and efficiency in typing the final draft of the manuscript. Last, but by no means least, I want to acknowledge the patient suffering and unswerving support of my wife while this book was being written.

Cambridge, Massachusetts
March 1969

Preface to the Second Edition

While it is still early to draw final conclusions on such a complex phenomenon as the Cultural Revolution, there are now enough indications to prove that during 1967 and 1968 the impact of the Cultural Revolution on Chinese foreign policy was grossly exaggerated. The record of Chinese foreign policy since August 1968 reinforces this interpretation. The limited and transitory effect of the Cultural Revolution on Chinese foreign policy points up the durability of basic Maoist themes, most notably self-reliance abroad and self-strengthening at home. The failure to lend heavy support to revolutionary movements in Vietnam and elsewhere, and the persistence of revolutionary rhetoric are not necessarily contradictory, although they are often perceived as such. Similarly, to postulate that ideology and national interest are opposite is misleading; no ideology based so closely on a specific revolutionary experience can systematically promote a policy which would destroy its homeland sanctuary. Self-strengthening at home protected by a cautious foreign policy can thus be seen as consistent with Maoism as a revolutionary doctrine.

If the Cultural Revolution *qua* social revolution had succeeded, China might have become a truly revolutionary power instead of a have-not seeking a bigger piece of the pie. Corresponding threat perceptions would have risen, and a new Cold War of unprecedented intensity might have erupted. By 1968, however, most nations correctly perceived that the Cultural Revolution had not led to a radical transformation of

Chinese society and politics. This perception prevented the transformation of growing concern into outright hostility.

Surprisingly, in spite of the self-imposed isolationism of 1967, and in spite of flagrant violations of diplomatic etiquette, support for China did not wane in key arenas of international politics. Outstanding examples include the United Nations and the diplomatic initiatives of such NATO members as Canada and Italy. In this respect the impact of the Cultural Revolution was neutral or even negative; China gained little, but she also lost little.

The present edition not only updates the book but also presents enough evidence to support the thesis that the Cultural Revolution did not have any enduring effects on Chinese foreign policy. Chapter Eight, entitled "Revolutionary Change and Foreign Policy: The Impact of the Cultural Revolution," is a completely new addition to the text. This chapter is concerned with the causes of the failure of the Cultural Revolution as a social revolution and demonstrates that the major inputs in Chinese foreign policy since August 1968 were external in origin. The consequences of the invasions of Czechoslovakia and Cambodia for Peking are discussed fully. At the same time, the continuity of basic goals of Chinese foreign policy is underlined and explored.

I owe an enormous debt of gratitude to the unflagging and expert assistance of Miss Elena Stein for research, reference, and typing. The new chapter has also benefited from exhaustive exchanges with Mr. Daniel Tretiak and with my wife Ellen.

Cambridge, Massachusetts
September 1970.

CHAPTER ONE

Historical Sources of China's Conduct

The impression that the Chinese are a people of "eternal stand-still" [1] has somehow endured the last three centuries of Western historical analysis. The picture held up for appraisal has usually remained the same, and Western responses have varied with the times. European conceptions of a supposedly static Chinese civilization shifted from deep admiration in the seventeenth century to growing revulsion in the eighteenth century. The age of Enlightenment, emphasizing rationalistic and humanistic values, voted squarely for some form of freedom and individual dignity. Seventeenth-century Europe had admired Chinese civilization for the wide-ranging and absolute power of its government, its class structure, and its seemingly lavish riches; the leaders of the Enlightenment attacked precisely these very things.

European admiration for the Chinese art of governance and for the wealth of Chinese civilization could not withstand the nineteenth century. Two hundred years earlier, the hardships endured by the common man in Europe and in China were probably similar. In the eighteenth and nineteenth centuries, however, conditions shifted in favor of Europe. The Western view of non-Western areas radically changed as industrialism endowed its homeland with a new civilization and a favorable balance of wealth and power.

1. Raymond Dawson, *The Chinese Chameleon: An Analysis of European Conceptions of Chinese Civilization* (London: Oxford University Press, 1967), pp. 65–89.

The balance was tipped primarily by the rise of the West rather than by the decline of China. The revolutionary pace of change in Europe and America further reinforced the notion of an unchanging China, making Chinese efforts seem insignificant by comparison. Seen through the prism of the Industrial Revolution, China was again distorted.

Other reports contributing to the decline of Chinese prestige in the West came from missionaries. The early Jesuits were impressed with China and wrote glowing accounts of what they found. Later missionaries, arriving from the increasingly industrialized West, looked upon China from their own economic perspective and could not but emphasize the poverty of the Chinese masses. In some cases the need to raise money in support of their activities led them to paint China in lurid and shocking colors. In most cases they made no attempt to adopt or even to understand Chinese civilization and its mores. They were like little Western islands transported to an alien culture. Their judgment reflected ethnocentric Western values.

Twentieth-century historians have tried to correct these imbalances. Yet consciously or unconsciously, the supposedly unchanging nature of Chinese civilization continues to obsess many laymen and specialists alike. Unfortunately several national histories of China have reinforced this tendency. Historians probing a single nation or civilization often emphasize peculiarities at the expense of comparative and balanced evaluations. The remedy for this dilemma lies in the development of comparative historical analysis.[2] The success of this approach depends on a careful appraisal of China's past.

China has the oldest uninterrupted civilization in recorded history. She has been the center of a major civilization for a longer

2. In the case of China, some recent attempts in this direction have already been made. Professor Benjamin Schwartz has tried to put the Chinese perception of world order in a comparative framework. Discussing other imperial centers of civilization, he has attempted to isolate the peculiarly Chinese variables from those which are common to all. See Benjamin Schwartz, "The Chinese Perception of World Order, Past and Present," in John K. Fairbank, ed., *The Chinese World Order: Traditional China's Foreign Relations* (Cambridge: Harvard University Press, 1968), pp. 276–288.

period than any other country. Until the mid-nineteenth century, her leaders practiced selective isolationism based on the premise that the Chinese Empire had little to gain from the outside world. Such an attitude did not prohibit extensive trade relations with Russia or the export of culture to countries like Korea.

Sinicization of frontier areas was based on the view that non-Chinese should pay homage to Confucian virtues and to the civilization which upheld them. This deference to Chinese virtue was never interpreted as homage to the Han race. It was not expressed in a racist equivalent of Kipling's "white man's burden" or "lesser breeds without the law." In this sense China did not deviate from the historical practices of other great civilizations before the era of the nation-state and the politics of racial self-expression. What may be unique about China is that such convictions about virtue survived into the twentieth century. Yet they did so because of all the traditional imperial centers of civilization, China was almost the only one left.

China's international thrusts were aimed predominantly at the export of culture. Territorial conquest was generally limited to frontier wars or to defense measures. Before the rise of the national territorial state, only hazy or undefined frontiers existed. The concept of rigid national boundaries was still relatively unimportant. The squabble for a few square miles of swamp and the concoction of *irridenta* had no place at a time when the politics of rage still belonged to the future. Dividing lines were mapped out not according to latitude and longitude but rather in terms of culture and virtue. Above all, the concept of a master race was absent from genuine centers of civilization like China. Unlike the concept of race, which glorified its members, the culture upheld by imperial statesmen was considered to transcend individual passions and to lie beyond the reach of the common man.

Even more important to premodern foreign relations was the fact that China's traditional culture discouraged economic activity and expansion, including foreign trade and economic growth. Like all parochial and traditional societies, China practiced self-sufficiency, smug self-satisfaction, and splendid isolation. Like many culturistic entities, she shunned the importation of foreign ideas and institutions. In fact, the whole idea of the interdependence of nations is a relatively modern concept and, as suggested by

George Modelski, a by-product of the communications revolution.[3] Only as mutual contact increased and as communications gained speed and reliability did the world witness the breakdown of isolation. From then on the notion of interdependence took root even in countries whose national well-being did not depend on extensive foreign trade. This whole scenario is a modern phenomenon.

To a certain degree, a superiority complex such as China exhibited arises in all centers of civilization, power, or techniques. The British have been and still are the most Chinese in this respect, but the French, the Germans, and even the Americans have had their own notions about the excellence of their virtue. Just as China looked down on the rest of the world as barbarians, so other nations at all times have glorified their socioeconomic system, their government, their material standards, and sometimes the color of their skin and the superiority of their genes.

Historians of China have often marveled at China's ability to absorb foreign invaders by a process known as "syncretism," or the inclusion of alien ideas and institutions without loss of identity. Yet this talent has been overrated, just as the voluntary adoption of Chinese ways by foreign conquerors has been underestimated. Before the nineteenth century, foreign invaders had little to contribute and a lot to learn.

Syncretism as an ideal type was never fully realized in China. Even in the Manchu era, a residual dualism remained between conqueror and conquered. Syncretism never resulted in complete integration. The first real test of syncretism as a practical device, the confrontation with the West, showed that China had no ability to syncretize those who did not admire her governmental system or the material welfare of her population.

Nineteenth-century Westerners were interested neither in total conquest nor in full-scale Westernization. They wanted to enjoy certain rights and privileges for the sake of promoting their economic activities. Here was a situation which had few precedents in Chinese history. It is small wonder that Chinese statesmen did

3. For an unusual discussion of the international relations of traditional systems, see George Modelski, "Agraria and Industria: Two Models of an International System," *World Politics*, October 1961.

not know how to respond and that most of their efforts were piecemeal. The question was not how to syncretize the West but how to modernize China. Only this recognition would have provided the proper framework for a realistic response.

The true significance of syncretism lies in its role as an integrative device designed to absorb any threat to the dominant themes of the civilization in question. By its very nature syncretism cannot be applied beyond the reach of its cultural influence. In India it was successfully applied toward the absorption of Buddhism, and in China toward unwelcome visitors from peripheral areas.

Similarly, sinicization beyond China's frontiers met with only limited success. The only case where it came close to its ideal was Korea. Nations like Thailand and Burma were never sinicized. The sinicization of Vietnam and Tibet is debatable at best. A twentieth-century counterpart would be the Americanization of certain portions of the world, with techniques substituted for cultural virtues. Both the advantages and the limitations of this trend are obvious. China's cultural impact along her East Asian periphery is no more unique than India's influence in Southeast Asia or the intermittent infatuation with French culture shared by such disparate elements as the tsarist court in Russia and intellectual circles in present-day Africa. In short, neither syncretism nor cultural dispersion is unique to China, and the significance of both has been exaggerated.

The dichotomy between Western and non-Western societies, increasingly less fashionable in contemporary social science, is useful for simultaneous comparison, but in the vertical time span of history it becomes less meaningful. Seen in a comparative light, the Chinese simply did what other nonindustrialized centers of civilization tried to do or succeeded in doing. To deny the particularities of Chinese civilization would be unfair to China's genius and creativity. Yet to emphasize them as sources of deviant behavior patterns confuses the issue. The terms of the argument would become dangerously rigid; to argue that "what has been will always continue to be" provides answers that are superficially convincing but ultimately harmful to a sound understanding of China.

The Chinese referred to their empire as *t'ien-hsia*, or "all-under-heaven" and even today the word for China is *Chung-kuo*, or "middle-country." These terms have served to bolster what might be called "the Middle Kingdom thesis." Emphasizing China's supposed uniqueness in international relations, the Middle Kingdom thesis points to the alleged continuity of traditional Chinese attitudes. These include belief in cultural superiority based on virtue (*tê*) and the corollary image of China as the center of the civilized world. Completely lacking is any notion of competition among equals or indeed of equality among nations. Paradoxically, both China's active diplomatic search for world influence in the mid-1950's and the Cultural Revolution's semi-isolationist withdrawal from normal diplomacy have been translated in terms of historical continuities in spite of the vast differences which they represent.

Nevertheless, a "middle country" or "Middle Kingdom" was essentially the basis of international relations for nonindustrialized empires, where contact with equals was almost unknown. Even in the modern world there is an element of the Middle Kingdom in the attitude of all great centers of power. The difference between traditional and modern civilizations does not lie in the disappearance of the Middle Kingdom complex but rather in the rise of more important variables. To limit the concept of the Middle Kingdom to China is to overlook an important motivation of all strong civilizations. Yet to overemphasize it denies the essence of historical change.

Historians of China have already dispelled the impression of a monolithic Chinese historical record. No civilization can endure for long in a perfect state of static equilibrium. The very fact of survival for such a long period means a certain inherent dynamism. China had its normal quota of challenges and met them successfully. Only when the challengers were both strong and convinced of their own superiority did syncretism break down. Such was the nature of the Anglo-Saxon challenge.

More brazenly than the Manchus and the Mongols, the Anglo-Saxons braved the Celestial Empire from the crusty shell of their own Middle Kingdom. When two Middle Kingdoms clash it is the defeated one which has to bow. In the latter half of the nineteenth century the maintenance of China as a Middle Kingdom and of syncretism as its pivotal weapon became increasingly difficult in the face of the superior technological civilization of the West.

It is not easy for a Middle Kingdom to fade away like an old soldier. The more convinced cultural elites are of their supposed superiority, the greater the agony and the more desperate the convulsions endemic to their decline. Such upheaval, ripping apart the very basis of China's societal existence, left marks on the social personality which may take centuries to heal. This process has left unique scars on modern China. Yet even the deaths of various Middle Kingdoms can be put in a comparative framework. The history of the impact of the industrial Anglo-Saxon model on nonindustrialized civilizations has repeated itself elsewhere. Other empires underwent the same agony. The best comparison in this respect is between China and the Ottoman Empire in the nineteenth century.

The Chinese and the Ottomans went through roughly the same stages of reaction. The first of these was the so-called "self-strengthening" phase, or *tzu-ch'iang* in Chinese. Both empires desperately tried to import techniques and to graft them onto the unaltered core of their civilization. These techniques were introduced selectively for the specific purpose of augmenting military power. As yet they did not realize that their survival depended on throwing away the baby with the bath.

This failure to realize the connection between techniques and social content is not confined to the Chinese or the Ottomans. It is so universal that conservatives of all countries have succumbed to it to some extent. Even progressives have been guilty of the same shortcoming. In the contemporary industrial Anglo-Saxon model, humanists often cannot make up their minds as to the compatibility between machines and human beings. To preserve the baby—a humanistic culture—it may be necessary to hold on to the bath. The survival of humanistic values may depend on a deliberate slowdown of technological growth.

This analysis refers to the creation of the industrial state as the Anglo-Saxon model. It is so named because the Anglo-Saxons invented industrial civilization and its institutional components, such as free enterprise and elections as the basis of mass participation in the political process. As the model spread, "Western" eventually became a synonym for "Anglo-Saxon." At one time or another those countries whose cultural heritage was not Anglo-Saxon were non-Western. In this sense, even the Latin countries of Western Europe were the first "non-Western" areas.

As yet, countries outside the Anglo-Saxon cultural heritage have only rarely adopted the Anglo-Saxon model without some kind of national trauma. Generated by the necessity to import a foreign model to ensure the very survival of the national unit, this trauma can be described as the politics of cultural despair. Even Western Europe and Japan, countries which evolved in an Anglo-Saxon direction, experienced anti-Western disturbances. Hitler was a classic example of a new figure in history: the anti-Western Western man. Glorification of the primitive denied the redemptive potential of Western industrial growth.

The rise of highly motivated ideological and political figures at the beginning of the twentieth century can thus be at least partially attributed to the politics of cultural despair. It was only after World War II that Japan and Germany finally accepted the political aspects of the Anglo-Saxon model and thus entered the Western system. On the whole, of course, this first tier of graduates realized the need to adopt the industrial aspects of the model from the start. Yet its social and political institutions were basically rejected. It took a hundred years and several catastrophic wars to implement these institutions once and for all.

Resistance to these institutional aspects of the Anglo-Saxon model, including free enterprise and democratic political institutions, can only be understood in the context of what might be called "culturism." This term denotes a nonterritorial concept defined here as preoccupation with the survival of a national culture. Both the intensity of the culturism and the anguish accompanying its demise depend to a great extent on the strength of the culture in question. The last one hundred years of Chinese history reflect an exceptionally virulent picture of cultural despair.

The phenomenon of anti-Western Westernization has produced not only such diverse leaders as Hitler and Mao, but also a whole spectrum of activities ranging from anticolonialist demonstrations in the Third World to the black power movement in American ghettos. The verbal violence of Mao, Sukarno, Nkrumah, Castro, Carmichael, or Malcolm X is derived, at least in part, from more or less the same source. "Soul" is only the latest expression of a real or imagined cultural identity reacting to economic superiority.

The bitterness and violence of the nations undergoing rapid modernization can be understood but never totally experienced by the Anglo-Saxon. Being the creators of the model, Anglo-Saxons never had to feel that they were forced to import a foreign way of life to ensure their very survival. The only near-exception took place in the seventeenth century, when the possible importation by the British of the Dutch commercial model stirred up great division and debate. If Britain had failed to create her own model, she might have suffered from cultural despair as well.

The self-strengthening movements in China during the 1860's and in the Ottoman Empire during the 1820's and 1830's were doomed to failure because of the halfhearted measures they employed. The major aim of these movements was military equality with the industrial states. Power was equated with armaments. The social and institutional reforms which generate the kind of power needed to confront Western nations were neglected. Neither the Chinese nor the Ottomans fully understood that they could not superimpose modern power upon traditional societies. Confucianism, a bulwark of the old society, became an obstacle of change.

Confucianism could not provide the dynamism necessary for modernization because it was primarily an ideology of an agrarian society. It was hostile to trade, industry, or economic development of any kind.[4] Although China had more social mobility than most other preindustrial societies,[5] the avenues to promotion lay neither in warfare nor, with certain exceptions, in money. The principal path consisted of a particular kind of knowledge. Suited to the needs of an agrarian society, this knowledge continuously contributed to its survival by extolling the virtues of social harmony and the limitation of needs. Confucianism thus provided a justification for both the economics and the politics of scarcity. In the Confucian framework each reinforced the other.

4. Mary C. Wright, *The Last Stand of Chinese Conservatism: The T'ung-chih Restoration, 1862–1874* (New York: Atheneum, 1966), p. 3.

5. Chung-li Chang, *The Chinese Gentry: Studies on Their Role in Nineteenth-Century Chinese Society* (Seattle and London: University of Washington Press, 1967), pp. 137–164.

The Confucian emphasis on happiness through harmony and the limitation of wants, at least for the common people, was naturally suited to an agrarian economy. In twentieth-century India, Gandhi tried to construct a similar philosophy through the so-called economic self-sufficiency of the individual. Yet the focal point of the plan was not the individual but rather the family, clan, or village. The link between individual gain and national GNP had to await the age of modern communications. In most traditional societies, the individual was supposed to be ascetic and self-sacrificing; harmony was another word for accepting one's assigned place.

In short, the power base needed to counter the challenge of the West could not be created on the basis of Confucian philosophy. The development of this power base depended on the economics of plenty and on a corresponding social and political philosophy which emphasized conflict, competition, innovation, and the creation of wealth. It required the release of individual energies by emphasizing the individual self. It also called for the demise of what Joseph R. Levenson has called "the ideal of the amateur." [6] In other words, it demanded the death penalty for Confucianism.

Even the diluted Confucianism of K'ang Yu-wei or Liang Ch'i-ch'ao could not supply the flexibility and horsepower needed for the creation of a modern society. In the Ottoman Empire, similar attitudes were found in Jamal al-Din al-Afghani and Muhammad 'Abduh.[7] Both K'ang and al-Afghani believed that national woes were to be blamed not on traditional institutions and philosophy but on the impurities which had crept into them over the centuries. These impurities were due to misinterpretation, bad rulers, or simple human deterioration. Given this hypothesis, the solution was obvious. Both K'ang and al-Afghani wanted to restore the pristine and correct forms of their institutions and beliefs. Thus the first stage, military self-strengthening, was followed by a deeper awareness of the need for change. This second phase, the effort

6. Joseph R. Levenson, *Confucian China and Its Modern Fate,* 3 vols. (Berkeley: University of California Press, 1965), Vol. I, pp. 15–45.

7. Albert Hourani, *Arabic Thought in the Liberal Age, 1798–1939* (London: Oxford University Press, 1962), pp. 103–160.

to return to a modified golden age, might be called "reformist revivalism."

The degree of reformism in this essentially revivalist attitude is what distinguishes K'ang and al-Afghani on the one hand from Liang and 'Abduh on the other. Yet none was prepared to recognize the extent of sacrifice needed for modernization. This sacrifice ultimately gives birth not only to the virulent politics of cultural despair but also to the psychology of revolutionary totalism. In an age of mass politics, the suffering and humiliation resulting from the transition to modernization can give rise to a negative backlash of revolutionary proportions. A fanatic search for scapegoats and relentless hostility to the symbols of oppression are characteristic of this total rejection of both past and present. In the face of this process the Chinese Revolution of 1911 and the Young Turk Movement, the last of the reformist revivalist movements, were merely grains of sand.

Probably the most important reason for Chiang Kai-shek's failure was his inability to understand that the stages of history cannot be reversed. It was when revolutionary Chiang slipped back into reformist revivalism and later into self-strengthening that the fate of the Nationalist regime was sealed. The cult of the Ch'ing statesman Tseng Kuo-fan, the restoration of Confucius to the pedestal of public veneration, and the acceptance of ideals from the T'ung-chih Restoration of the 1860's marked the transformation of the Kuomintang from a progressive to a revivalist force. Most of this transformation took place between 1924 and 1928.[8] Chiang's party relied increasingly on the army as a stabilizing force and attempted to indoctrinate the youth with the ideals of the Restoration.[9] Like its predecessors in the self-strengthening movement, the Kuomintang did not realize that abandoning Confucian ideals does not spell extinction. As Mary Wright so aptly put it, "Restoration statesmen were the last genuine Chinese conservatives. To them, to yield to the end of Confucianism was no alternative to extinction but extinction itself." [10]

8. Wright, *The Last Stand of Chinese Conservatism*, pp. 300–312.

9. John Israel, *Student Nationalism in China, 1927–1937* (Stanford: Stanford University Press, 1966).

10. Wright, *The Last Stand of Chinese Conservatism*, p. 312.

Thus the Kuomintang did not provide an alternative. What is more important is that after 1928 its leaders did not even think an alternative was necessary. This failure is not unique to China. In a broad sense, it has been and still is the dilemma of all non-Western societies. It is not easy to throw away one's past.

Prior to nationalism, the only binding force of political society is culturism. The most marked trait of culturism is that it can tolerate both foreigners and territorial concessions, but it cannot permit the importation of foreign cultural models. For this reason it was necessary for China, as it was and is for the rest of the non-Western world, to move from culturism to nationalism. By means of this transformation China could no longer tolerate foreigners or extraterritoriality, but the importation of foreign cultural models was no longer anathema. This giant step toward modernization could be justified in the name of national revival. To the Chinese the end of Confucianism no longer meant extinction.

To borrow from the West in order to answer the West is necessary but painful. In both past and present, the rise of the nation-state has provided a justification. Borrowing may mean the death of the old culture, but at least it permits the survival of the nation. The intellectual problem common to men as different as Yen Fu and Ch'en Tu-hsiu was to revitalize the Chinese nation. In this sense, all classes that took part in the May Fourth Movement of 1919, including the early Marxists, deserve the title of the first real nationalists.

At this stage the survival of the Chinese nation was equated with the creation of wealth and power. In turn, the wealth and power generated in the West was attributed to the release of individual energies[11] and to the adoption of science and democracy. To cultivate these trends in China, the Confucian framework had to become flexible in theory and to disappear in practice.

The key to this subtle dismantling of Confucianism was "lip service." To pay lip service to the past did not prevent the complete abandonment of traditional cultural mores. In fact, lip

11. Benjamin Schwartz, *In Search of Wealth and Power: Yen Fu and the West* (Cambridge: Harvard University Press, 1964).

service to historical symbols is a necessary component of progressive nationalism. By creating an illusion of historical continuity, it provides a sense of security as well as a sense of worth ascribed to antiquity. Once again, this remedy is common not only to developing countries in the contemporary world but to other national units as well.

It is true that in the early stages of revolutionary fervor, the psychology of totalism emphasizes a complete rejection of the past. Yet as the revolution mellows, lip service to certain aspects of the past tries to legitimize the new rulers by implying that they are the real inheritors of the past. Such was the case in China. A thorough analysis of Communist Chinese historiography reveals not a total rejection but rather a careful reconstruction of the past. For practical purposes, whether nationalist historiography adopts an attitude of acceptance, rejection, or reconstruction does not make much difference as long as one no longer believes in the past.

Conservative, reformist, and revisionist historians would all agree on the need to establish emotional and intellectual security by means of alleged historical continuity. It is in their interpretation of history that they differ. Yet none of them could fully practice what they preached. Whatever version of history they embraced, China's rate of progress would stagnate. In other words, a revolutionary regime must be selective, using history as a symbol rather than as a guideline.

A similarly doctored interpretation of history has made the Chinese Communists—at least to their own satisfaction—heirs to the revolutionary tradition of China. Assigning the responsibility for the Confucian tradition to the gentry and to other reactionary forces, the Communists dissociate themselves from the dead weight of historical refuse. They insist not only that the "true" heritage of China is revolution, but also that this specialty was reserved for the common people. In effect, they have created a new scenario of history from which their class enemies are excluded. This unique logic elevates Chinese Communism to the most consistent stage of revolutionary continuity.

The claim of historical continuity is a necessary prerequisite for psychological security. Yet a rigid interpretation of history would shackle the flexibility needed to construct the present. On this point dogmatists of both left and right are at an equal disadvantage. Although ideologically motivated historiography can leave some room for pragmatism, the dogmatic nature of ideology can also create a new kind of neo-traditionalism.

In sum, the historical sources of Communist China's conduct can be traced more to this reinterpretation of Chinese history than to the rejected Confucian gentry tradition. In practice, however, this new historiography can be applied to foreign policy more easily than to domestic politics. In contrast to procedures in a democratic state, specific foreign policy decisions in China are solely the product of ruling elites. For this reason it is not necessary for any historical reinterpretation to be internalized by a popular majority before it can be applied to the conduct of foreign affairs. Nevertheless, such acceptance, together with the legitimacy which it brings, may be essential to the success of China's domestic policies.

It has often been asserted that China has "sinicized" Marxism, that is, made it Chinese. This sinicization is held to be in line with the Chinese capacity for syncretism. Yet certain key factors surrounding the role of Marxism in China have not been sufficiently explored. If Marxism in its original form has more relevance to China than is usually believed, then the sinicization of Marxism, like syncretism, has been overrated.

First and foremost is the fact that Marxism claims to be a modernizing ideology. It places considerable emphasis on the creation of social wealth and even lauds the material achievements of capitalism. Being essentially a critique of early capitalism, however, it provides to many minds an alternative to the sufferings it deplores. Although Marxism mistook early capitalism for highly developed capitalism, and although it failed to foresee the evolution of modern capitalism into directions which have made this critique irrelevant, its relevance as an alternative model cannot be underestimated.

The appeal of Marxism is enhanced by the fact that it serves a triple purpose. In the first place, Marxism is a devastating Western critique of the West and thus falls into the category which has already been labeled anti-Western Western. It is a tool by which anti-Western Western man and society can criticize Western methods even while simultaneously adopting them.[12] It is a psychologically gratifying force suited perfectly to the politics of cultural despair.

In the second place, modernization involves the creation of new attitudes and new patterns of political behavior. Society must be organized not only to undergo rapid transformation but also to endure the sacrifices comparable to those of early capitalism. By emphasizing the creation of wealth, Marxism flies in the face of the agrarian ideology of Confucian tradition. Any syncretism of Marxism with Confucianism is neither possible nor conducive to modernization. Rather than sinicizing Marxism, the Chinese Communists have adopted those features most suitable to the needs of a developing country.

Since Marxism does not spell out a day-to-day checklist of postrevolutionary activities, programs adopted in the name of moderation are creative rather than heretical. One such measure is the *hsia fang* ("down to lower places") system of organization. Because of its hostility to routinized and hierarchical bureaucracies, this system contradicts the classical Weberian concept of advanced organizational development. Mindful that no one has a patent on modernization, Rensselaer W. Lee has remarked that:

modernization as a continuous process of capitalization and industrialization depends upon concomitant changes in elite attitudes, and it is in applying vigorous measures to create attitudes compatible with development that the Chinese Communists may probably lay claim to being the world's foremost modernizers.[13]

In the third place, even to introduce Marxism to China, the Chinese Communists needed a radical reinterpretation of history. As described above, this version substituted conflict and revolution for peace and harmony. A revolutionary tradition had to be dug up, and Marxism supplied the shovel. Even this historical grave-digging has not dispelled ambivalence on the part of the Chinese

12. Benjamin Schwartz, *Chinese Communism and the Rise of Mao* (Cambridge: Harvard University Press, 1961), pp. 1–27.

13. Rensselaer W. Lee, III, "The Hsia Fang System: Marxism and Modernization," *China Quarterly*, No. 28, October–December, 1966, p. 62.

Communist leadership. Nevertheless, such an effort is essential if Marxism in China is to serve as a modernizing force. A genuine sinicization of Marxism would result in its complete failure as a force of change. In purely sinicized form it would fare no better than past attempts at modernization.

The concept of historical continuity has also been applied to China's historical record in the East Asian world order. Before the Opium Wars forced her to enter the Western state system, China practiced what is known as the tribute system. Lacking any concept of equality in international relations, China is said to have assigned the states of the East Asian world order to places similar to those held by individual Chinese in the Confucian social system. It has also been asserted that this tribute system provides a sufficient rationale for Chinese expansionism in contemporary Asia.

The Chinese tribute system was nonexploitative in character. Economically, it was more a burden to the Chinese state than a source of wealth. The very idea of a Middle Kingdom would have prohibited the notion of Chinese dependence on foreign revenues. Tribute was not rendered to the Chinese state as such, but to the virtues of Chinese civilization.

The tribute system involved both rights and duties.[14] As John K. Fairbank and Ssu-yu Teng have pointed out, it was used for the investiture or recognition of a new ruler through the presentation of an imperial seal. Certain diplomatic courtesies were extended to tributary envoys. The system thus served as a diplomatic medium in which the number of tributaries and their geographical locale fluctuated and shifted. After the middle of the fifteenth century, for example, the tributary emissaries to the Ming court shifted from southern sea routes to northwestern land routes. Even the nature of the tribute system did not remain constant; Ch'ing rulers sugar-coated it to make it more palatable.[15]

14. Immanuel C. Y. Hsu, *China's Entrance into the Family of Nations: The Diplomatic Phase, 1858–1880* (Cambridge: Harvard University Press, 1960), pp. 3–20.

15. John K. Fairbank and Ssu-yu Teng, *Ch'ing Administration: Three Studies* (Cambridge: Harvard University Press, 1961), pp. 107–246. A more recent study of China's tributary relations with her neighbors, edited by Professor Fairbank further emphasizes their

By creating a zone of buffer states on their periphery, the tribute system was also a defensive measure. At times it became plain and simple bribery paid to the so-called "barbarians" in return for peace on Chinese frontiers. Other empires have employed similar measures; the British in India, for example, paid bribes or tribute to the tribes of the northwest frontier. When China was weak, tribute ceased; when strong, it was resumed.

The ceremony of submission or kowtowing naturally emphasized the nonegalitarian nature of the East Asian world order. Yet in any traditional hierarchical society, both individuals and rulers had assigned places. Individual and national dignity, a by-product of modernization, was unknown to any traditional imperial diplomacy. Common to the many different definitions of modernization is the effort to develop human potential in the service of some higher end. The very notions of development and change marked a break with traditional society.

As religion gave way to the search for national power, and as the Industrial Revolution unlocked the floodgates of imagination, the criterion of strength did not remain limited to military inventories. Modernizing leaders increasingly invoked individual potential as the primary impetus for change. Even in dictatorships this notion remains sacred in theory if not in fact. Only this conviction could justify the notion of individual dignity which was so conspicuously absent in traditional interstate relations.

Before the age of the national territorial state and international law, such nonegalitarian interstate relations were common. The concept of territorial sovereignty in the Austinian sense is relatively modern, and its application to all national units is a twentieth-century phenomenon. The world order of Rome, Christendom, India, and the various Islamic empires of West Asia all shared unequal interstate relations. The custom of bearing tribute is a product of this unequal distribution of power.

Even after the establishment of the European state system, the

---

flexible nature. As the analysis shows, the acceptance of a tributary relationship was proportional to the degree of sinicization. In a substantial number of cases on the Chinese periphery, sinicization was either absent or at best relative. For further reference, see John K. Fairbank, *The Chinese World Order: Traditional China's Foreign Relations* (Cambridge: Harvard University Press, 1968).

idea of equality was not extended to the non-European world for a considerable time. Although the Ottoman Empire was admitted to the system of Christian European states in the eighteenth century, the rest of the world remained less than equal until the end of the nineteenth century and beyond. Not until 1943 was China finally free from the burden of unequal treaties.

The numerous treaties drawn up by the British and other colonialist powers with the various principalities of India, Malaya, and other parts of the Afro-Asian world enjoyed no better status in the realm of international law than did the treaties between the United States government and the American Indians. To receive even theoretical equality required admission into the Western family of nations. Such admission depended in turn upon recognition and invitation. Even in the most modern period of international law, the categories of less than sovereign states and vassal states have been recognized.

Thus the unequal treatment which China accorded to other members of the East Asian state system is not without historical parallels. In the mid-nineteenth century, when the Western and East Asian systems confronted each other, each was essentially trying the same thing. Each wanted the other to follow its rules. In this sense, probably the most positive accomplishment of the so-called age of imperialism was gradually to unite the entire world into a single state system with similar conceptions of international law and diplomatic conduct. Needless to say, the system that triumphed was European in origin and Judaeo-Christian in inspiration. It was not easy for non-Western states to accept. In short, most of them entered the Western state system through the back door of colonialism or semicolonialism.

By comparison with the nineteenth-century West, the East Asian system, created and dominated by China, was the weaker. When confronted with the international etiquette of the industrialized West, China naturally balked. In part, the unequal treaties inflicted on China after her defeat in the Opium Wars stemmed from the desire of Westerners to bring China into their interstate system. It is ironic that the extension of the international legal order had to be achieved through the violation of those same legal principles.

Thus the force of superior arms taught China that the self-contained East Asian order had to lose its separate identity and merge with the Western state system. Ceremonies of the imperial court were to be replaced by the so-called rules of "civilized" states. For the first time in her history, China became the recipient of nonegalitarian treatment. Because of the force of culturism, adopting the diplomatic rules of another civilization was even more humiliating than military defeat. It is to the credit of Ch'ing statesmen, particularly Prince Kung, that China's adjustment to this new scheme of things took place in a remarkably short time.

The first major step marking China's entry into the Western state system was taken with the establishment of the Tsungli Yamen, or foreign office, at the beginning of 1861. Forced to accept resident ministers at the capital and elsewhere, China also had to develop new rules of diplomatic behavior in order to play the new game of international relations. As far as China was concerned, the traditional East Asian world order had come to an end.

The new system, of course, encountered the opposition of many Chinese statesmen. During her first major contact with the West between 1858 and 1861, China was seriously divided.[16] China's top leaders, however, constantly and painfully realized that the preservation of the East Asian tribute system by force was impossible. They even took steps to learn the Western law of nations. The early 1860's witnessed translations of both Wheaton's book on international law and the application of international law against Prussia when she detained Danish ships in Chinese territorial waters.[17] China took a second step in the modernization of her international conduct by sending out her first diplomatic mission in 1868.[18]

By this time, responsible Chinese statesmen had accepted the unequal treaties and understood the need to observe them if further Western encroachments were to be prevented. Significantly, opposition to China's knowledge and use of international

16. Masataka Banno, *China and the West, 1858–1861* (Cambridge: Harvard University Press, 1964).

17. Hsu, *China's Entrance into the Family of Nations*, pp. 109–137.

18. *Ibid.*

law came not only from certain backward-looking Chinese states-men, but from the foreign community as well. Westerners feared that if China mastered the subtleties and loopholes of international law, their rights of extraterritoriality would be jeopardized.[19]

By 1880, for all practical purposes, China had become technically a member of the Western family of nations. She had established diplomatic relations with all its leading members and had joined most of the existing international organizations. At the same time, the Chinese fought a major Western power practically to a stand-still. Although the Sino-French War cost China her sovereignty over Vietnam, she employed sophisticated diplomatic techniques to limit her losses and to avoid indemnity payments.[20]

By the end of the nineteenth century the Chinese could no longer keep up the pretensions of a separate East Asian world order. Not only did they suffer continuous losses at the hands of the West, but they swallowed their biggest humiliation when defeated by Japan in 1895. During a short period of twenty-seven years Japan had not only accepted the Western state system but had also modernized her entire economic and military power base. No Chinese could continue to think either rationally or emotion-ally in terms of an East Asian world order after such a humiliating defeat at the hands of one of its ex-members.

During the first two decades of the twentieth century China faced further defeat and shame. It is no exaggeration to say that after 1860 foreign policy took first priority and completely domi-nated China's domestic politics. In fact, domestic political life was totally shaped by the needs of foreign policy rather than the other way around. The major aim of all Chinese statesmen was to pre-serve China's existence as an independent unit. The subordination of domestic politics to the exigencies of foreign policy was dictated by this life-and-death struggle.

Thus, the self-strengthening movement of 1862–1874, the early modernization of the 1880's, and the rise of revolutionary national-ism during World War I were all related to China's humiliating defeats. The need for domestic reform, social justice, and economic

19. *Ibid.*

20. Lloyd E. Eastman, *Throne and Mandarins: China's Search for a Policy During the Sino-French Controversy, 1880–1885* (Cambridge: Harvard University Press, 1967), p. 202.

changes were grudgingly accepted. The purpose of these innovations was not to make China a better place to live but rather to make her better prepared to face her foreign enemies. Consciously or unconsciously, the need for national revival sprang not from the plight of the Chinese people but from the condition of the Chinese nation.

Such an international starting point is common to many nationalist movements. Although tasks dictated by domestic problems are usually announced, they do not always receive serious attention. Even when national leaders turn to internal affairs, the solution to domestic crises requires a strong and centralized government, one that can capture the loyalty of the population. Such allegiance demands a minimum amount of internal and external security. Efforts in this direction thus create a vicious circle as the government postpones domestic improvements and so prolongs the weakness of the nation as a whole.

In the case of China, no government from 1842 onward was able to provide such security. Serious internal rebellions, such as those of the T'ai-p'ings and the Boxers, were by no means the sole cause of the erosion of governmental power. The scarce resources of a nonindustrialized society were continuously transferred to inefficient industrial efforts, the cultivation of moral and selfless officials, or futile attempts at self-strengthening. No statesman fully understood the relation between domestic social and institutional reform and ultimate national power.

What was true of Ch'ing statesmen was true also of Chiang Kaishek. His ever-present excuse—namely, that domestic unity and the defeat of the Communists were prerequisites to reform—illustrates the error in his order of priorities. Nor is Chiang unique; from Louis XIV and Nicholas II to De Gaulle and Diem, a host of rulers have placed foreign policy above domestic needs. China's continuous decline can be traced in part to this incorrect emphasis.

Having passed through centuries as a great power and as the center of an international order, China was all the more humiliated by her defeats. Here China differs from India, which was ruled by foreigners for a millennium before regaining independence. India's memories of grandeur were dimmed by history and her national humiliation was softened by long practice. To China, whose independence was never totally lost, historical shame was recent enough to be galling. The Ottoman Empire presented still another picture, for Ataturk's statesmanship gave away all pretensions to the Empire and concentrated on the Turkish nation.

China was thus eager to regain her great-power status. This desire is often described as a peculiar heritage of Chinese history. A better explanation, however, lies in the drives of a nation trying to regain the power and status which its leaders consider appropriate to its size, population, geographical position, and historical heritage. To a considerable extent, this drive explains China's domestic and foreign policies of the twentieth century, including those of the Communist government. Whatever their ideological hue, foreign policy decision-makers have derived their ultimate motivation from the goal of regaining China's position as a great power. With the rise of mass nationalism the same goal has also motivated most of the Chinese people irrespective of political belief.

Nevertheless, this resurgent China is trying neither to dominate a resurrected East Asian world order nor to alter the diplomatic rules of the game. China now has world-wide pretensions. If and when Peking regains the status of a world power, its activities will never be confined to the East Asian periphery. Even if China succeeds in establishing a sort of Monroe Doctrine, her leaders will not withdraw their interest from the rest of the world. In any case, the East Asian world order cannot be revived, and the tribute system cannot be re-established.

The Chinese may not like all the rules of the present international order and may break many of them. Yet they can neither dominate the whole global system nor escape from it. In this case, history is irreversible. It has altered not only China and her periphery but the rest of the world as well. Just as the age of imperialism has bowed to the age of nationalism, so China as a Middle Kingdom has given way to China as a nation. If and when China develops superpower status, she will try to do all those things which other superpowers do.

The leaders of Communist China have not made their predecessors' mistake of giving foreign policy priority over domestic policy. They have realized the correct relationship between national power and the domestic base, between sociopolitical changes and economic modernization, and between the means and ends of power. Even the Cultural Revolution is attuned to the full mobilization of China's domestic base. The Chinese Communist government also understands that an inadequate domestic base places limits on the exercise of power. In spite of its verbal violence, Peking has in fact pursued a cautious foreign policy that accords with the continuing recognition of relative weakness. Concepts of people's war and self-reliance represent a clear-headed effort to strike the proper balance between a weak power base and a vigorous foreign policy.

In contrast to most other nationalist movements, Communist China's leaders had at least some foreign policy experience before they came to power. Even outside of the international Communist movement they maintained contacts with foreigners. In the 1940's, for example, an almost full-fledged foreign office, functioning under Chou En-lai's leadership, operated through communications outlets in Hong Kong and elsewhere. The Communists had their own territorial power base as well as their own armies in the northwest. They also acquired experience from negotiating with the Nationalist government at Chungking. Finally, they maintained their own news agency with foreign correspondents who gained some idea of what the diplomatic world was all about.

Many top Chinese officials of the foreign ministry and the diplomatic corps received their initial training during this period. By contrast, the nationalist struggles of countries like India, while concerning themselves with foreign policy, gained no practical experience. Thus Nehru, the foreign policy expert of the Indian National Congress, had developed his own ideas about India's foreign policy after independence but had almost no experience with diplomatic negotiations.

Nevertheless, although greater than those of other newly independent countries, China's foreign policy experience was far from well rounded. To a great extent, it was colored by the need for Communist survival. Chinese Communist attitudes toward Japan, the Soviet Union, and Chiang Kai-shek practically determined their view of other powers. They naturally resented all those who supported Chiang.

The intense Chinese Communist preoccupation with anticolonialism and anti-imperialism thus arises not only from the humiliations of modern Chinese history, but also from their intensely personal experience during twenty years of struggling for power. In this sense the Chinese leadership differs from the Soviets, who did not have to endure that bitter and prolonged period of civil war. Even their short civil war, as George F. Kennan has pointed out, gave rise to Soviet accusations of Western intervention and to considerable Soviet claustrophobia. In this light the bitter and resentful attitudes of Chinese foreign policy seem much more understandable.

The same twenty-year period also helps to explain why Communist China's leaders have sought to identify themselves with the cause of all other newly independent nations. Their preoccupation with imperialism and anticolonialism makes them see international relations in terms of the age of imperialism rather than the age of nationalism. For modern examples of imperialism they point to both the American presence in Asia and the Soviet invasion of Czechoslovakia. Their fear that a Soviet-American *entente* will divide up the world at China's expense is genuine. They do not even rule out the possibility of an invasion of China.

As they face a ring of American bases in Asia and a war in Vietnam, Chinese leaders conclude that the gunboat diplomacy which marked the age of imperialism lives on. For them, concessions wrung from the Opium Wars and American intervention in China's civil war (perpetuated by the protection of Taiwan) are part of the same spectrum.

For this reason they are naturally sympathetic to anyone who believes that the age of imperialism is not over. In other words, the search for historical continuities underlying Communist China's foreign policy would lead to the age of imperialism rather than to the Confucian past. On this point China does not significantly differ from the rest of the Third World, whose motive power springs from anti-imperialism rather than from semi-mythical golden ages.

Thus the historical sources of Communist China's conduct in international relations do not extend far into Chinese history. No one can deny that the Communists are Chinese. Yet they are a different kind of Chinese. They have accepted the need for modernization. They have realized that modernization cannot confine itself to armaments. They are prepared to make all the necessary sacrifices to make China a viable and influential nation. Aside from their efforts to establish their own legitimacy, they are also trying to create a new Chinese society and a new Chinese man.

China's present leaders will probably not succeed in casting a new society and a new man in the mold they desire. Nevertheless, their efforts have certainly changed the face of China. Elite attitudes have been altered to such an extent that the Confucian gentry tradition will never be acceptable again. For practical reasons, the signposts of this process are deliberately designed to resemble an unchanging tradition. Their content and use, however, are radically new and different.

It is not difficult to connect almost everything that China does or says with some aspect of Chinese history. Nevertheless, such connections are superficial and misleading. The fact that China's recent history was weighted down with humiliation and defeat means that historical continuity with this period is of a negative kind. This history serves China's rulers more as a guideline of what to avoid than as a beacon of inspiration.

The whole problem of historical continuity must also be examined from the viewpoint of the stages of historical growth. There are few historical continuities between an agrarian and an industrial society. Even when verbal respect is paid to the past, the erosion of traditional agrarian attitudes is so great that such continuity is almost meaningless. As China takes further steps in modernization, urbanization, and indoctrination, even recent historical experiences will match the irrelevance of the Confucian order. Even more than Communism or totalitarianism, modernization will relegate the past to the historical wastebasket.

CHAPTER TWO

The Nationalism of Cultural Despair

China's transition from culturism to nationalism demanded a major reconstruction of her belief systems. The thought process which typifies such intellectual efforts can be described as an "introspective revolution." A revolution of this type insists on a fundamental re-examination of all basic beliefs and institutions. The process is neither easy nor routine. In fact, only when a special combination of internal and external events have produced a crisis of confidence in an entire system of values does such an introspective revolution take place.

Every society periodically undergoes some kind of change. It occasionally reinterprets its beliefs. It often patches over its sore spots. Yet it does not skip lightly into a period of prolonged introspection concerning its very nature and its very rationale for existence. In the early stages of self-examination in such depth, intellectual elites feel a growing sense of dissatisfaction with the state of their society. This malaise can be temporarily checked if hopes for a rapid improvement are justified. In many cases, however, such hopes turn out to be only wishful thinking. Dissatisfaction then turns into profound disquietude.

Yet disquietude alone cannot generate action. Actually, the whole period of introspective revolution is marked at best by haphazard actions and at worst by total paralysis. As elites grope toward a solution and fail to provide clear guidance for action, they suffer from increasing disquietude, which in turn produces more uncertainty. In this period of insecurity it is not easy to determine the right course of action. The security of a culture which has outlived its relevance is left behind. Both present and future are cloudy. Meanwhile, uncertainty may produce irrational fears and hesitation which paralyze the will to action.

In this period of groping for a solution, the powers that be may undertake haphazard reforms, and the catalysts of change may respond with spontaneous and apparently aimless actions. The self-strengthening movement of the restoration period, the attempts at military modernization, and the Hundred Days' Reform all fall into the first category. The T'aip'ing and Boxer Rebellions, the general unrest on the part of foreign-educated Chinese students, and the Revolution of 1911 illustrate the second. In short, both the reforms and the revolts that initiate the period of introspective revolution are generally half-hearted and incomplete.

Although introspection demands turning inward, this process does not mean self-isolation or the creation of a hermit kingdom. It involves psychological conflict and psychological self-examination. Constantly asking the question "Why?" one often comes up with different answers. The people who have developed this sense of disquietude and who have started asking such fundamental questions have become transitional. In this context, a transitional person or society refers not only to the actual process of modernization but also to a prior sense of profound dissatisfaction with the status quo. It is difficult to become transitional, but it is nearly impossible to revert to established patterns. A person or society entering this transitional phase has taken an irreversible step.

To be satisfied with the status quo is to live in harmony with one's social conditioning. An intellectual in such a state does not suffer from a crisis of cultural or national identity. Only those who have achieved psychological mobility turn toward introspection. This psychological mobility can be described as a vague desire for change and as dissatisfaction with one's social and personal environment.[1] By itself, it does not connote any physical action or movement. By arousing the desire for profound introspection, such psychological mobility is a fundamental prerequisite of a personal or social revolution.

1. Daniel Lerner, *The Passing of Traditional Society: Modernizing the Middle East* (London: The Free Press of Glencoe, 1958), pp. 43–75.

The history of all major social revolutions provides some justification for this viewpoint. All are initiated by a period of intense intellectual conflict and psychological agony generated by an introspective revolution. While not all introspective revolutions lead to social upheaval, most social upheavals are preceded by prolonged periods of introspection. The French, Russian, and Chinese revolutions all illustrate this pattern. The intellectual history of France and Russia in the eighteenth and nineteenth centuries, respectively, reveal the degree and extent of debate and self-analysis which the intellectuals of these countries underwent. Similar introspective revolutions also stirred both the Islamic world and India in the nineteenth century.

The introspective debates which characterized India, the Middle East, and China bore certain resemblances to each other. All were concerned first and foremost with the modernization of their power base. Yet on a deeper and more fundamental level the question which elites really had to answer was whether religious and cultural values provided enough motivation for modernization. Such debates as those between al-Afghani and the French philosopher Renan over whether Christianity or Islam was more rational revealed an intense reluctance to discard tradition. Similar examples in India and China also missed the point. These exchanges focused on how to fit modernization into the traditional culture rather than on how to reconstruct the existing culture so as to make it suitable for modernization.

The history of China in the nineteenth and twentieth centuries revolves around a series of such introspective efforts. The reconstruction of fundamental values and institutions to suit the needs of modernization was painful and slow. As cultural predominance over the West lost its credibility, cultural eclecticism came to the rescue. The very admission that Chinese culture could not survive without massive doses of technological imports marked the first serious step from culturism to nationalism.

Within the first decade of the Western impact China's culturism suffered from a devastating attack from within. The T'aip'ing Rebellion can be described as China's first, albeit abortive, national and social revolution. Taking a step far ahead of their time, the T'aip'ings attacked and disowned the Confucian past, linked it with the gentry, and associated themselves with peasant uprisings. It is true that peasant wars and rebellions were frequent enough in Chinese history. Yet in the past they had usually been led by the gentry and were not directed at fundamental social revolution. The T'aip'ing Rebellion thus signified a serious reinterpretation of Chinese history, one of the first signposts of Chinese nationalism.

The T'aip'ings sensed that a new society had to be created at the expense of the gentry culture. Yet this modern idea was ahead of its time. The T'aip'ings' agrarian reform and family revolution, including the emancipation of women, were too radical for China and even for nineteenth-century Europe. They came at a time when Marx was still writing *Das Kapital* and when no Chinese had ever heard of him. The first rounds of an all-encompassing intellectual revolution had not yet been fired. The failure of the T'aip'ings demonstrates that a social revolution without a thorough introspective effort cannot succeed. Even apart from their weaknesses in institutions and leadership, the rebels did not really know what direction to take. What is surprising is not that they failed but that they achieved such a large measure of success.

The self-strengthening movement followed upon the end of the T'aip'ing Rebellion. Combined with the Western impact, the T'aip'ings constituted a national catastrophe which made the further procrastination of introspective revolution impossible. Foreign defeat and simultaneous domestic chaos meant that traditional values and institutions could no longer escape unscathed. Their analytical dissection, never easy in any culture, was even more difficult in the Chinese system. By placing faith in classical education and by relying on the moral virtues of China's leaders, Confucianism never paid sufficient attention to institutions and organizations. China thus needed not only leaders trained in new ways but institutions and organizations erected on new foundations as well. These tasks are precisely what the self-strengthening movement shirked. Yet admission of the need to borrow military technology from abroad amounted to a frank confession that the Confucian system was unable to protect itself. It was precisely for this reason that conservatives like Wo Jen opposed any steps in this direction.

From then on it was only a matter of time until cultural universalism, that is, loyalty to a culture with universal pretensions, yielded to cultural particularism. This transformation involved the realization that the universal validity of Chinese culture could no longer be sustained. The first step was to draw a distinction between Chinese culture and the Chinese nation. This distinction not only justified the reconstruction of Chinese culture but also rationalized this effort in the name of the nation. Henceforth the framework of Chinese culture was not the Chinese world of *t'ien-hsia*, "all under heaven," but the Chinese nation. The complacent universalism of the Chinese cultural tradition was chopped up and rearranged to suit the priorities of the nation.

The second step in the transition to nationalism was the application of anti-foreign attitudes toward the Manchu dynasty without fully realizing that this action amounted to disowning certain aspects of the Chinese past. Men like Chang Ping-lin, reviving the seventeenth-century Ming loyalism of Ku Yen-wu and others, led the way. In spite of the continuing dualism which marked the partial failure of syncretism, the Manchu dynasty had overcome Ming resistance and gone on to achieve legitimacy. Yet the period of the T'aip'ing Rebellion placed the sanctity of the Ch'ing court in question. The emergence of racial self-consciousness in China was similar to that which marked the formation of nation-states in Europe.

Especially during the Opium Wars, certain strains marred relations between Chinese and Manchu officials. On the question of Western encroachments, such friction resulted from two different attitudes: the Chinese usually took an uncompromising and unrealistic stand, while the Manchus were prone to capitulate to Western demands. Initially, however, this tension resulted not so much from racial conflict or Chinese nationalism as from the ignorance of Chinese officials. Not always taken into confidence, these men rarely received accurate intelligence reports. Yet by the end of the nineteenth century, anti-Manchu sentiments had aggravated and inflamed this long-standing dualism. Slogans calling for the ejection of the Manchus had become accepted tactics of Chinese nationalism.

This development meant that the process of syncretism, which was supposed to have made the Manchus a Chinese dynasty, was thrown overboard. If syncretism could not work with the West, the next step taken by the early nationalist was to reassess its role at home. The Manchus, previously supposed to be sufficiently Chinese, suddenly turned into foreign oppressors.

The lesson seems to be that xenophobia is a necessary by-product of an emerging nation in search of self-expression. Yet this attack was ultimately directed not so much against foreigners —Western or Manchu—as against the culture which had failed to protect China from foreigners. Westerners and Manchus, therefore, served as convenient scapegoats pending the completion of cultural introspection. The idea of nation, as opposed to that of culture, served as a device to soothe the pains of growing alienation from a defeated culture.

One of the great advantages of a distinction between nation and culture was that cultural continuities could now be defended in terms of a new and particularist nationalist culture rather than in the language of outmoded cultural universalism. Yet even this national culture could not be judged by its own standards but rather by what Joseph R. Levenson has called "cultural equivalence with the West." [2] More than anything else, this pressing need to place China on par with the West throws into clear relief the dilemma of the nationalism of cultural despair. Lacking the *a priori* assumptions and the unquestioned legitimacy which Confucianism had enjoyed, the new nationalism had to be justified. The very need for such a justification spelled the death blow to the universalist pretensions that Chinese elites had ascribed to their traditional culture.

As a necessary component of early nationalism, an awareness of racial identity followed the separation of culture and nation. The concept of race, generally absent from culturistic China, found a growing audience. Yet the partisans of racism were ambivalent. In confrontation with Westerners, race and nation tended to be equated. In confrontation with Manchus, hostility took the specific form of Han nationalism. Nevertheless, this Han consciousness limited itself to the Manchus and was not actively directed against China's Moslem, Mongol, or Tibetan population. Sun Yat-sen, however, rejected any form of Han chauvinism and spe-

2. For a detailed treatment of such concepts as cultural equivalence and cultural eclecticism, see Joseph R. Levenson's profound study, *Confucian China and Its Modern Fate*, 3 vols. (Berkeley: University of California Press, 1965), Vol. I, pp. 95–116 and 134–145.

cifically included Manchus within the fold of Chinese nationalism. In the long run Han nationalism, while still a problem in China today, yielded to a multiracial concept of the Chinese nation. Had it triumphed over Sun's vision, it probably would have fragmented China to an irreparable extent.

Ethnocentrism, therefore, is not the cause but the effect of emerging nationhood. Ethnocentrism without nationalism lacks both meaning and function. Only when the rallying cry is the nation does ethnocentrism emerge as a symbol of national identity and national exclusiveness. Since the era of syncretism had obviously perished, those outside of this nationalist culture could not be absorbed or even welcomed. The transition from cultural to racial or national exclusiveness characterizes the transition from cultural to racial or national identity. It rules out the hope of assimilation once and for all. While in the past the *kowtow* (*k'ou-t'ou*) or gesture of obeisance purchased a ticket for passive inclusion if not active participation, nothing short of a Chinese birth certificate can open the doors of the nationalist club.

The transition to nationalism also demands the nationalization of culture, which is a necessary step in the search for national identity. This process not only expresses the idea of cultural exclusiveness but also assumes that a culture will be able to protect and to assert the newly found identity of the nation. When culture is no longer an end in itself, it becomes a means to an end. It is here that nationalism differs most fundamentally from culturism. In essence, culturism assumes the inherent worth of the culture in question. Nationalism, which treats culture only as a means, demands from it a justification for its existence.

This justification depends on a culture's ability to provide the nation not only with assurance of its survival but also with pride. A nation must consider itself as virtuous as any other. Thus, the nationalism of great and powerful nations may sooner or later develop into what Hans J. Morgenthau has called the desire "to identify the moral aspirations of a particular nation with the moral laws that govern the universe." [3] Yet such claims to universalism differ fundamentally from those of culturism. The difference lies in the fact that culturism does not depend on the

3. Hans J. Morgenthau, *Politics Among Nations: The Struggle for Power and Peace* (New York: Alfred A. Knopf, 1966), pp. 10–11.

power of the nation, but on the excellence of its virtues. Foreign deference to cultural achievements is not equated with submission to the nation.

Nationalism requires the constant defense of its culture as equal or superior to other national cultures. Even to establish equality is not easy in a period of decline and defeat. In the 1890's and in the first two decades of the twentieth century Chinese intellectuals were not content with harnessing Confucianism to the yoke of national power. They constantly had to examine and re-examine it so that it could fulfill its assigned national purpose. The first step consisted of an effort to save as much of the traditional culture as possible, even in reconstructed form.

Since the aim of this reconstruction is the adaptation of the traditional culture to national needs, a process of selection was involved. The criterion for such selection is the need for a mythical nation. This new portrait of nationhood which mysteriously meets modern needs permits both rejection and importation. This simultaneous process, cultural pruning at home and importation from abroad, justifies cultural eclecticism.

Cultural eclecticism cannot be justified if it becomes a one-way street. The import of culture must be balanced by export so that eclecticism can be justified in terms of a cultural balance of payments. If China were to develop a tremendous cultural deficit, then cultural eclecticism would appear as cultural surrender and the age of nationalism would make this surrender intolerable. Such was the case of China; cultural eclecticism could not succeed. Although some modern nations borrowed some aspects of Chinese culture, they did not do so for the sake of national survival. For it is not merely the borrowing of culture which brings on the politics of cultural despair, but borrowing for national survival. The Chinese suffered from this painful process and the West did not. Under these conditions, cultural eclecticism could not establish China's cultural equivalence with the West, but could serve only as a smokescreen to disguise China's inferiority and surrender to the West.

China was comparatively the most qualified among all the nation-states who went through the transition from culturism to nationalism. She had historical continuity, racial homogeneity, and literary unity. At the end of the nineteenth century, she had started to develop the idea of Chineseness. Even now, of all the nations of continental size and proportions, China has the smallest percentage of national minorities. Although national minorities occupy roughly 60 per cent of China's territory, they constitute only 6 per cent of its population. Ninety-four per cent of its population, consisting of the Han race, is concentrated in 40 per cent of its land area. Although the large number of linguistic dialects hinders verbal communication, the universal identity of the written characters of the Chinese language establishes literal and cultural unity among the Han majority.

Thus China contained all those qualifications and prerequisites for nationhood emphasized so often by social scientists. The only thing which she lacked in the past was the impetus and ability to form a nation. It was the psychological component of nationalism which made up for the previous failure.

It is not easy to imagine the pain of this psychological transformation for a Chinese intellectual. It is easy to forgive him if he mistook the effect for the cause. Foreigners did not cause the need for this transformation. The real cause lay in the fact that Chinese political and social institutions and the philosophy which justified them were now only marginally relevant to China's national and international environment. Even if there had been no foreign invasion and consequent national humiliation, the Chinese would still have had to face this problem of relevance sooner or later. Foreign invasion simply acted as a catalyst and forced the pace of change.

The rate of social change must keep pace with the rate of psychological change. If and when the rate of social change falls seriously behind the rate of psychological change, alienation will result. The spontaneous adjustment of intellectual elites to the change in their environment will no longer be possible. There can be only two consequences from such maladjustment. Either the individual will have to make a superhuman effort of will to bridge the growing gap between his psychological conditioning and social reality, or he will sink deeper and deeper into the morass of frustration and alienation. If the second alternative is forced on him, then he will grasp at any solution. Considerations of ideological rectitude will no longer appeal to him.

The statesmen of the Restoration period made an effort to borrow military technology with the hope of establishing military equivalence with the West. The leaders, writers, and philosophers of cultural eclecticism went further in their desire to borrow so-called Western science and democracy in order to establish cultural equivalence with the West. Both of these groups failed because they wanted to borrow the forms and not the essence. Neither of them could understand that national rejuvenation cannot come from borrowing technology or even ideology but only from liberating the individual from inner cultural conflict.

Chinese nationalists of the early twentieth century desperately needed hope. They wanted to hope not so much for the survival of the Chinese race and its traditional values, but for the possibility that they would once again evolve toward greatness. Cultural eclecticism was supposed to provide the means for such an evolution. It was therefore justified in terms of evolution and of the idealistic aspirations of a new and all-encompassing world culture in which the best of all national cultures would merge. To this world culture China would have contributed its part and China would belong. Once again a rejuvenated China could feel like a part, if not the center, of world culture.

Both the statesmen of the Restoration and the leaders of cultural eclecticism knew that China had to borrow for survival. In both of these periods debate centered on whether Chinese culture should maintain its "base" or *t'i* upon which Western *yung* or "practical usage" could be grafted. Both of them failed to realize that to meet Western measure of wealth and power required Western *t'i* and Chinese *yung*.

From this perspective, it is not surprising that Charles Darwin became one of the most popular thinkers in China in the first two decades of the twentieth century.[4] The Darwinian concept of evolution was not as important in itself as in the rationale which it provided. The hope that the world was evolving toward a world culture gave the Chinese the proper rationalization to borrow from the rest of the globe. In other words, evolution would have justified the pruning of the past, the reconstruction of the present, and the hope for the future. Conversely, the doctrine of the survival of the fittest signified to Chinese intellectuals not only the

4. Jerome Ch'en, "China's Conception of Her Place in the World," *The Political Quarterly*, Vol. 35, No. 3, 1964, pp. 260–269.

urgency for national rejuvenation but also the clarity of the alternative fate which awaited them.

The last push toward polarization of the psychological conflict generated by the nationalism of cultural despair, was propelled by the events of World War I. Western cynicism toward Chinese national aspiration was the last straw. Japan's Twenty-One Demands in 1915, the exclusion of China from the application of Wilson's Fourteen Points, and the perfunctory treatment of Chinese nationalism at the Paris Peace Conference destroyed the hopes of Chinese eclectics. These events also confirmed their opinion that the age of imperialism was not yet over, a fact that made a permanent impression upon the young Mao Tse-tung.

In the face of an indifferent West, cultural eclecticism became a national liability. It was natural for the Chinese to doubt the value of borrowing from a civilization which had to be redeemed by a mammoth war. They probably believed, like Bernard Shaw, that World War I was necessary to rid the West of a social disease fostered by the incompetent statesmen of the previous generations. To the Chinese this war did not appear as a war in defense of democracy but as a nemesis of Western civilization. The period of cultural equivalence, like the period of military equivalence before it, was over. The anti-Western Western Chinese had started to arrive on the scene.

Disenchantment with the simplified Western model of what the Chinese called "Mr. Science" and "Mr. Democracy" was bound to come sooner or later. The West of the 1920's had not yet realized that admitting non-Western peoples and states into the Western state system required the concomitant extension of equality and the full benefit of international law and institutions. The Chinese were not far wrong in thinking that the age of imperialism was not over. Yet they were lacking in foresight in their inability to see that the transition from the age of imperialism had begun. All they knew was that the West, after admitting China into the international state system, was not prepared to grant her full membership. China remained a second-class member.

During this period greater emphasis came to be placed on the Chinese people and a new emphasis on populism began to grow. Unknowingly, the Chinese populists came very close to the doctrines of the Russian *narodniki* before them. This similarity is particularly striking in the case of Li Ta-chao, who went on to become one of the cofounders of the Chinese Communist Party.

Populism in nineteenth-century Russia meant an emotional faith in the revolutionary potential and creativity of the peasantry. It also signified the desire to avoid the mistakes and sufferings of early capitalism in the West. By linking populism to nationalism and by emphasizing the unique historical conditions of each nation, it mapped out a national path of development. In addition to formulating this national particularism, populists differed from Marxists on the question of class conflict. Populists denied the class struggle, not because it was not a valid concept, but because they thought it was valid only after industrialization. In their view, it could not be applied to preindustrial societies like Russia.[5]

Chinese populism lacked both a specific ideological motive and a reasoned, theoretical base. It arose from a vague desire to shift the focus of change from the statesmen to the people. It was concerned neither with the tactics of change nor with its direction. Its blind faith in the peasant masses assumed that they wanted change and would infallibly support revolution. Its adherents realized that China lacked not only a proletariat but even a sufficient manifestation of early capitalism to supply the necessary Marxist rationale for revolution. With its faith in the revolutionary potential of the peasantry, populism provided an emotional alternative.

A certain element of populism is apparent in the three principles of Sun Yat-sen. His emphasis on people's livelihood and nationalism represent vague but definite shifts away from China's traditional philosophy. The time had come when no Chinese politician or statesman could afford to ignore either the Chinese people or the Chinese nation. No one really knew how to make both nation and people yield their full strength, but almost every member of China's elite recognized their interdependence.

Yet it was difficult for China to organize on these principles. In 1916 and 1917 it was not only the monarchists who were thinking in terms of rule from above. Even the warlords, while knowing that the traditional political system could not be resurrected, were not prepared to go as far as relating the strength of the nation to its people. By 1920 China had entered a period of political dis-

5. Maurice Meisner, *Li Ta-chao and the Origins of Chinese Marxism* (Cambridge: Harvard University Press, 1967), pp. 71–89.

organization and conflicting political philosophies. A broad consensus had already been achieved on the need for nationalism. Monarchists, warlords, nationalists, and even Communists were all agreed on this point. Yet nationalism by itself did not suffice. The problem lay rather in how to translate the hopes of national rejuvenation into reality.

Another important group at this time consisted of intellectuals. In underdeveloped countries the word "intellectual" should be defined in the broadest terms. In this analysis an intellectual denotes any educated person who is conscious of and concerns himself with the social, economic, and political questions of his time. Both populism and Leninism hold the somewhat romantic belief that the revolutionary potential of the people in general, and the peasantry in particular, can be released by intellectuals. In this regard the role of intellectuals should never be underestimated. The very nature of transitional society and the agony of the introspective revolution make the role of the intellectuals much more central than elsewhere. These conditions also make it impossible for them to escape. Given their sensitivity and their capacity to feel the suffering of others, they must provide answers to the psychological conflict not only within themselves but all around them as well.

Most intellectuals naturally come from various student groups. Yet building a national political movement on the basis of such mercurial and sensitive people is like building a castle on a sandy beach. Students seem to pass through cycles, alternating between elation and depression, extreme involvement and extreme alienation, exhilaration and despair. Capable of great enthusiasm and reckless sacrifices for a short period of time, students somehow cannot keep up the momentum.

The record of Chinese student movement was similarly sketchy and erratic. The May Fourth Movement of 1919, the May Thirtieth Movement of 1925, and the outraged spirit of student nationalism after the Japanese invasion of 1931 were all followed by periods of profound despair and frustration.[6] It is hardly surprising that Mao, while recognizing the importance of mobilizing students

6. For a detailed account of the student movement, see John Israel, *Student Nationalism in China, 1927–37* (Stanford: Stanford University Press, 1966).

into the revolutionary movement, referred to them as "fair-weather friends of revolution." In this sense, Chinese students are by no means unique, for similar cycles of reaction can be traced in the student movements of most other countries.

Not only did China's students lack revolutionary staying power and a consistent will to action, but they were also incapable of disciplined sacrifices. China lived in her villages. It was there, according to both populists and Maoists, that revolutionary potential lay ready to be plucked. In the populist period of his intellectual development, Li Ta-chao strongly urged students to go to the villages. While some did, most did not. Those who did were often appalled and dismayed.

Students also failed to grasp fully the truth of Mao's dictum that revolution is not an invitation to a dinner party. They did not see that it demands organization, patience, discipline, self-sacrifice, and the capacity to absorb failures. In 1931 students returned to the countryside to mobilize national feeling and to shape national resistance against the Japanese. Encountering apathy and indifference, they did not stay long. Official China, lying above this vast network of silent villages, thus continued in its state of paralysis.

Nevertheless, the value of intellectuals in the process of change should not be dismissed. In their importance to the national population they still form a disproportionate group. They are particularly influential in their role of articulating national aspirations. Over a period of time, they can induce the people to accept a large measure of social change. Yet because of their very nature, intellectual elites can neither organize themselves nor achieve consensus on the nature and direction of this change.

More than industrial states, traditional and transitional societies place great emphasis on the capacity of philosophical and theoretical knowledge to solve social problems. While industrial states try to tailor knowledge to the needs of the industrial model and industrial society, traditional and transitional states pay undue reverence to knowledge that lacks practical usefulness. Such knowledge is not useless merely because it is unrelated to technology. Its real drawback lies in the fact that it is oriented toward stating problems rather than solving them. While taking the lead in sensing national feeling and articulating national needs, Chinese intellectuals still could not provide the tactics and strategy needed to translate hopes into concrete realities.

It was in the literary revolution that the intellectuals made their most valuable contribution to the process of social change. They tried not only to bring literature to the common people, but to make them the subjects of their literary creations as well. By breaking away from traditional forms of writing, they took a step toward a more popular culture. They abandoned *wen-yen* or literary language in favor of *pai-hua* or "plain talk." They satirized both past and present, thus undermining traditional social bonds. They made many Chinese recognize and mock the shallowness of what they had always considered sacrosanct. Perhaps the greatest example of this kind of writing is Lu Hsun's *The True Story of Ah Q*.

Thus the writers of the New Culture Movement and later of the new left accelerated the erosion of the old and the formulation of the new. Perhaps more important, they helped in easing the process of social change by making the psychological conflict more bearable through satire. They played a very important role in the crystallization and articulation of the introspective revolution. They expressed what others only felt. They clarified issues which were confusing. They thought the unthinkable and expressed ideas that struck a chord in the hearts of a people filled with disquietude. In short, they eased the trauma of social identification, lit a social spark, generated a will to action, and paved the way for revolutionary change.

It is generally assumed that evolution is preferable to revolution and that the former may forestall the latter. The psychic costs of the evolutionary path are said to be much less than those of revolution. Proponents of this view point mainly to the overt violence of revolution but also to the fact that revolutions never achieve their desired ends. Conversely, the covert and scattered violence of the evolutionary process has led social scientists to believe that a slow pace permits people to see where they are going. Yet there is no guarantee that evolution can solve pressing national and social problems. If such was the case, history would not be full of abortive and successful revolutions.

In fact, most major upheavals are preceded by evolution. A revolution is the conscious expression of hitherto unconscious trends. In short, both revolution and evolution may sometimes be complementary instead of contradictory. In some cases one cannot succeed without the other. Revolution does not aim at reaching an end but rather at initiating a beginning. Its greatest significance lies in clearing the emotional and psychological barricades which block the starting point. By itself, a revolution cannot achieve the implementation of all the philosophical and human values which it professes. Yet it can silence those who oppose such changes and coerce others into trying them.

Revolution is social vomit. Yet sometimes this vomiting is necessary to cure social illnesses and to clear the social system. It is only after the revolution has installed a new group of leaders professing a new philosophy that the job of reconstruction begins. This reconstruction will always be evolutionary. The pace of such evolution will depend upon both the leadership and the philosophy of the revolution. Without revolution, evolution might never start to roll. The history of China from 1850 to 1920 was not a history of evolution in a forward direction but a history of haphazard and semi-paralyzed writhing.

From this perspective, only two of the various political parties competing for the spoils of power deserve serious consideration as agents of change. One was the Nationalists after 1920, acting through the revised and reconstituted Kuomintang; the other was the Chinese Communist Party (CCP) after the debacle of 1927 and the subsequent rise of Mao. In general, warlords did not qualify.

It is true that some warlords, notably Yen Hsi-shan of Shansi Province, tried their hand at administrative and social reforms. It is also true that most of these men owed their rise to the mobility of military life rather than to traditional social pedigrees. Yet the methods which they adopted resembled those of the Restoration statesman Tseng-Kuo-fan. Like Tseng, Yen advocated the introduction of Western technology to bolster traditional values and institutions. His progressive efforts, such as the abolition of foot-binding and universal education, failed to confront the need for a fundamental social revolution.[7] Handicapped by their reliance on

7. For a stimulating analysis of Yen's career, see Donald G. Gillin, *Warlord: Yen Hsi-shan in Shansi Province, 1911–1949* (Princeton: Princeton University Press, 1967), *passim* and Conclusions.

an unpopular army and a hidebound bureaucracy, warlords like Yen lacked both the will and the capability to initiate such an upheaval.

It cannot be denied that many warlords took steps to industrialize their domains and trod on the toes of the gentry along the way. In many cases their relatively humble origins meant that they did not share the gentry's traditional Confucian outlook. To a certain extent, their pragmatic awareness of the mainsprings of personal and military power permitted them to break loose from the mental confines of the Restoration. Yet even they did not leave the Chinese *t'i* sufficiently far behind. Social revolution could be initiated only by an agent who was ready to adopt fundamental and revolutionary measures to reconstruct individual and social attitudes. In short, such changes required leaders dedicated not only to power but also to a revolutionary vision.

Even the Kuomintang and its leaders, including Sun Yat-sen, had never completed the transition from culturism to nationalism. From 1894 to 1916, for example, Sun placed considerable hope in Japanese support. Even after Japan's Twenty-One Demands of 1915, Sun refused to take the final step from culturism to nationalism and continued to look to Japan for help.[8] Meanwhile, the anti-Japanese feelings of large segments of China's urban population demonstrated the frequent lesson that the people are often ahead of their leaders in their readiness to change. The Chinese had rejected culturistic nationalism to a greater degree than Sun had realized. As opposed to culturism, nationalism could tolerate foreign ideas but not foreign occupation of its territory. In this sense the Kuomintang never really dissociated itself from a nationalism which was still permeated with culturism. This trait would not have been a serious handicap in itself if the degree of culturism could have been minimized.

By 1920, the leaders of the Kuomintang finally agreed on the need for organization and discipline. Significantly, this realization came from an anti-Western Western source, namely, the Russian Revolution. The Sun-Joffe Agreement of 1923 supplied the Kuo-

8. For further information on the transformation of the Kuomintang, see George T. Yu, *Party Politics in Republican China: the Kuomintang, 1912–1924* (Berkeley: University of California Press, 1966).

mintang with advice and expertise on the organization of institutional power along Bolshevik lines. Yet neither this arrangement nor the meager resources of the Comintern could have moved the majority of the Kuomintang to abandon a Chinese *t'i* in favor of any foreign one, let alone Marxism. Although neither the left wing of the Kuomintang nor the Chinese Communist Party fully realized what would happen, the philosophy of the Restoration period was bound to resurface in the Kuomintang sooner or later. By 1928 this revival had taken place.

Both the Canton Massacre of 1927 and Chiang's break with the Comintern thus had a double-pronged effect. Both events made the CCP realize that it must develop its own national strategy rather than rely on the faulty judgments of the Comintern. It also made most of the other Chinese elites realize that the Kuomintang had never really moved away from the Chinese base incorporated in the philosophy of the Restoration. If the Kuomintang had imported a foreign *t'i*, that of the democratic West, it could have provided a serious alternative to Communism. If it had fully accepted the social substructure of the Anglo-Saxon model, it could have become the principal agent of change in China. Its failure to meet China's needs in this respect inaugurated a search for alternatives and a twenty-year series of desertions.

In moving away from Comintern dictates, CCP leaders met a dual need. They were forced not only to develop a national strategy of capturing power but also to reconstruct China's social revolution on the basis of a Marxist base and a Chinese superstructure. The importance of this step can hardly be exaggerated. It is true that international exigencies, such as the Japanese invasion, did play a part in ensuring Communist success. Yet this catastrophe might have propelled China in any direction, not merely toward Communism. What really counted in the Communist victory was the absence of an alternative foreign *t'i* on the basis of which a new Chinese superstructure could have been erected.

By adopting a Marxist base the Chinese Communists were well armed with rationalizations. They could justify cultural eclecticism in terms of the universal validity of Marxism itself. They were not borrowing the dominant Western model—Anglo-Saxon industrial capitalism—but rather a critique of it. At least in the period of the Russian Revolution, they could paint Marxism in universal evolutionary colors, defending it as the wave of the future. Although attitudes toward the Soviet Union were later modified, this view continues to form a basic part of Chinese Communist thought.

By reconstructing Chinese history, the Communists could also establish cultural equivalence between this anti-Western Western *t'i* on the one hand and Chinese culture on the other. Identifying feudal and reactionary aspects of Chinese culture with the gentry, Mao restructured and redefined the meaning of China's history and placed it on the shoulders of the poor and the dispossessed. In short, this version stood China's history on its head. By translating Chinese history into class terms, Mao simultaneously satisfied the standards of Marxism at least to his own satisfaction. The entire philosophy of the Restoration and the sacrosanct tradition of Confucianism could now be brushed aside as decadent and outmoded aspects of gentry culture.

The fundamental advantage of this reconstructed history was that the Communists could now identify themselves with the Chinese people and the Chinese nation rather than with an imported culture. They could embrace Marxism without appearing to surrender to the land of its birth. This kind of cultural eclecticism, which syncretized Marxism with Chinese history, added a dynamic dimension to nationalism. China's glory could now be said to have consisted not so much in her cultural heritage as in her revolutionary tradition. In short, pride in being Chinese, linked with the motor force of revolution, reinforced each other in an upward spiral.

In this new framework, every revolt against constituted authority could be interpreted as a blow to free China and her people from the oppressive Confucian gentry culture. Those historical figures who had sought to offer alternatives now received special attention. To cite an example, the Communists could now look with greater affection on the Taoists, not because they believed in Taoist philosophy, but because they opposed Confucianism. Their favorite group, of course, was the T'aip'ings. The reason is obvious. Although ignorant of Marxism, the T'aip'ings were the first to reject the Confucian culture on the grounds that it was not the culture of the Chinese people.

As Barrington Moore has suggested, it is doubtful that the Confucian culture of the gentry class ever thoroughly permeated the Chinese peasantry.[9] In both its metaphysical and material aspects, Confucian culture was patronized, created, amended, and surrounded by a very restricted elite. In the case of China, this elite consisted of the gentry. At best, the common people could only adapt this culture to previous patterns of superstition and mysticism. Yet the restrictions of Confucian culture to a minority did not ease the pain of discarding it, for introspective revolution is by nature an elite phenomenon. Even for nonintellectuals, the collapse of Confucian authority left an unsettling vacuum.

With the Chinese Communists came a nationwide Marxist-populist ideology affecting all classes. The role of this ideology with respect to Chinese goals and Chinese nationalism has often been debated. For me, the function of ideology is to provide and rationalize a new belief system. It must also inspire faith and hope. In terms of modernization and rejuvenation, Communist ideology has activated the previously paralyzed will to action and breathed into China a new life force. It has led to rigidity and to the clichés of Marxist-cum-Maoist orthodoxy. While closely overshadowing every aspect of China's political life, it has managed to maintain its own distinctive identity.

What this identity is and to what extent it determines China's national goals are legitimate questions. In this case, the fact that ideology and national interest are so difficult to separate represents not analytical fuzziness but the deliberate policy of the Communist leaders. Mao, taking the ideology of Marxism-Leninism, has not so much sinicized it as nationalized it. Nationalization should not be confused with sinicization. Even if some features of sinicization remain, they pertain to the Communist reconstruction of Chinese history rather than to Chinese history as it was.

The nationalization of ideology did not merely meet the needs

9. Barrington Moore, Jr., *Social Origins of Dictatorship and Democracy* (Boston: Beacon Press, 1966), Chapter IV.

of Chinese nationalism and cultural eclecticism. Its anti-Western Western nature also established China's cultural dignity and justified the adoption of Western goals. In other words, China can declare that her national goal is to overtake Great Britain's industrial output or to match the military power of the United States without compromising the anti-Western spirit behind these tasks.

Nevertheless, while giving the impression and probably believing that they are creating a new Chinese man and nation, the Chinese Communists are actually building the industrial basis of the Anglo-Saxon model without its sociopolitical features. Their efforts to erect a model of economic and political development along new lines incorporate many Western traits and look for justification to Marxism's anti-Western Western critique. Once again, they are fulfilling the needs of Chinese nationalism without giving the appearance of cultural surrender. The key to this achievement, and the source of Maoist energy, is ideology.

Ideology has long been held to determine the framework for decision-making and to set limits on the number and type of options in policy-making. Yet the nationalization of ideology adds a dynamic dimension. For if the requirements of ideology and national interest are virtually synonymous, then every aspect of national policy becomes charged with ideological electricity.

The theme that unites this dualistic emphasis is the Chinese "people," formally defined as the proletariat, the peasantry, the petty bourgeoisie, and the national bourgeoisie. Instead of representing loyalty to a fixed territorial unit or to all members of a given race irrespective of politics, membership in the "people" is always subject to change. In fact, inclusion in the "people" depends upon acceptable political behavior.

In one fundamental respect, acceptable political behavior can be defined as acceptance of socialism and modernization as they are defined from time to time by the Communist leadership. Those who fail to meet this test are automatically transferred into the category of "nonpeople" and as such are no longer members of the Chinese nation. Communist ideology, not content to redefine Chinese history, has also made membership in the Chinese nation dependent upon political acceptability. Although Mao's vision of modernized society is unique, its basic tenet is insistence on continuous change. If this attitude toward change is a pre-requisite for modernization, then ideology contributes to national development in a very concrete sense. On a more general level, it also serves as the medium through which modernization and nationalism intermingle.

Reliance on the concept of the Chinese people further signifies that patriotism and revolutionary behavior are two sides of the same coin. Since nation and people have become synonymous, someone whose behavior prevents him from qualifying for membership in the Chinese people is a traitor by definition. This mixture of nationalism and revolution has made the nationaliza tion of ideology simultaneously an integrative tool and a divisive force.

Ideology also serves as an integrative communications process. Starting with an initially prepolitical and prcindustrial population, it has sought to mold a united Chinese citizenry through standardized channels of communication. By providing its believers with a new and unified pattern of words and symbols, it has speeded up the process of national integration. Through the lateral geographical mobility of Communist cadres it has partially offset regionalism. It has widened the circle of loyalty and trans-ferred it from such restrictive and traditional units as the family, clan, or village to the Communist Party and the Chinese people. If nationalism is a precondition for the cultural borrowing needed for modernization, then the transfer of loyalty from the clan to the nation is a prerequisite for nationalism.

Mao does not regard the Chinese people as a monolithic and conformist whole. Ever since 1937 he has held that "contradic-tions" may exist within the ranks of the Chinese people even in the future utopia. Nevertheless, they are said to be "nonantago-nistic," that is, able to be resolved without violence. Such non-antagonistic contradictions may even arise between the leaders and those led. Accordingly, strong emphasis is placed on the rec-tification of incorrect ideas among Party cadres. The Cultural Revolution is only the latest and most spectacular effort to purify China's leaders.

Seen through Mao's ideological spectacles, the equivalent of several centuries of political and social development can be com-pressed into a few decades in China. Ideology, the vehicle of this process, must therefore remain dynamic. To this end the active promotion of conflict is considered a necessary ingredient. The notion that conflict is creative is an improvement over both the classical Marxist utopia and the united front platform of wartime Chinese Communism. What was initially an ideology of unity against Japan has thus become an ideology of struggle. It provides unity against foreigners without destroying the tensions that stimulate creative development.

Insisting that the Party must keep in touch with the masses, Chinese Communist ideology constantly redefines the role and validity of theory in terms of concrete revolutionary experience. The correct application of ideology to suit the practical needs of the people is part and parcel of the so-called "mass line." Besides reliance on practice, the other twin pillar of the mass line is voluntarism. In Mao's view, voluntarism, however imperfectly elicited, is the means of arousing mass enthusiasm as well as of guaranteeing that China's development does not culminate in revisionism. By constantly emphasizing spontaneity and popular participation in the political process, Chinese leaders hope to avoid the bureaucratic rigidities and popular alienation which they attribute to the Soviet Union.

A revolutionary culture, marked by a secular faith extending into all spheres of human endeavor, leads elites to express themselves in ideological terms. Because of its terminological complexities, ideology can be used either as a sophisticated weapon against its critics or as a crude tool of mass manipulation. Because of its crucial importance in long years of training, ideology can become the mainstay of elite communication. Secret documents seized by Kuomintang agents in Fukien in 1964, for example, revealed essentially the same ideological structure of thought.

As in the case of Li Ta-chao, another important ingredient of Mao's ideological outlook is populism. For strategic reasons, of course, the Chinese Communists were much more dependent upon the peasant population than their counterparts in the Soviet Union. Without going into the considerable and hair-splitting debate regarding Mao's originality on the question of the peasantry, it is obvious that Mao always insisted on good relations with the Chinese masses. Populism and the glorification of the common people radiated from Mao's writings even before he began his organizational work among the peasants. As previously suggested, this populism helped him launch a crippling attack against Confucian tradition while simultaneously cultivating pride in being Chinese.

The political consequence of Chinese populism is the "mass line," which can be defined as a manipulative device to make the Chinese people accept changing revolutionary policy. Yet besides being a means of control, it is also a listening device for China's ruling elites. Cadres are expected to listen to the masses, to record their grievances, and to rely on education and persuasion rather than coercion in the implementation of Party policies. Yet the application of the mass line places the average cadre on the horns of a difficult dilemma. The cadre is expected not only to serve the Party and to enforce unpopular decisions but also to act as friend and representative of the Chinese masses. The Cultural Revolution has dramatized the dangers of trying to tread this thin line.

In spite of the mass line's identification between the Chinese nation and the Chinese people on a redefined basis, Communist China still shows signs of the transition from culturism to nationalism. Ambivalence toward the West, toward Chinese history, and toward territorial and populist conceptions of the nation is still apparent. Mao's ideology is inseparable from China's national and international position.

Like all other new nations aspiring to great power status, China insists on national identity and national sovereignty. Her leaders cannot tolerate any violation of land, air space, or territorial waters. They demand absolute respect to such symbols of sovereignty as Chinese embassies and the Chinese flag. While denying much of China's heritage, they nevertheless insist on all the rights and privileges of a successor government, including a seat in the Security Council. While denouncing the diplomacy of China's imperial era, they are reluctant to abandon their claim to boundaries which the imperialist era erased from the maps.

The case of Communist China's boundaries illustrates that most new nations aspiring for international power must pass through three stages of national aspirations. In the first stage their leaders must clearly redefine national boundaries. Because of their aversion to imperialism, the Communists challenged boundaries drawn up in the pre-Communist era. But Chinese Communist *irredenta* derive less from imperial China than from Western intervention. Thus, instead of demanding the reassertion of complete sovereignty over ex-tributary states, China has only demanded the renegotiation of all those boundaries drawn up by Western powers in the age of unequal treatment.

The second stage seeks to establish a sphere of influence around a nation's periphery. Even this goal is partially negative, ensuring mainly that bordering areas not totally succumb to the influence of other powers. Thus, China's minimum demand on her Asian neighbors is that they should not be used by any other power to threaten China. Her maximum demand would require a pro-Chinese foreign policy and full support for China's interests in the international state system.

The third stage reached by aspiring world powers, including China, transcends territorial security and a regional sphere of influence. It consists of a search for a world role. In this sense China's efforts toward Western Europe and the Third World should not be underrated. The satisfaction with regional supremacy that marked the days of the tribute system is gone forever.

China, no less than other aspiring powers, illustrates that the three stages often overlap. All of them basically, lie in the area of nationalist goals. In terms of past history, and in comparison with other powers, these goals would probably have been considered legitimate if they had not been intermingled with Communist ideology and the tensions of the Cold War. All of these topics will be examined in the next chapter.

CHAPTER THREE

China and the Western World Order

The Western world order, which China was finally forced to enter, evolved from the breakdown of medieval Christian universalism. The new framework rejected the universalist pretensions of a Christian moral order and gave up the search for a rational world order based on natural law. In their place it substituted the concept of the national sovereignty of the territorial state.

In its initial phase this new international system corresponded to the rise of strong and centralized monarchies based on the divine right of kings. Its central element, the national territorial state, was founded on territorial impermeability, that is, the defense of territorial boundaries. The corollary to this notion was noninterference in the domestic politics of another state. This arrangement brought to a close the era of religious cold war.

The new form of international politics no longer considered religion as the basis of a just war. It also moved away from the concepts of abstract justice and moral justification. Power and reason of state became enshrined as the new deities of international relations. To obtain and augment power became ends of statecraft rather than means. As the West moved away from teleological concepts of world order, the ultimate purpose of power was forgotten or ignored.

Once emancipated from the confines of medieval notions of moral universalism and natural law, international politics also pushed aside the human ends of power. The rejection of religion, while extracting some of the dynamite from interstate relations, also drained them of humanism and morality. The removal of emotionally divisive issues left behind a dry shell of businesslike self-interest.

Another feature of the new world order was voluntarist positivism. As De Visscher has pointed out, the twin notions that nations were free to act and that written law was the only source of obligation were logical consequences of the break with medieval tradition. Natural law had previously been invoked to sanction certain types of warfare but had also forbidden others. Its disappearance signified the removal of limitations on military action. Unable to agree on a definition of aggression, international treaties and conventions confined themselves to minute details of river navigation and diplomatic conventions. While such arrangements established the institutional uniformity necessary to unite a state system, they left the fundamental issues unanswered.

The Congress of Vienna followed the world's first real revolution, the rise of ideology, and the explosive expansionism which accompanied it. Yet except for the question of slavery, it shut its eyes to all but the nuts and bolts of international decorum.

The century which followed the Congress of Vienna was marked by gigantic systems. The Concert of Europe dominated the continental order, and the blanket of imperialism covered the rest of the world. The established international order recognized the special responsibility of the great powers to uphold the "public law of Europe" while simultaneously refusing to extend this law to non-European areas. For all practical purposes the nation-state had acquired a legal personality, an achievement confined strictly to the Western family of nations. Meanwhile, the peoples of the non-Western world were treated as legal wards.

It was during the nineteenth century in particular that Western man developed a self-image based on the monopoly of reason. He saw himself in the role of a rational liberator of non-Western man, who was defined as superstitious and therefore nonrational. He considered himself a free agent, a master of his own destiny. Non-Western man, by contrast, was held to be bound by tradition and paralyzed by fatalism. Yet the self-styled hero of the West failed to realize that he was often looked upon as an agent of oppression rather than an angel of liberation, a mouthpiece of an alien ideology rather than a spokesman for truth.

The growing emphasis on a rational world order, now reduced to secular terms, exploited the fear of anarchy to disguise the hegemony of the great powers. From the Concert of Europe to the veto principle of the Security Council, this common theme remains. The assertion that international law is "law by courtesy" applies only to the great powers, for only the consent of the strong permits its application. As for the rest of the world, the great powers can impose international law on lesser states by coercion if not by consent. The international state system of the nineteenth and twentieth centuries has rested on a double standard.

By emphasizing the sanctity of treaties and the notion of *pacta sunt servanda*, great power hegemony tended to perpetuate the status quo. It did so not only because great powers wish to retain their status as long as possible, but also because of the specific nature of the international treaties drawn up by the Concert of Europe. Once devoid of moral purpose, international conventions lost all excuse for movement and concentrated solely on a frozen network of state relations. The international law which they embodied was thus identified with a status quo which served the great powers and ignored the dispossessed.

In contrast to the world view embodied in the Western state system of the nineteenth century, China's outlook continued to reflect moral universalism. Although relations between the states of the Chou Dynasty (ca. 1100–221 B.C.) resembled those between the Italian city-states of the fifteenth century,[1] China had outstripped the West in the formation of a centralized monarchy by more than a millennium. Yet this important domestic development led to different results. The centralization and administrative unity of the Chou era yielded not the concept of national sovereignty but rather the attitudes of culturism. Moreover, the social dynamism that accompanied the territorial unification of Western nation-states was lacking in China. This absence of social and political consciousness on the part of the masses was reflected

1. K. J. Holsti, *International Politics: A Framework for Analysis*, Prentice-Hall, Englewood Cliffs, N.J., 1967, pp. 27–42.

in the stability of the East Asian world order. Such was the nature of the difference between the two state systems that confronted each other in the nineteenth century.

Devoid of moral content and deflected from humanistic aims, Western international law, initially a regulator of international politics, deteriorated into being its instrument. Nowhere is this more apparent than in the functioning of international organizations. Such organizations do not run on the basis of universal legal principles but on the concepts of prevailing world politics, reflecting not abstract law and justice but the realities of the political world order. Members of international organizations are concerned with manipulating rules of procedure, publicizing grievances, and maximizing the political ends of national power. Like the League of Nations, the United Nations has become an extension of national diplomacies. Acting on the principle that politics is the art of the possible, they have also shown a healthy and realistic respect for power in international relations.

International organizations, reflecting world realities, require great power consensus. But they must face the inadequacy of enforcing their decisions without such agreement. The majority principle cannot and does not work if the great powers do not belong to this majority. It is natural that great power majorities, rarely attained, reflect not so much law and justice as political manipulations.

The minorities in such organizations do not have to be convinced about the majority's sense of justice. Nevertheless, countries in the minority must be persuaded that they will receive a proportionate share of power and influence. Minorities challenging the status quo, whether in a domestic society or in an international order, have learned from long historical practice that manipulated majorities often deny them a rightful place in the sun. What the great powers are actually doing today is of very little consequence. The legacy of suspicion is too strong. It is the historical experience of past injustices, real or imagined, which shapes the attitudes of the present and determines the course of the future. Minorities, whether in the United Nations or in Harlem, aspire not so much to moral superiority as to a finger in the political pie.

Understanding the motivations of a minority challenging the

status quo requires an analysis of the members' view of historical continuity. They are generally bursting with a vivid sense of outrage,[2] arising not so much from a sense of injustice as from the frustration that they are powerless to do anything about it. Their view of historical continuity has taught them the lesson that power and influence go hand in hand. They believe with Thrasymachus that justice is the interest of the stronger. This view of historical continuity, even if distorted, motivates challengers of the status quo to seek power in their own right.

Outraged minorities believe that their interests are at worst trampled by power and at best ignored by indifference. They can thus be forgiven if they make a strong connection between interest and power. To them, power is the only logical means to the maintenance and promotion of their interests. What separates the developing areas from the ghetto dwellers of American cities, however, is the difference between the nature of law and power in a national state and that of an international system. The modern state can suppress its domestic dissidents to a far greater extent than the loosely knit international community.

China, whose freedom from foreign aid permits her to surpass other developing areas in the vocal expression of bitterness, is thus a principal challenger of the status quo. Her leaders constantly emphasize both the drive for power and the need for justice. Very often they tend to confuse the two. Since China has been bullied in the past, the argument runs, it is somehow just that she should augment her strength as rapidly as possible. The power wielded by great powers is considered immoral. By the same token, weakness, however undesirable, is somehow more moral. This attitude, expressed so fervently by the Nehrus and Sihanouks of the 1950's, illustrates what can be called the politics of weakness.

Such ambivalence, which condemns the power wielded by the great powers but embraces it for international minorities, leads to contradictory action. On the one hand, China castigates nuclear testing while simultaneously straining every resource for the development of nuclear power. She opposes every intervention while simultaneously recommending people's wars. In a sense China

2. Mark Mancall, "The Persistence of Tradition in Chinese Foreign Policy," *The Annals*, September 1963, pp. 14 and 23.

shares this ambivalence with all the nations in the international state system, especially the great powers. Nevertheless, China's sense of moral outrage, like that of the advocates of the black power movement in America, is all the more vehement and genuine because it demands a fundamental alteration of the status quo. The reconstruction of history which both movements have undertaken lends them all the more dynamism.

The lesson that "political power grows out of the barrel of a gun," so aptly learned and so often reiterated by Mao, was taught to him by the Western powers. Even Chiang Kai-shek was quick to appreciate this reality, as even a rapid reading of *China's Destiny* reveals. Chiang's failure lay not in any naïveté but in an inability to draw a proper correlation between political and military power.

To China, as to the rest of the Third World, important declarations of international law which emphasized humanistic ends appear as cynical and callous machinations. Chinese leaders see them as means to gain their support, which will then be discarded when such support is no longer needed. Weak nations expect the strong to take advantage of their position but do not believe in grandiose rationalizations. Yet the humanistic platitudes which they scorn raise false hopes and publicize the gap between theory and reality. In this sense declarations like Wilson's Fourteen Points and the Atlantic Charter contributed far more to the disillusionment and anti-Western Westernism of the developing areas than all the treaty ports, rights of extraterritoriality, and acts of alleged economic exploitation put together.

Thus the Paris Peace Conference, which gave birth to the most idealistic and humanistic trends in international law and organization, was also the principal instrument of disillusionment. It crushed the visions of the leaders of China and the Arab world, as well as of people like Gandhi. The years following 1919, therefore, mark not only the beginning of the Chinese Communist movement but also the thrust of national revolutions in countries as far apart as China, Turkey, the Arab world, Egypt, India, and Indonesia.

China's experiences in the supposedly humanistic period of international law and order, from 1919 to 1943, were not designed to strengthen her faith in the Western sense of justice. The principal Western powers did not protect her from Japanese demands, nor did they surrender Germany's rights in Shantung Province, lost after World War I. Wilson's Fourteen Points could not even free China from the unequal treaties of the nineteenth century. In spite of the unanimous report of the Lytton Commission, branding Japan as an aggressor and earning the concurrence of the League's members, nobody came to China's aid. More than anything else, the fate of Manchuria taught China the lesson that in a world of power politics a nation must ultimately rely on its own strength.

With this view of betrayal as their immediate historical heritage, the Chinese Communists came to power. Their experiences from 1949 onward served not so much to correct their views as to reinforce them. In 1943 the Cairo Declaration of the Big Three, at the encouragement and insistence of the United States, had declared that at the end of the war with Japan, Taiwan would return to China. In 1950, however, President Truman questioned the legality of the Cairo declaration with respect to Taiwan by declaring that "the determination of the future status of Formosa must await the restoration of security in the Pacific, a peaceful settlement with Japan, or considerations by the United Nations." [3] These contradictory statements did not prevent the United States from placing a military buffer around the island of Taiwan and thus intervening in the civil war. Washington still continues to recognize Taiwan as an integral part of China by insisting that the Nationalists in Taipei are the only legal government of China.

The arguments used to buttress this legal standpoint are varied. One line of thought runs that the Chinese Communist victory resulted from Soviet aggression in violation of the wartime agreements. In actual fact, however, the amount of Soviet aid that reached the Communists was small. Mao Tse-tung boasted that the Red Army's main supply of weapons came from American arms captured from Kuomintang troops. Furthermore, Moscow apparently underestimated Communist strength and signed a treaty with Chiang Kai-shek as late as 1945.

Yet even if Soviet aid had been substantial, proving that inter-

3. Statement of President Truman, June 27, 1950, *Department of State Bulletin*, No. 5, 1950.

national assistance constitutes intervention or aggression is difficult at best. Besides, such a claim could have a boomerang effect on American policy because of its reliance on radio broadcasts, military aid, and the like. In fact, the Soviet objection to Eisenhower's "Captive Nations Week" was based precisely on these grounds. In the Soviet view, the tools of American policy toward East Europe, notably Radio Free Europe, amounted to intervention in domestic affairs and thus violated the Charter of the United Nations.[4]

Another argument asserts that Communist China's acts of domestic violence deprived her of any claim to recognition by the international community, although China's record in this respect compares favorably with many other Communist nations. Quincy Wright has pointed out that the very idea of basing international recognition on domestic policies adds up to bad politics and doubtful legality.[5] Even the concept of legitimacy itself, originally developed in Europe to uphold the principle of monarchy, has been largely abandoned by the Americans themselves. In its place, Washington's hostility to military juntas in Latin America has relied on Jefferson's criterion, "the will of the nation substantially declared." [6] The meaning of this phrase is extremely fluid, to say the least.

Communist China's perception of international law is conditioned not only by historical experience but also by Peking's observations in the contemporary world. Watching other powers play the game has convinced the Chinese that no country either interprets or follows international law with any consistency. By contrast, the Chinese, impelled by their sense of moral outrage and unaware of their own ambivalence, insist on a fundamentalist version of international law. This attitude leads them not only to a strong emphasis on national sovereignty but also to a demand

4. An excellent discussion of this issue can be found in Quincy Wright, "Subversive Intervention," *American Journal of International Law,* Vol. 54, No. 3, July 1960.

5. Quincy Wright, "The China Recognition Problem," *American Journal of International Law,* Vol. 49, No. 3, July 1955.

6. J. P. Jain, "The Legal Status of Formosa," *American Journal of International Law,* Vol. 57, No. 1, January 1962.

for the strict observance of international law by other powers.[7]

It is often asserted that Communist China does not believe in international law and therefore cannot be trusted to observe it. Actually, scholars who have made a thorough examination of China's attitude toward international law have concluded that Peking, while dissenting from Moscow on several points, is still far from indifferent. On the diplomatic level, China appears to recognize technical rules that facilitate international exchange. Moreover, her spokesmen agree with the Soviets that treaties are the principal source of international law. Although they differ from the Soviets in insisting that international organizations are not subjects of international law and thus cannot conclude treaties in their own right,[8] their arguments are directed against an international body from which they are excluded. It is thus natural that their response to international law has been reactive rather than innovative.

In practice, China has usually fulfilled those obligations which international law has required. A recent article points out that after the only known crossing by unarmed Chinese of the Military Demarcation Line in Korea, in violation of the Armistice, China quickly expressed regret. Similarly, Peking has generally met the terms of trade and fisheries agreements to the letter.[9] If anything, China has a healthy respect for those aspects of international law which her leaders feel have been negotiated on a just basis, such as the so-called Five Principles. It is the manipulation of international law by status quo powers which China scorns. In the eyes of her present leaders, justice is equated with sovereign consent.

7. For further thoughts on this viewpoint, see Jerome Alan Cohen, "China's Attitude Toward International Law—And Our Own," *Proceedings of the American Society of International Law*, Vol. 61, 1967, pp. 108–116.

8. Hungdah Chiu, "The Theory and Practice of Communist China with Respect to the Conclusion of Treaties," *Columbia Journal of Transnational Law*, Vol. 5, No. 1, 1966.

9. Luke T. Lee, "Treaty Relations of the People's Republic of China: A Study of Compliance," *University of Pennsylvania Law Review*, Vol. 116, No. 2, December 1967, p. 271.

The infusion of ideology into interpretations of international law adds still another dimension to Communist Chinese attitudes. From a Marxist-Leninist viewpoint, law represents neither a rational world order nor objective truth. Instead it reflects merely the interest of the ruling class and is thus the tool of the state through which that class exercises power. For this reason, the Communist Chinese interpretation of national and international law is one in which power, interest, and law are intermingled. Rather than clarifying the issue, however, this formula places them on the horns of a very serious dilemma.

The very necessity for survival, communication, trade, influence, and the protection of national interest demands that a state will sooner or later have to follow rules which are acceptable to others. No state, not even Communist China, can do without international law. In the formulation of treaties, in diplomatic notes of protest and commendation, and in verbal attacks on nations with which it is in conflict, a nation must invoke international law. China thus complies with a system which she basically resents.

The problem arises when a nation asks, "Which international law?" China's answer to this query differs significantly from both the Western concept and the Soviet variant.[10] While her differences with the West can be attributed in part to her historical perception of the role of international law in the Western state system, her quarrels with the Soviet Union can be blamed on different foreign policy objectives. Although both Moscow and Peking are interested in peaceful coexistence, Chinese leaders want such a relationship with the West on their own terms.

While different foreign policy objectives do comprise part of the contrast between Chinese and Soviet attitudes toward the West, other factors should not be ignored. The Soviet Union does not have an irredentist problem like Taiwan, while China has. In her own way, the Soviet Union has become a status quo power, while China is trying to challenge the present state of affairs in both the socialist and the nonsocialist worlds. Peking's

10. For an illuminating discussion of the debates and dilemmas of Communist Chinese writers on international law with respect to China's official position, see Hungdah Chiu, "Communist China's Attitude Toward International Law," *American Journal of International Law*, Vol. 60, No. 2, April 1966, pp. 245–267.

diplomatic isolation, its frustration and resentment against a system which excludes it, and its consequent insecurity further exacerbate its grievances with respect to international law. On a theoretical level, Communist China has attacked the idea that international law is only for "civilized states." This hostility is understandable from both an emotional and a historical viewpoint. As a tool of diplomacy, such criticism is also bound to gain considerable applause from Afro-Asian jurists.

In short, China must live within the confines of international law and attack it at the same time. She must conform to it as an insider and castigate it as an outsider. As suggested above, one solution to this dilemma might be to accept the technical aspects of international protocol while seeking to reformulate the essence of natural law on the basis of equity and consent.

By taking a class view of law in general and international law in particular, Chinese theorists must answer the question of whether or not there is a universal international law. They cannot on the one hand subscribe to the Bandung Declaration, which insists that peaceful coexistence between states with different social systems is possible, and, on the other, to the view that international law expresses the will of the ruling class of particular states.

To avoid such an obvious contradiction, the Soviets have modified their position since 1956. From regarding all law as a tool of class rule, they have moved to the concept that international law represents "the agreed will of a number of states." The Soviets also believe that the source of a unified international legal system stems primarily from treaties and secondarily from custom. Although they continue to emphasize the socialist contributions which have supposedly made international law more progressive, they have not yet succeeded in formulating a specifically socialist system of international law. In the meantime, they concede a sort of peaceful coexistence between socialist and capitalist concepts. They have thus bridged the gap between the class conception of law and the practical need for a general international legal framework.

The Chinese do not share this point of view, but as yet they have not reached agreement on an alternative. Writing in 1957, Professor Ch'iu Jih-ch'ing of Fu-tan University in Shanghai insisted on the existence of two systems of international law—one socialist and the other general. According to his analysis, socialist international law regulates the relations between socialist countries, while general international law governs the relations between both socialist and bourgeois countries and between bourgeois states themselves.[11] He probably did not recognize the contradiction expressed in this attitude, for such a definition of a general international law would largely conform to the Western concept of a universal system of law.

Probably aware of the flaws of Ch'iu's logic, the writer Lin Hsin responded by arguing for two separate systems of international law, one bourgeois and the other socialist, which peacefully coexist. Taking a more fundamentalist and ideological line, he insisted that since socialist and capitalist value systems are so different, there could never be a general international law which could incorporate both. Seen in perspective, Lin's article threw into clear relief the dilemma posed by a strict application of Marxism-Leninism.

To resolve this controversy and to come to some kind of decision, an article published a few months later criticized Lin's position. The writer, Chou Fu-lun, emphasized that international relations must be based on common agreements. Since this common system of international law must accommodate the interests and policies of ever-changing centers of power, it must be in a constant state of flux. According to Chou, Lin's solution would harm China's interests and seriously undermine her struggle for international rights. It would also put China in a weak position by depriving her of the legal right to complain about the infraction of international law by capitalist countries.[12]

In February 1958, the Conference on the Systems of International Law, organized by the Shanghai Law Association and the East China Institute of Political Science, failed either to clarify or to resolve this debate. While opposing Lin's view, most of the participants could not arrive at any consensus. This uncertainty continues to characterize China's position. Chinese criticism of the Soviet invasion of Czechoslovakia, for example, almost ignored international law altogether. The few legal references

11. *Ibid.*, pp. 252–275.
12. *Ibid.*, p. 255.

called the move a "monstrous crime against the Czechoslovak people" and an example of "imperialist jungle law." [13] While castigating Soviet-style "internationalism," the Chinese offered no substitute and seemed to feel that international law was insignificant in comparison to national sovereignty.[14] The Albanians were only slightly less vague, branding the invasion as a "flagrant contravention of all norms governing the relations between states." [15]

Underneath the indecisiveness of the debate and the reticence of Peking's public pronouncements, however, China's official view of international law rests on the assumption that whatever legal order exists at present is inadequate. Whether there are one, two, or three types of general international law, none of them can meet the exigencies of China's international relations or protect China's national interests. In the formulation of treaties, therefore, China's leaders usually stress particular concepts or documents, such as proletarian internationalism, the Five Principles of Peaceful Coexistence, or even the United Nations Charter. Most basic, however, is China's insistence on the full panoply of rights of national sovereignty.[16]

13. "Beset With Difficulties at Home and Abroad and Finding Itself in Tight Corner, Soviet Revisionist Renegade Clique Blatantly Sends Troops to Occupy Czechoslovakia," Hsinhua Report, August 22, 1968, *Peking Review*, Vol. 11, No. 34, August 23, 1968, Supplement, pp. vi and viii.

14. See, for example, Chou En-lai's speech at Rumania's National Day Reception and the article by *Jenmin Jihpao's* Commentator, "Total Bankruptcy of Soviet Modern Revisionism," in *ibid.*, pp. iii–vi.

15. "Brutal Aggression by Soviet Revisionist Renegade Clique Against Czechoslovakia Resolutely Condemned," Statement by the Central Committee of the Albanian Party of Labor and the Council of Ministers of Albania, *Peking Review*, Vol. 11, No. 35, August 30, 1968, p. 9.

16. For more detailed discussions of China's stand, see two articles by Hungdah Chiu, "The Theory and Practice of Communist China with Respect to the Conclusions of Treaties," *The Columbia Journal of Transnational Law*, Vol. 5, No. 1, 1966, pp. 1–13 and "Certain Legal Aspects of Communist China's Treaty Practice," *Proceedings of the American Society of International Law*, Vol. 61, 1967, pp. 117–130.

Even the view that treaties are the principal source of international law conforms to this emphasis on consent. The very fact that Peking has included the Five Principles in virtually every treaty concluded since 1954 reveals a disproportionate emphasis on freely negotiated treaties as the basis of the international legal order. Most Chinese writers try to give the impression that the Five Principles are a major contribution to general international law.

The content of the Five Principles closely corresponds to China's own attitudes. One of them, noninterference in internal affairs, reflects the strict emphasis on national sovereignty which is particularly typical of Chinese nationalism but also of nationalism in general. Even in the international application of this attitude, Peking's attitude is fairly consistent. China's criticism of South Africa, for example, calls not for United Nations action but for a domestic revolution. The need for self-reliance, the slogan of the Mao-Lin group, is used to defend the paucity of China's aid to revolutionary movements abroad, including the Vietcong.

Another one of the Five Principles, mutual benefit, is even more indicative of China's concept of international justice. Regardless of legal etiquette, no treaty which bestows a benefit on one country at the expense of the other can be called just. Even if the treaty bears the signatures of representatives of two sovereign governments, its content may be unjust. This point of view completely rejects the argument that China's "unequal treaties" were not really unequal because they were signed between two sovereign powers. To China's leaders, consent by gunpoint can never be the basis of international law.

Peking's insistence on genuine consent does not differ significantly from the attitudes of other great powers. In fact, consent is the bedrock of the Security Council. In the ultimate analysis, China's point of view should not affect her role in the world order. Many of her ideas are already gaining importance in international law. Customary law is a prime example.

At one time in history, customary law was created by common consent and the usual practice of nations. It thus forms part of the Western historical heritage and represents historical continuity for those nations who were a party to its creation. In historical perspective, customary law evolved from the consent of those nations fortunate enough to be original members of the Western family of nations. What is customary today must have received the consent of nations yesterday. To China's satisfaction, it is this customary law which is gradually being incorporated into conventions dependent on the consent of all. In this sense the Chinese insistence on consent is not a significant departure from the practice of all nations.

Nevertheless, Peking's stress on consent has sometimes amounted to an obsession. Responsible for serious foreign policy complications and setbacks, this obsession also bears partial blame for China's image as a power which cannot be trusted to carry out its commitments. In the entire scope of Chinese foreign policy, nowhere has it influenced China's behavior more than in her border problems. Her leaders have consistently demanded not so much a change of boundary lines for their own sake as their renegotiation on a free and equal basis. Except for the final border arrangements with India and the Soviet Union, settlements with China's neighbors were actually unfavorable. Thus, China's performance with respect to her borders is motivated not by territorial expansionism but by this fanatical obsession with sovereign consent.

One clue to Peking's behavior arises from the desire to dissociate China from historical continuity with the age of imperialism. More than almost anything else, China longs to be recognized as a sovereign power capable of formulating its own boundaries. In this sense, China is like an adolescent in the family of nations who wishes to assert his adulthood and his identity with a rather heavy hand. To brand this adolescent as a juvenile delinquent would be unfair to both him and his family.

If this analysis is correct, then China can be depended on to respect those boundaries which she had renegotiated herself and to follow those laws to which she has consented. As she develops her own customary law through consent, and as custom is incorporated into conventions, present practices will acquire historical solidity. It has therefore been argued that the more treaties China enters into and the more agreements that China negotiates, the greater will be the integration of China with international law.[17] This line of reasoning would point toward a historical convergence between China and former challengers of the status quo, notably the Soviet Union.

Through the principles of national sovereignty and consent, China also wants to emphasize that she is a contributor to international law and order as well as a recipient. It is in this sense that the nationalism of cultural despair influences her attitude toward international law. Specifically, the principle of consent permits China to establish her equivalence with the West, at least to her own satisfaction. In this way China seeks not to discard and defy the world order but to belong to it. Understanding this point requires a clear understanding of China's motivations. For her leaders, belonging must not be understood as a mark of surrender but as a badge of acceptance on terms of equality. In the international legal order China wishes to be a participant and not a client.

China's record in the field of treaty implementation has also shown this willingness to live up to freely negotiated commitments. Except for the period of the Cultural Revolution, she has fulfilled all her trade obligations. Even the delays or cancellations produced by the Cultural Revolution can be attributed to political problems of domestic law enforcement rather than to backtracking on international pledges. Even international law recognizes a state's limitations in the fulfillment of international obligations during a period of political turmoil.

China has also shown a willingness to enter into trade and other agreements with nations with which she has no diplomatic relations. The most important example is Japan. Treaties between Japan and China are usually to Japan's advantage, such as the Fisheries Agreements of 1959 and 1963. Although there had been cases of harassment and confiscation before 1959, no serious incidents of any kind took place between 1959 and 1966. This record shows that China willingly and scrupulously fulfilled an agreement with a nation which failed to grant her diplomatic recognition.

17. Luke T. Lee, "Treaty Relations of the People's Republic of China," *loc. cit.*

Similar cases include the wheat agreements with Australia and Canada and the trade agreements with West Germany. In all these cases, agreements were signed by organizations which have no international legal personality. Specifically, agreements with Canada were concluded between the Canadian Wheat Board and the China Resources Corporation. The Canadian Wheat Board, an autonomous body created by an act of 1935, reports to the Minister of Trade and Commerce. No Canadian, Australian, or West German source has ever complained that China has not met her deadlines. Sometimes she has even fulfilled her commitments ahead of schedule.

In short, China's credit and credibility as a trading partner are among the highest in the world. This fact is all the more remarkable when one considers that since 1960 China is probably the only developing country which has not received aid. She is also a rare example of a developing country which has solved the balance of payments problem through remarkable self-discipline. To attribute these feats to tight domestic control is relevant but not entirely adequate, since other dictatorships cannot boast of such a record.

China's attitude toward the United Nations is quite complex and flexible. As the Communists moved toward power, they hoped that victory in the civil war would lead to admission in the United Nations. Judging from international practice, these hopes were justified. The Chinese Communists had even sent a delegate to the San Francisco Conference in 1945, which drafted the United Nations Charter. Yet in spite of this auspicious beginning, the Korean War made it increasingly clear that China's admission to the United Nations would be blocked by a pro-Western majority. When this majority passed a resolution branding China as an aggressor, Peking's hopeful expectations turned into frustrated antagonism.[18]

The admission of Communist China to the United Nations has gradually become more a symbolic than a legal issue. As stated in Article 23 of the Charter, "China" is an original member. The question is not whether to admit Peking as a new sov-

18. See Wang's article, "Communist China's Changing Attitude Toward the United Nations," *International Organizations*, No. 20, 1966, p. 677.

ereign entity which has only recently acquired an international legal personality. It is rather whether to recognize Peking or Taipei as the legal government of China. The provisions of Article 4, therefore, which deal with the admission of new members, do not apply. Similarly, Paragraph One of that article, requiring new members to be "peace loving," is irrelevant to this issue.

The problem is complicated by the fact that each of the forty-odd organs of the United Nations is entitled to solve the recognition problem by itself. Except for the Security Council, none of these organs contains the veto principle, so that none of its great power representatives is capable of blocking the admission of any particular government of China. According to surveys, the majority of delegates to the United Nations favor recognizing Peking and consider its exclusion legally wrong. In 1961 this pressure grew so strong that the United States was forced to switch from urging postponement of the issue to declaring it sufficiently "important" to require a two-thirds majority in the General Assembly.[19] A large number of polls have also indicated that the majority of American citizens would prefer to see the United Nations recognize the Communist Chinese government.[20]

Ever since the French Revolution, ideological divisions have persisted in the international community. To avoid the breakdown of this community and to continue some kind of dialogue between members who are on ideologically opposite sides of the fence, recognition of governments and states came to be based more on *de facto* control than on *de jure* considerations. Accordingly, most states do not inquire into the question of the constitutional legitimacy of a government before awarding it recognition. They are usually more concerned with whether or not it effectively controls its territory and population. American recognition of military juntas in Latin America, no matter how offensive to Washington they may be, has followed this line of reasoning.

Furthermore, neither the Covenant of the League of Nations

19. Sheldon Appleton, "The United Nations China Tangle," *Pacific Affairs*, Vol. 35, No. 2, Summer 1962.

20. A. T. Steele, *The American People and China* (New York: McGraw-Hill, 1966), pp. 94–111.

nor the Charter of the United Nations makes it a precondition that a government must be democratically constituted on the basis of democratic legitimacy before it can be admitted into an international organization. If such were the terms, membership would be pitifully small. For all practical purposes, therefore, the consent of the people must be judged in negative and passive terms. In these cases the "will of the nation substantially declared" refers to a government's ability to control its subjects rather than the reverse.

For obvious reasons bestowing the title of legitimacy cannot be confined to ideological preferences or democratic systems. In the League as well as the United Nations, both Communist governments and right-wing dictatorships have masqueraded as democracies and enjoyed the full and unfettered rights of membership. In the final analysis, a government's ability to represent a nation should be appraised in the Austinian sense of receiving "habitual obedience from the bulk of its population." In this respect, it must be admitted that the Nationalist government controls Taiwan and that the Communist government holds similar sway over the mainland. Each seems to enjoy at the least the passive consent of its citizenry.

Another criterion often brandished in discussions is whether a candidate for admission to the United Nations will follow the letter and spirit of the Charter. Actually, there is hardly any choice but to take the prospective member's word for it. Moreover, there is hardly any member of the United Nations who does not feel that other members have violated the Charter at one time or another. Yet it is often argued that since the General Assembly branded China an aggressor in Korea, she is ineligible for membership.

In answer to this viewpoint, a considerable degree of debate surrounds China's role in the Korean War. Korea has traditionally been the invasion route to China, used most recently by Japan. Furthermore, China's entry into the Korean War took place after United Nations troops crossed the 38th Parallel and thus changed the nature of the war from the defense of South Korea to the political unification of Korea as a whole. One scholar has argued, therefore, that China intervened not to commit aggression but to protect her security by defending her buffer state, North

Korea.[21] Even if aggression could be proved, those countries who have been condemned as aggressors after joining the United Nations have not been expelled.

The other objection to the implications of the United Nations resolution on Korea questions whether it can block China's admission forever. Most scholars would probably agree that the principle of *rebus sic stantibus* may be applied to this resolution in the course of time. It has been argued here that such a step might be taken if and when China changes her course and assures the international community that she will abide by the Charter. Yet this is circular reasoning. After all, such an argument returns to the original position. If such an assurance is a precondition to China's admission, the United Nations will have to take her word for it. As a possible token of good faith, the record of China's foreign policy reveals a cautious attempt to avoid a repetition of Korea. Nowhere is this attitude more clearly demonstrated than in the case of the Vietnam War.

Even if admitted, China has declared herself unwilling to accept membership in the United Nations as long as Taiwan continued to hold a seat. The "two Chinas" solution is anathema to both Taipei and Peking. Communist China has repeatedly gone on record to assert her militant hostility to such a solution.[22] Even apart from the Chinese, the "two Chinas" idea would fly in the face of America's wartime pledges to the effect that Taiwan is an integral part of China. Although it appears to be a perfect compromise, neither side will settle for less than complete victory. Ultimately Washington may have to sit back and let other members of the United Nations handle the problem as they see fit, even if their solution involves the exclusion of Taiwan. Judging from past experience, nothing would prevent the United States

21. Tang Tsou, *America's Failure in China, 1941–1950* (Chicago: University of Chicago Press, 1963), pp. 555–591. See also Allen S. Whiting, *China Crosses the Yalu: The Decision to Enter the Korean War* (New York: Macmillan Co., 1960), pp. 151–162.

22. See, for example, Kung Pu-sheng, "A Conspiracy Against the Chinese People," in Chinese People's Institute of Foreign Affairs, *Oppose United States Occupation of Taiwan and the "Two Chinas" Plot: A Selection of Important Documents* (Peking: Foreign Languages Press, 1958), pp. 160–161.

from continuing to aid and foster the Nationalist government if American policy remained the same.

Communist China's admission to the United Nations would probably not change her foreign policy to any significant degree. If the United Nations remains an extension of national diplomacy, then Peking will utilize it as an instrument to secure foreign policy ends. There is no reason to expect China to behave any differently from other members in this respect. The mere question of admission or nonadmission does not determine China's national drives or vital national interests. What is at stake is granting China a world role proportionate to her new strength. The question of membership in the United Nations is only frosting on the cake.

China's admission is thus no more of a panacea than the admission of the Soviet Union, Cuba, or any other nation. People who feel that the United Nations can solve most of the world's problems understand the true nature of neither international organizations nor international politics. Expectations from international law and international organizations should be kept at the minimum possible level so that disillusionment may not lead to complete loss of faith. Hope is inversely proportionate to frustration. The danger of idealism turning into cynicism is much greater than that of realism turning into passive acceptance. In and out of the United Nations, countries will try to promote their foreign policy aims through diplomacy, power, law, and organization.

Because of similar frustrations, China turned from a receptive attitude to bitter denunciations of the United Nations. She did so partly because she felt herself in the minority and because she shared the philosophy of sour grapes. From this standpoint her leaders constantly attacked the United Nations as a manipulative instrument of American policy. To a considerable extent, their view in this respect was determined by the Korean War, where China fought American troops under a United Nations umbrella. Peking is also convinced that the majorities which exclude China from United Nations membership are also manipulated by Washington. Needless to say, this opinion is shared by many other governments.

Whenever she could participate as an equal, China has taken every opportunity to attend and participate in any international conference. Both Bandung and the preparatory meetings for Afro-Asian conferences are noteworthy examples, as are the Geneva Conferences of 1954 and 1962. These conferences show not only that China is willing to confer with other powers on international disputes, but also that her presence is essential to the long-term solution of problems with which she is connected.

Contrary to popular impression, China has placed great emphasis on keeping the channels of communication open, even with its principal enemies. Ever since 1955, China has continued to hold talks with the United States on the ambassadorial level. The present cancellation is probably a tactical delay rather than a long-term cessation. In spite of loud complaints, she has never gone to the extent of unilaterally closing her embassies and suspending diplomatic contacts with any country, including the Soviet Union, India, and Indonesia. She has made every effort to establish some sort of contact with every country, regardless of ideological preferences or sociopolitical patterns. In sum, Peking fully recognizes the value of diplomatic contacts in the promotion of foreign policy aims.

In the ultimate analysis, the United Nations also provides a multidimensional channel of communication and widespread diplomatic contacts. Therefore, as far as China is concerned, the United Nations would serve her foreign policy goals as well as those of any other nations likely to remain in a permanent minority for some time to come. In this sense, admission can only be an attractive prospect, especially since it will symbolize victory over a long-standing American policy.

However, Peking does not grant admission to the United Nations such an overwhelming priority as to overrule its basic foreign policy aims. Given the choice between admission to the United Nations and irredentist claims to Taiwan, therefore, China would choose the latter. In 1945 the United States had to make a similar decision. The question was whether to choose complete sovereign freedom and safeguard America's vital interests or to join a United Nations in which Washington's efforts might be modified by a United Nations majority. Initially, American leaders chose the former. Both Cabot Lodge in 1919 and Senator Vandenburg in 1945 preferred freedom of action to membership in an international organization. Only the veto principle made

Washington's participation in the United Nations possible. It almost seems as if China has carefully read the proceedings of the United States Senate.

China's noisy search for an alternative to the United Nations has borne little fruit. On balance, both her vociferous support of Indonesia's withdrawal from the United Nations and her recommendations to Cambodia to do the same are manifestations of frustration rather than genuine steps to form a rival organization. Clearly, such an organization would not suit her foreign policy goals. China wants not segregation but integration. In order to influence the majority and to achieve world-wide involvement and participation, China prefers the United Nations to a rump organization. All indications point in this direction.

China's disillusionment with the United Nations may not have resulted only from what she sees as American manipulation. She also believes that changes in the spirit of the Charter which were inspired by the United States have corrupted the organization as a whole. Like Moscow, Peking considers that the Uniting for Peace Resolution of 1950, which was meant to bypass the Soviet veto in the Security Council by transferring important peace-keeping decisions to the General Assembly, tampered with the terms of the Charter. To China, it was no coincidence that this deviation led to her condemnation as an aggressor.

China also remembers that this charge of aggression followed her intervention in Korea, which took place after repeated warnings that United Nations troops must not cross the 38th Parallel and threaten the political independence of Korea. Both the United States and other members of the United Nations have apparently taken this sequence into account during the course of the Vietnam conflict. The United Nations is not eager to enter the fray nor is the United States in a hurry to cross the 17th Parallel. This reluctance signifies a possible ex post facto recognition that China's entry into Korea sprang not so much from aggression as from a desire to safeguard national security. The right to preventive military action in the name of self-defense has often been claimed by other nations. A recent and classic example would be the Cuban missile crisis, when the United States argued, and her allies agreed, that the mere presence of missiles in Cuba was a threat to American security.

To comprehend China's actions, to analyze her motivations, and to formulate her view of the Western world order requires understanding of her past history, her ideological perspective, and especially her version of recent experiences with the West. Her leaders feel not only that her exclusion from the United Nations is unjust. Their evaluation of international law and organization is also shaped by what they consider to be a number of violations of international legality. In their views these injustices are committed both inside and outside the United Nations, by Western powers in general and the United States in particular. One potent example is Washington's protection of Taiwan, a policy that the Chinese interpret as a continuation of interference in China's civil war.

China can well be blamed for outmoded conceptions of national sovereignty. She continues to cling to an interpretation of power and law which is more characteristic of the age of imperialism than of the contemporary world. Furthermore, her moral outrage does not prevent considerations of both power and ideology from outweighing the strict dictates of legality. Challenging the international establishment permits China to clothe herself in moral superiority, but this garment might appear threadbare if China achieved the rank of a status quo power herself.

Yet such arguments bear only marginal relevance to the solution of the "China problem." To the Chinese this phenomenon probably appears to be more of a "Western problem." China holds outmoded conceptions because she has been excluded from the world community and because she has not yet acquired the status of complete equality. She cannot move away from the stage of nationalism and national sovereignty until she has fully grasped such equality and until her achievement has been fully recognized. To expect China to do so is to expect her to be more mature and more sophisticated than other nations were in their own respective stages of historical development.

It is also true that China places more political and ideological emphasis on her foreign policy than some of the other powers. Yet this trait is more a matter of degree than a difference of kind. In modern times, motivated by calculations of national power and deflected from humanistic or religious ends, the Western world order can surely tolerate China's attitude. Her entry does not demand any qualitative changes in the pattern of international politics. What is needed instead is a fundamental reappraisal of China's behavior coupled with a major blow at the mythology which surrounds her. China's emergence as a nuclear power means that the architects of the Western world order should postpone this task no longer.

CHAPTER FOUR

Sino-American Misperceptions

Harold Isaacs has divided American attitudes toward China into two distinct periods. He terms the first, from 1840 to 1905, as the age of contempt. The second, from 1905 to 1937, is called the age of benevolence.[1] A third period can be added to this list; the years from 1941 to the present might be known as the age of misperceptions.

American relations with China span the entire existence of the United States as an independent state. The first American commercial clipper, *Empress of China*, visited the Orient in 1784. By the time the statesmen at Philadelphia finalized the Constitution in 1789, there were fourteen American ships in Chinese harbors, and the Chinese trade was already considered as one of the most lucrative.[2] For a century, American contacts with China were limited either to seamen or to missionaries. Both of these groups were thus responsible for the creation of the popular images which provided the principal motive force of the age of contempt.

The first group, the traders, indulged in all the seamy aspects of Oriental trade. Transactions dealing with both opium and coolies passed through their hands. Yankee clippers were mainly

1. Harold Isaacs, *Scratches on Our Minds: American Images of China and India* (New York: John Day, 1958), pp. 140–164.
2. A. T. Steele, *The American People and China* (New York: McGraw-Hill, 1966), p. 8.

responsible for the transportation of most of the Chinese who emigrated to the Western hemisphere. The great majority of these people were transported under subhuman conditions and arrived as indentured laborers. Their living conditions in the New World were usually appalling. In America, they were mainly used for railway construction. Meanwhile, upper class Americans showed a certain appreciation for Chinese *objets d'art* but little respect for the civilization which created them.

Most of these traders came in contact only with port life and their view of China was determined to a great extent by this perspective. The coolie trade and the starvation which encouraged indentured labor did not improve China's image. It was natural for Westerners in general and Americans in particular to judge China from their limited and distorted range of vision. Port life was hardly typical of China. Lacking any knowledge of Chinese history, Americans concluded that the disturbances and famines which plagued the Celestial Empire were characteristics of permanent incompetence rather than a symptom of recent decay.

The second group, the missionaries, faced the need to raise money at home. To gain support for their efforts they probably exaggerated the poverty, the lack of popular culture, and the general absence of humanistic values among China's lower classes. On the positive side, however, Professor John K. Fairbank has correctly pointed out that missionaries helped to create modernizing attitudes and to make many Chinese transitional.

In this respect, missionaries probably performed a eufunctional role. By contributing to the transitional nature of Chinese society they helped to create a cultural conflict. It is true that this conflict polarized traditional and transitional groups which may have contributed to the xenophobia of the Boxer Rebellion. Yet in the long run, it was beneficial in that it taught the Chinese that their cultural system was not suited to a modern environment.

As Walter Lippmann has pointed out, nineteenth-century America was expanding her commitments without a concurrent expansion of power. Beginning with the Monroe Doctrine of 1823, American commitments in both the Western hemisphere and the Pacific were constantly increasing. The United States ended Japan's isolation, bought Alaska, took over Hawaii, and participated in the benefits of the Opium Wars with China. While pursuing territorial expansionism at home, America's efforts in the Pacific were mainly commercial. One exception was the acquisition of the Philippines after the Spanish-American War. All in all, the United States had more commitments at the end of the nineteenth century than power to fulfill them.

This imbalance between commitments and power led the United States to follow in the footsteps of other great powers. The development of American national interest demanded not only an independent foreign policy, but also the national will to translate that potential into power. It is a matter of historical record that Washington started to develop an independent foreign policy long before it made the necessary transition from potential strength to actual power. Thus, while the United States started the move toward an independent foreign policy at the end of the nineteenth century, it took another fifty years before the power and will to back it up developed.

With the exception of World War I, the dichotomy between United States policy and power existed from 1900 to 1940. This period coincided with the age of benevolence toward China. American policy in the Far East differed from that of European powers but lacked either the will or the power to be translated into action. From Secretary Hay's notes of 1899 and 1900 enunciating the Open Door policy with respect to China to the Stimson Doctrine of 1931, Washington sought to maintain China's territorial integrity and sovereign independence while taking little concrete action in her defense.

Naturally both official and national historians of American policy in the Far East took the position that these were years of benevolence. They gave the United States the credit for preventing other great powers from parceling China into a number of spheres of influence. Dissenting from this complacency, both the "realist" and "revisionist" historians argue that America's attitude was not based on moral aspirations. They point out that by the end of the nineteenth century, American trade with China had reached substantial proportions. America could not afford to permit the closed door policy characteristic of European spheres of influence to damage a profitable business. In this sense, Open Door policy meant an open door for American commerce.

Although the question of American benevolence is still open to debate, it is clear that Washington failed to support China in the 1930's beyond a declaration of policy. During the Sino-Japanese confrontation in Manchuria and elsewhere, the United States was more concerned with avoiding a war with Japan than with aiding China.[3] Ironically, the only nation which helped China in that period was the Soviet Union. Moscow's actions were dictated strictly by the need to maintain a buffer state between the Soviet Union's Far Eastern frontier and Japan's vigorous imperialism.

It was only during the period of World War II that Americans really became emotionally involved with China. Yet from 1941 on, American public opinion and American foreign policy objectives in the Far East had one point in common: relative indifference. As far as official policy was concerned, wholehearted support for China occupied a low rung in the ladder of commitments. The primary aim was to win the war, but American policy-makers were divided on the question of assigning priority to the Atlantic or the Pacific. In either case, however, the Chinese theater of operations occupied a lowly status in the general strategy of World War II. The national goal was victory over Japan; China was a marginal problem. This situation would have remained more or less the same, and American public opinion would have continued to regard China with the same indifference as it did in the 1930's, if certain qualitative changes had not occurred in American policy and in American attitudes.

First and foremost, the United States did not embrace the isolationism and the passionate neutrality so typical of the period following World War I and of the 1930's. American involvement in the world became permanent. Washington was no longer formulating policies as a regional power but as a world power. Areas like Latin America and China, which had previously re-

3. For a comprehensive account of America's Far Eastern policy at this time, see Dorothy Borg, *The United States and the Far Eastern Crisis of 1933–1938* (Cambridge: Harvard University Press, 1964).

ceived disproportionate verbal attention in such declaratory policies as the Monroe Doctrine and the Open Door, were now
relegated to an inferior status. After 1946 their task became one
of finding their place in a foreign policy which was mostly concerned with the Soviet Union. America's China policy thus
became an adjunct to her policy toward the Soviet Union. In
this sense China had become a casualty of the Cold War.

Two further developments need to be examined in depth.
One was the growing disillusionment of several American policy-
makers and diplomatic personnel assigned to China. The most
important name in this category was that of General Joseph W.
Stilwell. Fully realizing the inherent weaknesses and the increasing
disintegration of the Kuomintang regime, Stilwell's efforts to
modernize China's armed forces naturally led to serious conflicts
of personality and principles with Chiang Kai-shek. He also
realized the full seriousness of the Communist threat and was
frustrated by Chiang's assertion that the Communists had no
support. Thanks to men like him, the American public caught
some glimpses of the reality and the gravity of the situation in
China during 1943 and 1944.

In the meantime a second force started to emerge. The year
1943 marks the beginning of emotional support for what might
be called the "Chiang myth" in the United States. It was in
this year that Madame Chiang Kai-shek visited America and
received a tremendous welcome. Among other things, she addressed both houses of Congress. These efforts succeeded in projecting a new image of China—that of a helpless nation valiantly
trying to uphold its freedom and independence against heavy odds.

One reason why this appeal met with such a sympathetic
response concerns American attitudes. America's traditional idealism and sense of fair play impelled her citizens to support the
country which they considered to be the underdog. Consciously
or subconsciously, they even drew a vague parallel between the
two countries. After all, both had grievances against what they
considered to be a cynical and selfish clique of European statesmen. Although America's growing wealth and power made this
self-image increasingly irrelevant, the traditional underdog mentality continued to grip the American imagination.

Yet this attitude did not prevent American public opinion from splitting into two camps. One was pro-Chiang and the other was anti-Chiang. Both of them felt sympathy for their particular image of the Chinese people, but they disagreed in their respective estimations of China's leadership. With certain modifications, both of these groups have survived until the present day. Both of them displayed various degrees of euphoria regarding the China problem, and both failed to realize that America could only play a marginal role in its solution. They could not perceive that a long-run answer to China's dilemma could only spring from a sound domestic base and from a government which could mobilize China's potential to the full.

Both American foreign policy and public opinion, like those of most other nations, were more concerned with the foreign policy interests of the United States than with the domestic realities of Chinese politics in the 1940's. Chiang's weaknesses, his quasi-Confucian philosophy, and even the anti-Westernism which he revealed in *China's Destiny* were ignored or side-stepped. The main concern of the pro-Chiang group was that anybody was preferable to the Communists.

Another complicating factor at the time was the general belief that the Soviet Union was giving heavy support to Mao's forces and that Moscow was the principal architect of the Communist victory. Most Americans viewed the situation as a case of Soviet aggression and expansionism rather than as a genuine civil war. The Soviet occupation of Czechoslovakia in 1948 solidified this belief. In actual fact, however, Soviet aid to the Communists was inconsequential, particularly when compared to American aid to the Nationalists.

During the same period the establishment of the China lobby, backed up by considerable publicity on behalf of the Nationalists, was instrumental in the creation of pro-Chiang fervor. This stance was marked by an uncritical acceptance of the Nationalist government as the right and lawful government of China. The so-called "fundamentalists" who clung to this faith refused to permit the possibility of a major accommodation with the Chinese Communists under any circumstances. Fundamentalist positions are promoted by organizations which take a strongly emotional anti-

Communist stand, of which one example is the Committee of One Million.[4] A few people from the universities adopt similar attitudes, but they do not form an important segment of that part of the intellectual community which is concerned with China or Chinese studies.[5]

The fundamentalist approach toward China is based on the assumption that the Chinese Communist government is neither durable nor representative. Advocates of this point of view deny that Chinese Communism is a genuine product of domestic forces. They consider that China is an agent of the Soviet Union and thus a part of the international Communist conspiracy. Even now, they downgrade the Sino-Soviet dispute quite dramatically. In their view the split between the two countries is a fraudulent pose designed to make the Western powers weaken their defenses. This failure to distinguish between Russian and Chinese Communism is paralleled by an inability to differentiate between China and other Asian Communist movements.

The belief that a majority of the American people supports such a position is not corroborated by public opinion studies.[6] Nevertheless, many congressmen and senators take varying fundamentalist positions because of their belief that their constituencies support them.[7] Such misrepresentation helps to thwart any proposed changes in America's China policy.

A second broad category which has been gaining strength in the 1960's is that of the so-called "gradualists." In contrast to funda-

4. See Robert Hunter and Forrest Davis, *The New Red China Lobby* (New York: Fleet Publishing Company, 1966). For a more scholarly description of the same groups, see Freda Utley, *The China Story* (Chicago: Henry Regnery Co., 1951).

5. See the testimony by David N. Rowe in *U.S. Policy with Respect to China*, Hearings Before the Committee on Foreign Relations, United States Senate, Eighty-Ninth Congress, March 1966, pp. 496–512.

6. For a summary of these studies, see A. T. Steele, *The American People and China* (New York: McGraw-Hill, 1966).

7. For a classification of the members of Congress regarding the China question, see the Appendix to Hunter and Davis, *The New Red China Lobby*. It contains the 1966 declaration of those members of Congress who opposed any change in policy.

mentalists, gradualists believe that some concrete steps should be taken to ensure the eventual normalization of Sino-American relations.[8] Their position can be expressed in Professor A. Doak Barnett's phrase, "containment without isolation." [9] They would begin with an exchange of journalists, scholars, doctors, and the like, leading to *de facto* recognition of the Communist government. They support their case by emphasizing that to some extent *de facto* recognition already exists. They point not only to the fact that both governments participated in the Geneva Conference of 1962, but also to what Kenneth Young has called the "subdiplomatic system." [10] This term refers to the bilateral talks between the two governments which have taken place ever since 1955.

Gradualists stress that the trade embargo on nonstrategic goods should be relaxed as soon as possible. As far as a seat in the United Nations is concerned, however, they want to wait and see. Believing that China is inherently expansionist, they attribute to Peking the so-called Middle Kingdom or self-centered ethos of international relations. In their view, China is more orthodox and more rigid and thus compares unfavorably with the Soviet Union or with Eastern Europe.

Proponents of gradualism agree with the fundamentalists on the need for military containment, but most of them are beginning to downgrade the direct military threat and to upgrade the threat of indirect aggression and political subversion. Just as Communist commentators tend to blame all setbacks on the C.I.A., so gradualists attribute to China a superhuman capacity to initiate, support, and control guerrilla movements or "people's war." They disagree with the fundamentalists in their denial that China is an agent of the Soviet Union and in their insistence that the Chinese Communist government is highly durable. In the long run, they favor a "two Chinas" solution.

Within these broad categories, individual scholars and policy-

8. For easy access to all the gradualist views held by American scholars, see *U.S. Policy with Respect to Mainland China* (Washington, D.C.: Government Printing Office, March 1966).

9. *Ibid.*, pp. 4ff.

10. Kenneth T. Young, *Negotiating with the Chinese Communists: The United States Experience, 1953–1967* (New York: McGraw-Hill, 1968), p. 393.

makers display different conceptions of China and her foreign policy intentions. Certain so-called "realists," such as Walter Lippmann, Hans Morgenthau, George Kennan, and Arthur Schlesinger, Jr., believe that China could enter the status quo if given a legitimate sphere of influence. These writers point out that although America's China policy has hitherto denied the legitimacy of China's interest, corresponding American aims have long been established in the Western hemisphere.[11] They feel that a similar arrangement might constitute Communist China's legitimate interest in Southeast Asia. Significantly, Secretary Rusk has agreed that China's legitimate interests will have to be recognized.[12]

The people who cautiously argue that China should be permitted to enjoy legitimate interests along her periphery have not provided any clear indication as to what these interests are. Historically, legitimate political interests for most great powers have taken the form of a sphere of influence along their borders. The minimum demand which a great power has made is that the nations in its sphere of influence should follow a strategy of denial with regard to the military forces of another great power. In the period following World War II, this demand has meant a refusal to permit the establishment of military bases. The maximum demand in this connection is the exclusion of hostile ideologies, political systems, or foreign policies.

To what extent these historical conceptions are valid in the present stage of international relations is debatable. In the era of nuclear overkill it can be argued that only superpowers should have spheres of influence which extend far beyond their peripheries. The instantaneous communications of the atomic age argue against geopolitical considerations in the designation of spheres of influence. China, which is only an aspiring great power, cannot realistically expect to have any sphere of influence. With their

11. Arthur Schlesinger, Jr., "Origins of the Cold War," *Foreign Affairs*, October 1967, pp. 32–52. See also the testimony of George Kennan and Henry Steele Commager to the Committee on Foreign Relations, United States Senate, in January and February 1967, respectively.

12. Dean Rusk "Statement Before the House Subcommittee on Far Eastern Affairs on United States Policy Toward Communist China," *The New York Times*, April 17, 1966.

nineteenth-century concepts, this is very hard for the Chinese to realize. The world is no longer in such a clear-cut stage as to confine the United States to the Western hemisphere and China to Southeast Asia. Thailand is in the American sphere of influence in the same way that China tried to bring Cuba into hers.

American scholars in the 1960's have displayed an increasing tendency to recognize that China will not militarily occupy Asian countries on her periphery. What they worry about is whether China will keep within the minimum or maximum limits of any legitimate political interest that she may be said to have either in Asia or elsewhere. They often hint that China's new capabilities entitle her to a greater voice in Asian or world affairs. Yet they subconsciously fear that such an accommodation will be at the expense of American influence. They are reluctant to admit publicly that this change would place a proportional limitation on America's freedom of action in Asia.

Given the progress of contemporary Chinese studies in the United States, at least American intellectuals and policy-makers are entering an era of sophisticated analysis. The Chinese Communists are no longer considered in such simplistic terms as mere agents of the Soviet Union or as agrarian reformers. Such sophistication might have sprouted in the 1950's if the McCarthy era had not dealt the study of contemporary China such a serious blow. China scholars suffered from the intense search for a scapegoat for what the fundamentalists believed was a serious American defeat in the Far East. McCarthy supporters failed to realize that responsibility for the "loss" of China did not lie in the United States. It was not that America abandoned China and thus failed to fulfill her moral duties. Blame lay instead with America's ally—Chiang Kai-shek—who never really understood the true nature of China's domestic politics.

A generation of social scientists had put democracy and totalitarianism on opposite poles. They had considered totalitarianism more as a pathological political disease than as a system which could have its own normal physiology. Under these circumstances, it was difficult to grasp that given a very special combination of factors, Communism could enjoy a sufficient measure of domestic support. This misperception and the mythology which surrounds it continue to be responsible for the view that Communism in

China is imported or imposed. While the importation of ideas and their imposition by force were indeed involved in both the Communists' rise to power and their pattern of government, no system, not even a totalitarian one, can survive without at least passive consent.

A totalitarian system which is trying to modernize cannot rest only on such passive consent. It must generate sufficiently active consent and political participation to implement its designs for social change. Although often overlooked, the question of political participation, at least at the level of policy implementation, is extremely important to a Communist state which seeks to be a modernizing system. To uproot traditional attitudes and to cultivate the self-sacrifice needed for rapid economic development, active consent is essential.

Another argument which is often emphasized is the violent cost and the repressive nature of the Chinese Communist government. It is often forgotten that the Communist revolution in China was and is a peasant revolution. As such it is trying to telescope the stages of modernization and therefore to crystallize the cost of the modernizing revolution. There is simply no painless way to modernize.

The cost of modernization can be paid as it was during the development of the Anglo-Saxon model—through legal violence or self-repression and "holy watching." In many senses the Puritan revolution was not only a revolution in politics but also a social revolution which emphasized individual responsibility reinforced through communal inspection. Profound self-examination was accompanied by overwhelming social repression.[13] Like the Puritan revolution, most modernizing movements emphasize asceticism, puritanic attitudes, holy watching, conformity, and an entirely new belief system. (In both Cuba and China, for example, almost the first step of the new revolutionary governments was to abolish prostitution.) In this sense the Chinese case is a variant of the Puritan revolution. Carrying the analogy a little further, one finds that a witch hunt is a common characteristic of both.

13. For a profound analysis of the Puritan revolution, see Michael Walzer, *The Revolution of the Saints: A Study in the Origins of Radical Politics* (Cambridge: Harvard University Press, 1965).

The Chinese revolution has kept the cost of modernization low by emphasizing the eufunctional nature of conflict and by stressing persuasion rather than coercion. By contrast, the cost of the Soviet revolution, with its Stalinist model of repression and coercive change, compares highly unfavorably with the Chinese model. Nevertheless, all modern political systems arose in the context of physical force and were nurtured by violence. The present generation of Americans tends to forget this fact. Recent disturbances only make it clear that modernization is by no means complete and that whole groups have been left out of the modernizing process.

Another reason for the misunderstanding of violence in contemporary Chinese politics is that the study of individual countries has been overemphasized at the expense of comparative studies. Beyond a certain point, sound knowledge of any given country must take into account a comparative perspective. Social science must even integrate comparative Communist studies with the analysis of other political systems. In the field of Soviet studies, this effort is already being made.[14]

A similar order of misperceptions exists in China. Many Chinese are passionately convinced that the West destroyed the Chinese soul and the Chinese personality.[15] As Professor John K. Fairbank has often emphasized, the Western expansion, although beneficial to the West and ultimately to China's modernization, destroyed

14. For further thoughts on this problem, see "Symposium: Comparative Politics and Communist Systems: Introductory Remarks," *Slavic Review*, Vol. XXVI, No. 1, March 1967, pp. 1–28; Chalmers Johnson, "The Role of Social Science in China Scholarship," *World Politics*, Vol. XVII, No. 2, January 1965, pp. 256–271; H. Gordon Skilling, "Interest Groups and Communist Politics," *World Politics*, Vol. XVIII, No. 3, April 1966, pp. 435–451; and John A. Armstrong, "Sources of Administrative Behavior: Some Soviet and West European Comparisons," *American Political Science Review*, Vol. LIX, No. 3, September 1965, pp. 643–655. Barrington Moore, Jr., *Social Origins of Dictatorship and Democracy* (Boston: Beacon Press, 1966).

15. For a historical account of how the Chinese viewed the nineteenth-century West, see Arthur Waley, *The Opium War Through Chinese Eyes* (Stanford: Stanford University Press, 1958).

Imperial China.[16] Perhaps the most hated symbol of the age of imperialism was the destructive opium trade, to which American merchants certainly contributed their share. Although it is true that the opium trade could not have existed if the Chinese government had rationalized and modernized its bureaucratic apparatus and its enforcement agencies, the issue of whether China or the West deserves more blame is still under debate.[17] Quite obviously, the Chinese Communists do not want the memory of the alleged offenses to fade away.[18]

Nor does the list of Chinese grievances stop here. To the leaders in Peking, the United States "Open Door Policy" forms part of an unbroken spectrum of aggression. For evidence of this crime, the Chinese point to the American presence on China's periphery, the American trade embargo, Washington's attempts to keep China excluded from the United Nations, and the American government's hostility to what they consider to be their legitimate aims in foreign policy.

The Maoist view of international politics has generally been described as that of a rigid bipolar world composed of socialist and imperialist camps. Actually, this analysis is not quite accurate. It is true that to Mao no nation can be really neutral in the long run. It must "lean to one side." [19] China thus refuses to accept any criticism of her foreign policy from countries like Yugoslavia and India while still granting them the status of neutrality. Any na-

16. John K. Fairbank, "Why Peking Casts Us as the Villain," *The New York Times Magazine*, May 22, 1966. For a detailed study of Sino-Western contacts in the mid-nineteenth century, see Fairbank, *Trade and Diplomacy on the China Coast: The Opening of the Treaty Ports, 1842–1854* (Cambridge: Harvard University Press, 1964).

17. For an exhaustive study of this issue, see Hsin-pao Chang, *Commissioner Lin and the Opium War* (Cambridge: Harvard University Press, 1964).

18. See, for example, "How to Understand the United States," Shih Shih Shou-ts'e (*Current Affairs Handbook*), Vol. I, No. 2, November 5, 1950, in *Current Background*, No. 32, November 29, 1950, p. 3.

19. See Mao Tse-tung, "On the People's Democratic Dictatorship," *Selected Works of Mao Tse-tung* (5 vols., New York: International Publishers, 1954–64), Vol. V, p. 415.

tion which claims to oppose colonialism and neocolonialism must align itself with Peking.

This obsession with imperialism has dominated Chinese foreign policy and cannot help but distort China's perception of America's world role. Although Mao has sometimes propounded his concept of "intermediate zones" to include West Europe and Japan, moving away from the United States is a precondition for membership. The inevitability of eventually siding with one camp or the other still dominates China's diplomatic attitude.

Yet a description based on a dichotomy between socialist and imperialist camps is no longer relevant. Ever since the rapid deterioration of Sino-Soviet relations, China has increasingly substituted the concept of "revolutionary camp" for "socialist camp." Judging from Chinese commentaries, "revolutionary camp" is a euphemism for China, Albania, and a few selected protégés. Most emphatically, it does not include the Soviet Union. To side with the revolutionary camp is to side with China against the United States, the revisionist powers of the Bloc, and the wishy-washy neutrals of the Third World. China is quick to encourage the anti-imperialist aspects of neutralism, but she does not expect it to last.

China's ideological attitude, therefore, is shaped by opposition to America as the leader of the imperialist camp rather than of the capitalist world. In the final analysis, it is not a Marxist-Leninist evaluation of international relations which shapes the attitudes of Chinese leaders and molds their perceptions of the United States and the world. It is rather their reconstruction of Chinese history and their sense of continuity with the age of imperialism.

It has often been argued that China feels special hostility toward America. This is true to a limited extent because China perceives America as the principal threat to her security. Yet China's resentment of the United States is based equally on a general diplomatic outlook which her leaders apply to the entire world. They consider that the age of imperialism has not yet ended. For that reason, they oppose anybody and everybody whom they consider to be "soft on imperialism."

Students of Chinese foreign policy have often been puzzled by China's simultaneous hostility to the West, the Soviet Union, and

India, especially since the latter is supposed to be a leader of the Third World. The only measurement justifying such hostility to these disparate sociopolitical systems with their conflicting foreign policy aims is the yardstick of imperialism. In this sense the Chinese are much more similar to fundamentalist Americans than either side realizes. Just as the Chinese world view is determined by who is "soft on imperialism," so the American fundamentalists base their decisions on who is "soft on Communism."

It is often argued that Sino-American relations have remained frozen for twenty years. Probably the fact most responsible for this impression is that neither China nor America has made any serious effort to clarify their respective foreign policy goals toward each other. Each has acted as if the other occupies the lowest order of priority. Each has perpetuated a level of vague confusion which is almost unmatched in international relations. Neither side has ever expressed these bilateral relations in concrete terms. Both have treated their relationship either as subservient to their general world view or as a means to their domestic needs.

Nevertheless, Communist Chinese hostility toward the United States since 1949 has varied sharply in its intensity. Initially, Peking almost seemed to be trying to give Washington a chance. These feelers were retracted when Truman extended American protection to Taiwan, a move which showed that Americans had made their final choice. During the Korean War, anti-American press attacks constantly stressed the threat of an American invasion of China and launched increasingly bitter tirades against the United States. Taking General Douglas MacArthur as the spokesman for American policies and dismissing President Harry Truman as a "faithful running dog," the Chinese saw the United States as ruled by a small clique of capitalists who actively promoted a massive attack on China. This view corresponds more to the so-called "devil's theory" of international relations than to an orthodox application of Marxism-Leninism. It showed once again that the Chinese look upon the United States primarily as an imperialist power rather than as a capitalist bastion.

The Chinese also used the threat of an American invasion for domestic consumption. It was undoubtedly a useful instrument in promoting unity and in partially counteracting the disruptive influence of the Agrarian Reform Law of 1950. In some cases the possibility of an American attack was used to justify both the acceleration and the retardation of various regional land reform schedules.[20]

Toward the end of the Korean War, the so-call "Three-Anti" and "Five-Anti" (san-fan and wu-fan) movements, together with the acceleration of agrarian reform, started to overshadow the anti-American campaigns. At the same time, an overall easing of Chinese foreign policy could be discerned. By the time of the Bandung Conference of Afro-Asian nations in 1955, Chinese comments on relations with the United States assumed a new height in mildness. Rather than being rabid warmongers, American leaders were now seen as divided between peace and war, with the international situation definitely favoring peace.[21] Whether this viewpoint was deliberately expounded to harmonize with the spirit of co-operation which China tried to project at Bandung or whether it represented a genuine shift in Chinese attitudes is still open to debate. In either case, however, Peking would have been hard put to rebuff a favorable American response.

A number of indications suggesting that Chinese attitudes toward the United States and toward imperialism were softening were evident as early as 1953. As China experienced strains with the Soviet Union and began to move away from the Soviet model, her leaders began to soften their criticisms of both the United States and the Third World. Probably the first example was the change in attitude on the part of Chinese negotiators at the Korean Armistice negotiations. Another was the Geneva Conference of 1954, where China put pressure on North Vietnam to accept the 17th Parallel as a military demarcation line.

Among other things, these indications could be attributed to the Chinese desire to disengage from a hostile foreign policy for domestic reasons. Deprived of guaranteed Soviet military support, Chinese leaders faced the tasks of consolidating the new political

20. See, for example, "Land Reform in East China To Be Accelerated," *Shanghai News*, December 16, 1950, in *Survey of the China Mainland Press*, No. 35, December 21, 1959, pp. 7–8.

21. Chou En-lai, "The Present International Situation, China's Foreign Policy, and the Question of the Liberation of Taiwan," Report to the National People's Congress, June 28, 1956, in *Current Background*, No. 395, July 5, 1956, pp. 2–15.

system and tackling the tasks of rapid modernization with large-scale outlays on defense. A high point of the rapidly increasing conciliatory attitude was Chou En-lai's offer, repeated twice at Bandung on April 23 and 24, 1955, to negotiate all differences, including Taiwan, with the United States. It is often overlooked that the subdiplomatic system of bilateral talks at the ambassadorial level began at this time.

The initiation of these talks was neither smooth nor easy. The United States was then under a Republican administration. Its foreign policy architect was Secretary John Foster Dulles, an intense believer in moral universalism. The first serious steps in this direction were taken by a third party. In February 1955 the Burmese Prime Minister U Nu visited China and tried to mediate between Peking and Washington. By translating the Chinese view to Secretary Dulles when he visited Rangoon shortly thereafter, he played an important role in getting the talks underway. Another influential figure was Krishna Menon of India, who played the role of a persistent irritator by insisting on being a mediator. A further consideration on Washington's side was the need for an excuse to avoid including Communist China at the summit meeting scheduled for July 1955. In fact both sides have found the talks useful in combating accusations of unwillingness to compromise.

As it turned out, Great Britain played the role of actual mediator in getting the talks started. Upon receiving a nod from Washington, London negotiated the mechanics of the first meeting. On July 25, 1955, China and the United States issued a joint communiqué announcing the initiation of this subdiplomacy. Quoting its diplomatic reservation of 1954, Washington made it clear that any talks with China did not involve diplomatic recognition. In spite of this reservation, however, the bilateral talks represented a great advance from Panmunjon and Geneva, where all human and social contact was forbidden. At Geneva, the British delegation had continued to act as a go-between.

Talks between the United States and China started in Geneva on August 1, 1955. The day before, in order to seize the diplomatic initiative and to create a favorable atmosphere for the talks, Peking had released eleven American airmen previously imprisoned in China. Washington made no official comment on this gesture.

At the same time, Chou En-lai made another conciliatory move by issuing a statement expressing hope that the talks would lead to a peaceful settlement, at least on the question of the return of civilians on both sides.[22] Dulles' press conference on August 2 responded favorably to Chou's remarks.[23]

In spite of this cordial beginning, the only agreement which has ever resulted from thirteen years of sporadic negotiations came on September 10, 1955. It is a pity that neither side ever considered this agreement on the exchange of civilian personnel as a sufficient foundation upon which diplomatic contacts could be strengthened or extended. Each has continually accused the other of misinterpreting this agreement and therefore of not fulfilling it. The Chinese assumed that the exchange would not extend to those Americans who had violated Chinese law. This reservation meant that nineteen Americans held in Chinese prisons could not leave China without a thorough review of their cases. In a similar category were twenty-four Chinese serving prison sentences in the United States.

Nevertheless, both sides retreated from their original position. On January 29, 1956, Chou En-lai hinted that the judicial review which was then in process would affect the American prisoners favorably. Similarly, Washington finally announced that any Chinese serving a prison sentence in the United States was free to leave. Only two out of the twenty-four chose to do so; one opted for Communist China, and one chose Taiwan. Out of a total of sixty-six Americans in China at the time of this agreement, including nineteen in prison, only four were still in China in 1966. As late as 1964, however, Dean Rusk continued to complain that China had never fulfilled her commitment in this regard. The Chinese have continuously countercharged that the Chinese in the United States feared going back to China because of American intimidation.

The problems of transportation and visas for Americans in China were handled by the British Embassy in Peking. Similar arrangements for the Chinese in America were covered by the

22. *The New York Times,* August 2, 1955.

23. *Department of State Bulletin,* Vol. XXXIII, No. 842, August 15, 1955, pp. 260–262.

Indian Embassy. Neither of these two embassies has ever given any indication that unusual obstructions were placed in the path of those who wanted to leave. In fact, practically every post office in the United States carried a general notice informing all Chinese who wanted to go to Communist China that they should contact the Indian Embassy. Very few Chinese took advantage of this offer. Most Chinese, even while serving prison terms in America, were naturally unwilling to return either to Taiwan or to the mainland.

Further efforts to relax Sino-American hostility and to widen the contacts between the two countries took place on August 6, 1956, when Peking suddenly offered visas to fifteen American journalists and invited them as guests of the Chinese government for one month. This move apparently caught Washington by surprise. The reaction was immediately negative. On the following day, the State Department announced that there would be no relaxation of its ban on travel to China and that its passport policy would continue to reflect this decision. On August 20 President Eisenhower lent his official endorsement.

By September of 1957, when Washington finally came around to accepting China's offer, the situation had already changed. This time it was the Chinese who turned down the American offer. In 1966 and 1967 Washington unilaterally relaxed the passport requirements which had previously banned travel to China. Although a number of bona fide professionals concerned with China were now permitted to go, the Chinese have continued to treat this offer in the same manner as Washington responded to the unilateral offer of 1956.

During this period of conflict, Peking held that increasing contacts in the form of both trade and the exchange of visitors should not await a general settlement of Sino-American relations, diplomatic recognition, or admission to the United Nations. Unfortunately, America's position at that time was all or nothing. Beginning with the Kennedy Administration and continuing through Johnson's presidency, the positions of both sides underwent a complete reversal. Now it is the Americans who favor gradualism and a piecemeal approach, while the Chinese have developed a totalistic attitude.

The Cultural Revolution has further dampened the prospects

for improved relations. Although Washington has made a number of offers, China has not even responded. In part this silence can be attributed to the confusion surrounding domestic upheavals and to the urgency of coping with more pressing matters. Yet a more fundamental reason goes back to the Sino-Soviet dispute. Moscow has repeatedly charged that the Chinese do not practice what they preach. Soviet commentators accuse Peking of being fiery in word but passive in deed, particularly with respect to Vietnam. Other Communist parties privately echo this suspicion, with some justification. For China to respond to American overtures while the Vietnam War continues to rage would only corroborate this charge.

The history of Sino-American relations thus illustrates the vagaries of international relations. When the Chinese were ready for gradualism, America was totalistic. When America adopted gradualism, the Chinese had swung to totalism. Making concilia tory gestures that the other side will not accept is often a clever diplomatic trick. In arms control negotiations, for example, the Soviet Union has sometimes announced a dramatic offer, thus getting the credit for easing the deadlock while remaining confident that Moscow's bluff will not be called. Yet in the Sino-American case, a genuine matter of timing was at stake. A good deal of tension could probably have been eased if the moods and desires of both parties could somehow have been synchronized.

From 1955 to 1957 the biggest stumbling block facing Chinese gradualism was the American insistence that no improvement in Sino-American relations was possible until China signed an agreement renouncing the use of force in solving international problems. During this period the Chinese were willing to submit to this condition, but they insisted that it could not extend to Taiwan. From the very beginning, they have contended that Taiwan is a domestic question and not an international problem. Any American pressure on behalf of an agreement covering Taiwan would thus constitute unwarranted interference in China's domestic politics.

China's willingness to renounce force except with respect to Taiwan conformed to the policy expressed in the Five Principles of 1954. In other words, the Chinese were prepared to extend the Bandung spirit to the United States but not to Taiwan. They were ready to accept that outstanding differences between nations whose social and political systems were considered to be poles apart could be settled through negotiation. They merely reserved the right to use force within what they held to be their sovereign boundaries.

Significantly this attitude toward Taiwan corresponded to a similar position taken toward Tibet in 1950. The tone and rationale of the Chinese reply to India regarding the use of force in Tibet also rested on the argument of domestic jurisdiction. In other words, as we shall see in Chapter Six, China's recalcitrance does not spring from the desire to use force in international relations but rather from insistence on the full and maximum limits of national sovereignty, including complete independence in matters of domestic jurisdiction. Once again, even if this is a nineteenth-century attitude, no major power has yet abandoned it.

As far as the United States was concerned, the only major problem through which Sino-American hostilities could erupt into open war at that time was the question of Taiwan. Not only had President Truman put the Seventh Fleet in the Formosa Straits to act as a buffer between Taiwan and the mainland, but in January of 1955 Washington also signed a specific treaty with the Nationalist government promising American protection. This legal commitment, however unwisely undertaken, and the policy background preceding it naturally inhibit the State Department's freedom of action.

From the American point of view, a Communist Chinese agreement to renounce the use of force without the exception of Taiwan would have had several diplomatic benefits. It would have eased Washington's worry regarding an open military confrontation with China over Taiwan. Legally and diplomatically, it would have strengthened the position of the Nationalist government. It would have also paved the way for both China and Taiwan to accept a two-Chinas solution. As far as the United States was concerned, such an agreement would have led to a realistic solution of the Sino-American conflict in the Far East. In fact, the United States and China are still debating the issue.[24]

24. For a very detailed account of Sino-American negotiations, including the various drafts and positions adopted by both sides on

Each side immediately tested the limits of the other's intentions in the Taiwan crisis of 1958. Besides testing both Soviet intentions and the Sino-Soviet alliance of 1950, the Chinese were also exploring the nature of America's alliance with the Nationalists. In addition, they were reinforcing their point that Taiwan could not be included in an agreement to renounce the use of force. In this respect China's attitude during the Taiwan crisis was almost a gesture of defiance.

The most surprising thing about the Taiwan crisis of 1958 was that Washington, Moscow, and Peking all understood the limits of the flare-up. All of them made every effort to avoid direct confrontations. Neither the United States nor the Soviet Union used or even threatened force until it was clear that direct negotiations, then temporarily suspended, would be resumed. Thus Moscow waited until September 7 before threatening the United States. Soviet decision-makers already knew that a decision to resume the talks had been taken on September 4. Similarly, the United States waited until the night of September 14 to break the Chinese blockade—after the talks had already started.

Meanwhile, the Chinese continued to announce that they bore no hostility to the people of Quemoy and Matsu. Instead, they asserted that the bombardment was a symbolic protest against the American imperialists and their henchmen in Taiwan. They used this pledge of friendship to the population of the islands as a convenient excuse for suspending the bombing periodically. Marshal P'eng Teh-huai's orders to the Chinese armed forces signified that the bombing halts were intended to permit the people of Quemoy and Matsu to replenish their supplies. Furthermore, by bombing only on alternate days they could avoid unnecessary casualties. It is worth noting that during the crisis both Mao and Liu Shao-ch'i were away from Peking on an inspection tour of the provinces.

In some ways the Chinese achieved the goals that motivated their attitude toward the Crisis. Specifically they discovered the definite limits of the Sino-Soviet alliance. Although Eisenhower misinterpreted the Soviet notes of September 7 and 19, the Chinese did not. Soviet leaders appeared to be threatening the United

the question of the renunciation of force, see Kenneth T. Young, *Negotiating with the Chinese Communists* (New York: McGraw-Hill, 1968).

States, but they were actually informing Peking that the Sino-Soviet alliance of 1950 would not provide China with a nuclear umbrella to achieve her national goals. Once the Chinese received this message, they decided to build their own nuclear umbrella.

As for American intentions, the Chinese also discovered that the United States was firmly committed at least to the defense of Taiwan if not to the offshore islands. In spite of tremendous pressure exerted by friendly and neutral governments on behalf of a conciliatory position on the Taiwan crisis, the American government could neither permit the fall of Taiwan nor risk a direct military confrontation with China, thus repeating Korea on a vast scale. Under these circumstances there was nothing for both Chinese and Americans to do but to go back to Warsaw, resume their talks, and continue to argue over the renunciation of force.

Most analysts of Sino-American relations have labeled Taiwan the most important stumbling block to a Sino-American rapprochement. This problem is so fundamental that it deserves an analysis of various underlying factors. Obviously Taiwan cannot be regarded as simply a matter of a border adjustment entailing the loss of territorial irridenta. Other irridentist problems, including that of Outer Mongolia, have been settled in a manner unfavorable to China's territorial claims. Taiwan would not be the first case where China reluctantly agreed to an adverse settlement. The central fact is that Taiwan is not primarily a territorial problem. It is a symbolic and political problem. As such it does belong to the category of border settlements with Outer Mongolia, Burma, Nepal, Pakistan, and Afghanistan.

Taiwan signifies to China the existence of a rival government. It poses a fundamental challenge to the legitimacy of Communist rule on the mainland. Outer Mongolia did not constitute such a threat. The only solution, therefore, is either to return Taiwan to China, which would be impossible under the present balance of world power, or slowly to strip Taiwan of its status as an alternative symbol of legitimacy. This latter possibility would require both internal and external changes in Taiwan's position. Externally, Taipei would have to give up its claim to the mainland, just as Peking would have to give up its claims to Taiwan. Internally, a Chinese government would gradually have to give way to a Taiwanese government.

The United States can influence both of these changes. Yet even Washington has its limitations, both domestic and foreign, with respect to the pace of such changes. China might be able to tolerate a Taiwanese Taiwan and might even permit an adverse territorial settlement, but a Chinese Taiwan would be a constant threat to the legitimacy of the Peking government. With a Taiwanese Taiwan, Communist leaders might settle merely for the return of the offshore islands. As far as the United States is concerned, there are no legal obstacles to this type of arrangement. In fact, the Eisenhower Declaration of 1958 already placed the offshore islands outside the pale of the American commitment.

In the years following 1950, the United States has never promised to help the Nationalist government re-establish itself on the mainland. American policy-makers have promised protection and aid against a Communist Chinese takeover. They have been very careful not to use Nationalist troops in any conflict with China where their presence might be misconstrued. Thus Nationalist forces were used neither in Korea nor in Vietnam.

A Taiwanese Taiwan would improve America's moral and diplomatic position in the world. It is true that the Han Chinese, like the Ibos in Nigeria, enjoy higher standards of education, job opportunities, and living conditions. Relegating them to minority status might involve serious setbacks for Taiwan's economic growth. Yet the American example proves that the rapid creation of wealth does not lead to the equal distribution of benefits. In the case of Taiwan, those excluded from the bulk of wealth and power are not a minority but a majority. Their independence might thus satisfy advocates of self-determination while simultaneously removing a major irritant in Sino-American relations. Just as the Chinese Communists were forced to accept the independence of Outer Mongolia, pressure from the great powers might bring about a similar future for Taiwan. This step might blossom into the normalization of Sino-American relations in particular and the Far Eastern situation in general.

Another area which deserves careful examination is the increasing American involvement in Vietnam. Communist China's perceptions of this entanglement exert a profound influence on Sino-American relations. Ever since 1964 Vietnam has occupied a central place in Chinese discussions and debates. It has also occupied a key position in the internal factional disputes over foreign policy during the period of the Cultural Revolution.

As the American involvement in Vietnam escalated during 1965, China witnessed a serious controversy regarding its possible consequences. Chinese policy-makers probably revived the image of Korea in 1950. From February 1965 to August 1966, at least two well-defined factions illustrated different Chinese perceptions of the Sino-American confrontation in Vietnam.

One faction was apparently led by Chief of Staff Lo Jui-ch'ing and Peking's Mayor P'eng Chen, joined by Liu Shao-ch'i in early 1966. This group drew a clear parallel with Korea and expected the United States, sooner or later, to cross the 17th Parallel. They also expected that if China intervened to protect her buffer state of North Vietnam, the United States would extend the war to China. They therefore emphasized greater military preparedness at home and rapprochement with the Soviet Union abroad. It is possible that these men, who suffered most from the Cultural Revolution, were using Vietnam to forestall political attacks and to strengthen their position by cultivating good relations with the Soviet Union.

By September 1965, another faction, led by Defense Minister Lin Piao and supported by Chairman Mao, was urging the Vietnamese to practice self-reliance. This group, which constituted the motive force behind the Cultural Revolution, was forced to argue that the Vietnam War would not be escalated into China. They also insisted that the Vietnamese could get along perfectly well without massive Chinese aid. From their point of view, Vietnam could not be used as an excuse for postponing the Cultural Revolution or for strengthening their opponents. Nevertheless, the first eight months following the first American bombing raids on North Vietnam witnessed no major political moves. In short, it is difficult to ascertain whether the positions of both these groups sprang primarily from domestic considerations or from international realities.

Whatever their motivations, the former group can be called "interventionists" and the latter "noninterventionists." The interventionists claimed that some form of cooperation with the Soviet Union was the only way to defeat the United States. This strategy would at least guarantee the survival of North Vietnam and the avoidance of a direct American attack on the Chinese mainland. For China to intervene in North Vietnam without invoking an American retaliation would require a Soviet umbrella. However strongly they doubted Soviet reliability, they felt that America could not afford to take the risk.

Their opponents, while agreeing that the possibility of an American attack required some kind of preparation, still stressed that China should not follow a strategy of the type adopted by the Soviet Union during World War II, that is, cooperating with an enemy in order to achieve some larger purpose. Instead, they urged a return to the self-reliance practiced by the Communists in the period of anti-Japanese resistance and civil war.

The Mao-Lin group thus emphasized that the United States could never defeat a revolutionary and self-reliant Vietnamese population. Chinese aid, therefore, should be limited and conditional. It should be augmented only if the guerrilla movement seemed to be on the verge of collapse or if the United States actually crossed the 17th Parallel. In the event of Chinese entanglement, China still had to follow her own advice, that is, self-reliance. The noninterventionists also attached a further rider on Chinese assistance to Vietnam. They offered only as much aid from China as "international circumstances would permit." This is an old and familiar escape clause often used by major powers to evade firm commitments.

When the United States began the bombing of North Vietnam in February 1965, the Chinese press began to publish a re-evaluation of the military aspects of the Vietnam conflict. In particular, Chinese commentaries began to emphasize that the United States had shifted strategic gears from the "special war" to a "limited war" of the Korean type. They also interpreted the American strategy of "flexible response" to mean gradual escalation from limited warfare to global nuclear warfare. The regular bombing of North Vietnam seemed to be a prelude to a ground attack on North Vietnam and therefore a repetition of Korea. Throughout 1965 the Chinese were trying to make up their minds as to the significance of the bombing with respect to China's foreign policy and national security. The only historical precedent they could use as a guide was Korea.

Yet the circumstances of the Vietnam War were entirely different from Korea. The United States had made it clear that crossing the 17th Parallel was out of the question. China had also threatened to extend the fighting anywhere in Asia if the United States attacked North Vietnam and China. Although similar warnings had circulated during the course of the Korean War, communications had not been quite so clear. For one thing, the Chinese have continued to carry on the Sino-American talks at Warsaw throughout the duration of the Vietnam conflict. They have become less and less eager to publicize these talks or to place any importance on them because of Soviet, Indian, and generally anti-Chinese accusations of a Sino-American deal over Vietnam.

Furthermore, even if the Chinese were ready to intervene in Vietnam, the logistical problem would differ from the Korean case. There were only two highways and two railroads leading into North Vietnam. This difficulty would hinder the Chinese from moving substantial amounts of manpower and material resources to fight a limited war. Intervention was thus less of a strategic possibility in Vietnam than in Korea.

Finally, the Chinese were also convinced that if China did intervene, the ensuing war would not resemble Korea. Peking could no longer calculate that China would be treated as a sanctuary. In other words, the Chinese had to be prepared not for a limited war in Vietnam, but for a general war. This realization sparked a great debate on how to fight a general war against an enemy who might even use nuclear weapons. The interventionists believed that the war could still remain limited if they could secure a sufficient nuclear umbrella from the Soviet Union. From their point of view a sufficient Soviet involvement would inhibit the United States from expanding the war. Noninterventionists pointed to the difficulty of extracting such a commitment. They reasoned that firm Soviet support would require a concession of such order and magnitude that China would have to become a satellite. This prospect would certainly weaken the hand of the Mao-Lin group.

The self-reliance faction in China has also been called the "people's war" faction. In a series of articles and editorials, this group began to react strongly to Lo Jui-ch'ing's emphasis on the strategy of cooperation pursued during World War II. Asserting that the United States would neither escalate the war nor get out of Vietnam, they stressed that the fate of Vietnam was ultimately in the hands of the Vietnamese. The support for the National Liberation Front expressed by this faction has always remained conditional.[25] Emphasizing China's own civil war and the war of national resistance and pointing to China's revolutionary traditions, advocates of this position minimized the importance of outside assistance.[26]

Among the opponents of this view of self-reliance was Lo Jui-ch'ing, who felt that the Vietnamese conflict would certainly spill over into China.[27] In the face of such a grave risk, he hinted that the socialist countries might have to come to the aid of Vietnam.

25. These views started to come out in the spring and summer of 1965. See editorial. "The Great Victory of Leninism," *Hung-ch'i* (*Red Flag*), No. 4, April 30, 1965, *Survey of China Mainland Magazines* (*SCMM*), No. 469, May 17, 1965, pp. 1–7; and *Commentator*, "Drive the US Aggressors Out of Vietnam," *Hung-ch'i* (*Red Flag*), No. 4, April 30, 1965, in *SCMM*, No. 469, May 17, 1965, pp. 7–10.

26. See Shih Tung-hsiang, "The Deciding Factor of Victory or Defeat in War Is Man, Not Matter," *Hung-ch'i* (*Red Flag*), No. 7, June 14, 1965, in *SCMM*, No. 477, July 6, 1965, pp. 1–13; Kuo Li-chun, "On Dialectics of Paper Tiger and Real Tiger," *Che-hsueh Yen-chiu* (*Study of Philosophy*), No. 3, May 25, 1965, in *SCMM*, No. 481, July 26, 1965, pp. 5–21; Ho Lung, "The Democratic Traditions of the Chinese People's Liberation Army," *Hung-ch'i* (*Red Flag*), No. 8, July 31, 1965, in *SCMM*, No. 483, Aug. 9, 1965, pp. 1–15; Yang Ch'eng-wu, "Seizure of the Luting Bridge," *Hung-ch'i* (*Red Flag*), No. 9, Aug. 21, 1965 in *SCMM*, No. 489, Sept. 13, 1965, pp. 9–17; editorial, "Inherit and Develop the Great Revolutionary Spirit of the Long-March of the Workers and Peasants Red Army," *Ch'ien-hsien* (*Front*), Peking, No. 19, Oct. 10, 1965, in *SCMM*, No. 572, Apr. 17, 1967, pp. 15–19.

27. Lo Jui-ch'ing, "Commemorate the Victory over German Fascism! Carry the Struggle Against US Imperialism Through to the End!" *Hung-ch'i* (*Red Flag*), No. 5, May 1965, *SCMM*, No. 469, May 17, 1965, pp. 11–22. A different viewpoint was expressed by the editorial department of *Jen Min Jih Pao* (*People's Daily*), May 9, 1965, in their article "On the Historical Experience of the War Against Fascism." It did not link World War II strategy with the war in Vietnam. For further support of Lo Jui-ch'ing's position see Ch'ang Kung, "The Bankruptcy of US 'Special War' in South Vietnam," *Shih-chieh Chih-shih* (*World Knowledge*), No. 12, June 25, 1965, in *SCMM*, No. 481, July 26, 1965, pp. 1–4.

To support his case, he cited what he called the Stalinist strategy of "active defense." As applied by Stalin in World War II, "active defense" could develop into a "strategic offense." Such a strategy would naturally presuppose some form of Soviet cooperation.

It is surprising how little Lo Jui-ch'ing grasped either the essence of Mao's self-evaluation or the fundamental nature of the Sino-Soviet dispute. After Stalin's death, and once de-Stalinization had become routine, Mao was not interested in evoking Stalin's name in support of strategic or ideological programs. Instead he has been relying on Lenin and on himself to legitimize his innovations. Either Lo made a serious misinterpretation of this aspect of the Sino-Soviet dispute or he was lulled into security by an overestimation of his power and position.

Probably another reason for Lo's analysis was the growing belief that in the face of the massive land, air, and naval involvement of American forces, the strategy of people's war as practiced by the North Vietnamese and by the National Liberation Front could not win by itself. As Lo pointed out, the "South Vietnamese Liberation Army" would face the difficult task of fighting "regular" as well as "guerrilla" wars at the same time. The only alternative, therefore, was counterescalation combined with either Chinese or Sino-Soviet support.

In 1965 and 1966 there were some hints that the Soviets were prepared to cooperate to a limited extent with the Chinese, and thereby to present a joint Sino-Soviet front in support of North Vietnam. According to Edward Crankshaw, writing in the London *Observer*, the Soviets demanded facilities for air transport and personnel in South China near the Sino-Vietnamese border. Not only were such requests turned down, but according to recurrent press reports, the Chinese have been constantly interfering with Soviet shipments to North Vietnam.

A number of hypotheses can be advanced in this connection. The people's war faction in China may have wanted to keep the Soviet supplies at a low level and therefore to control the level of counter-escalation by the North Vietnamese and the NLF. They may also have wished to force the Soviets to transport their aid by sea and thereby to use the harbor facilities at Haiphong, thus increasing the risk of a direct Soviet-American confrontation. Actually, such a confrontation would help both factions. To those who wanted greater Soviet participation, it would seriously jeopardize the Soviet-American détente and increasingly commit the Soviet Union to a joint Sino-Soviet venture. To the people's war faction, it would mean that the Soviet Union would join China on Chinese terms.

In spite of this debate and the uncertainty of Chinese policy toward United States involvement in Vietnam, great emphasis was placed on preparedness for war in China throughout 1965. The Chinese recognized that if a general war did come, it would lead to great destruction. They acknowledged that the United States could inflict heavy casualties and that China would have to mobilize vast reserves of manpower. They believed that the United States would be able to destroy "at one stroke, our military strength, economic centers, and communications hubs by launching sudden raids, and thus try to deprive us of the ability to resist." The escalation of war to China was regarded as highly probable.[28] The Chinese also believed that the war would be fought in three dimensions, "rear, front, and everywhere." All this made it imperative that everyone must be a soldier.[29]

To achieve this goal, intensive militia training and constant preparedness were emphasized. The fear of conflict probably gave a great impetus to the rapid attainment of nuclear research and weapons capabilities. A growing emphasis was placed on the destructiveness of modern conventional and nuclear weapons and also on the necessity to produce them. There was growing fear

28. Chang Ching, "How to View the Enemy's Opposition," *Hung-Ch'i* (*Red Flag*), No. 2, Feb. 27, 1965, in SCMM, No. 462, Mar. 29, 1965; "Hold High the Great Red Banner of Mao Tse-tung's Thought and Courageously Drive Ahead," *Peking Review*, No. 40, Oct. 1, 1965, pp. 8–11; "Complete All Preparations for Smashing Aggression by US Imperialism," *Chung-kuo Ch'ing-nien* (*China Youth*), No. 23, Dec. 1, 1965, in SCMM, No. 508, Jan. 24, 1966, pp. 39–42. Fang Mu-hui, "A Militia Force of Returned Overseas Chinese on the Front of Coastal Defense," *Ch'iao-wu Pao* (*Overseas Chinese Affairs Journal*), No. 6, Dec. 1965, in SCMM, No. 510, Feb. 7, 1966, pp. 1–3. According to some reports, it was during this period that China started to fortify the island of Hainan.

29. Lin Yun-cheng, "The Role of People's Militia," *Peking Review*, No. 6, Feb. 5, 1965.

that the Japan-Korea treaty would be used to bring Japan in on the American side in the event of any North Korean-American or Sino-American war. According to the Chinese interpretation of the "Three-Arrow Plan" and the "Flying Dragon Plan," Japan was to support the United States and to put her forces under American command within thirty days of such hostility.[30]

During the height of this debate, Lin Piao's famous article on people's war came out in *Jen-min Jih-pao* (*People's Daily*) on September 3, 1965. Contrary to the assumption that this was Peking's clarion call to world revolution, this document should be considered as a major foreign policy statement by the Mao-Lin group on Vietnam and indirectly on Sino-American relations. Among other things, it emphasized that massive American intervention had changed the status of the Vietnam conflict from a guerrilla war to a war of national resistance. Because of this transformation, the National Liberation Front was following an incorrect line. To fight a war of national resistance, the Front was told to follow a united front policy. Finally, Lin's article gave notice to the National Liberation Front that China's assistance would vary according to international circumstances. Primarily addressed to the North Vietnamese and to the National Liberation Front, Lin emphasized that the Chinese prefer to follow what had been called the "low-risk policy of indirect conflict." [31]

30. Lin Yun-cheng, *op. cit.*; Liu Hua-ch'iu and Shih Chen, "Look How US Imperialism Is Stepping Up Preparations for Attack on China!" *Chung-kuo Ch'ing-nien* (*China Youth*), No. 23, Dec. 1965, in *SCMM*, No. 507, Jan. 17, 1966, pp. 1–3. Curiously enough, this article also mentioned, among other bases, two U.S. bases in India, although it did not give any troop figures for these bases.

31. Lin Piao, "Long Live the Victory of the People's War!" *Peking Review*, Vol. VIII, No. 36, September 3, 1965, pp. 9–30. For a reasoned analysis of this article, see D. P. Mozingo and T. W. Robinson, "Lin Piao on 'People's War': China Takes a Second Look at Vietnam," Rand Memorandum RM-4814-PR, Nov. 1965, especially p. 18. It must be kept in mind, however, that Lin Piao's article by no means ended the debate in China. At most, it would be considered as an authoritative statement of the Mao-Lin position. The debate over whether to intervene or not to intervene continued for another year.

At the same time, Lo Jui-ch'ing published an article which again took an opposite view on the nature of the American threat in Vietnam. Clearly the debate had not yet been settled. By October 1965 the Maoist strategy was being glorified in the Chinese press without mention of the danger of escalation to China. Lo's downfall appears to have begun at this time, for he never gained prominence again. Finally, the Maoist position was expressed by Chou En-lai, who merely offered conditional support for both North Vietnam's Four-Point Plan and the National Liberation Front's Five-Point Plan for peace negotiations.

As of early 1966, the debate over Vietnam and the Sino American confrontation was still undecided. Liu Shao-ch'i, who had kept out of this dispute throughout 1965, stated that China would support North Vietnam regardless of the nature and extent of American involvement and American escalation.[32] In February 1966 he even administered a public rebuke to Ghanaian President Kwame Nkrumah for indulging in peacemaking. In his words, Afro-Asian nations must not take a middle position between the aggressor and the victim of aggression.[33]

Throughout the first half of 1966, Chou En-lai played an increasing part in the Vietnam debate. His most important statement on this question came at a press conference in Karachi in April 1966, when he warned that war with China would not necessarily be confined to one geographical area. In retrospect it seems certain that Chou threw his weight behind the Maoist policy of nonintervention and conditional support. His frequent speeches and his importance to the Mao-Lin coalition, at least in foreign policy, have led some observers to believe that he may be the sole beneficiary of the Cultural Revolution.

By August 1966 this new coalition in foreign policy won the policy debate at the Eleventh Plenum of the Eighth Central Committee of the Chinese Communist Party. The final communiqué

32. Liu Shao-ch'i, "Chairman Liu Shao-ch'i's Replies to President Ho Chi Minh," January 30, 1966, in *Peking Review*, Vol. IX, No. 6, February 4, 1966, pp. 5–6.

33. Liu Shao-ch'i, "Chairman Liu Shao-ch'i on Vietnam Question," Speech in Honor of Nkrumah, February 24, 1966, *Peking Review*, Vol. IX, No. 10, March 4, 1966, p. 5. It was during this trip that Nkrumah fell from power in Ghana.

of the gathering gave less attention to American imperialism than to Soviet revisionism and emphasized only conditional support for Vietnam. Even the war threat was minimized with the perfunctory statement that should the Americans start a war against China, the Chinese were ready to meet them.

After eighteen months of serious debate, the present Chinese leadership has apparently decided that at present, as in the past, China must continue to practice a low-risk strategy of direct confrontation. Following this type of conflict management, China has avoided two pitfalls. On the one hand, she has escaped the serious losses which would result from a general war with the United States. On the other, she has not been forced to pay the price of Sino-Soviet cooperation. The Mao-Lin-Chou strategy is essentially cautious. It does not wish to perpetuate the gap between policy and power in Chinese foreign policy and is thus making every effort to bridge it. Three nuclear tests since 1966 and two thermonuclear weapons tests in June 1967 and December 1968 prove that the Maoist stress on guerrilla warfare does not preclude a strong emphasis on nuclear weapons. They also indicate that China is determined to correct the serious imbalance in the Sino-American power relationship.

Until this imbalance is rectified considerably, China will continue to follow a cautious, noninterventionist policy in order to avoid a direct confrontation with the United States. The Chinese nuclear deterrent is not aimed at Asian countries, but rather at gaining relative freedom of action in foreign policy without risking instant and total destruction by a nuclear superpower. The Chinese have interpreted American statements that no sanctuary will be granted to China in the event of Chinese intervention in Vietnam to mean that there is no possibility of a limited war of the Korean type between a nuclear and a non-nuclear power. Most Chinese foreign policy statements dealing with nuclear weapons thus emphasize their value in breaking the nuclear monopoly of the superpowers.

A look at the past nineteen years suggests that vehement anti-American attacks partly serve to maintain a high degree of internal unity and a rather exhausting level of patriotic fervor. To further these ends the Chinese leadership is apt to use the United States as a "filler" between intensive ideological campaigns. On the whole it would seem that a certain degree of Sino-American tension is useful or even necessary to Peking.

In spite of almost two decades of anti-Americanism and a host of misperceptions on either side, both sides have been essentially cautious. The only major military confrontation with the United States took place in Korea. Both sides learned the lessons of bad communications and not believing each other's messages. Since then, in spite of more than four hundred "serious warnings," Peking has avoided direct Sino-American hostilities, probably because of the great realism with which it estimates American military strength. Thus, it is ill-advised to adopt what might be called a "Munich Complex" which views Mao as an expansionist fanatic and which dismisses compromise as appeasement, and to equate the present day Chinese leadership with Hitler or Chinese Communism with German Fascism.

Nor is it wise to overlook the military realities behind Chinese resentment of the American presence in Asia. China is surrounded by a ring of bases that help to explain Peking's somewhat claustrophobic anxiety. Yet the real heart of the matter is Peking's drive to gain world status commensurate with China's new strength.

This goal may not be incompatible with American foreign policy aims, for such an adjustment might bring China into the status quo group. Only a vested interest in the status quo has any chance of bringing about a more complacent attitude on the part of the Chinese rulers. Although there is no guarantee of instant success, it is reasonable to suppose that the longer China is treated as a pariah, the more she is tempted to cast herself in the role of challenger of the status quo.

Judging from this perspective, Sino-American relations have remained frozen because they are based on circular reasoning. China cannot be permitted to become a member of the present world order because she challenges it. Yet as long as she is not a part of the status quo, she will continue to do so. On China's side, America's role in excluding Peking from the international power club simply feeds a growing spiral of anti-American misperceptions.

At least the gradualists have recognized that at some point the circle has to be broken. In the past China has made certain efforts in this direction, just as the United States has done in the present.

It is ironic, tragic, and perhaps deliberate that such gestures have not coincided. If and when a coincidence occurs, a more realistic period of Sino-American relations will begin.

The Recent New York conference, sponsored by the National Committee on United States-China Relations, revealed a growing mood of realism and a new impatience with previous gradualist policies. At this gathering Senator Edward M. Kennedy advocated the establishment of American Consulates in China as a first step toward normalizing Sino-American relations. Theodore Sorenson declared that the United States should adopt a policy of not increasing China's insecurity. In the academic world, the appearance of the Committee of Concerned Asian Scholars (CCAS) points to a new orientation for China scholarship, one which seeks a radical redefinition of American foreign policy as well as a more sympathetic interpretation of China's grievances. Now that the Ninth Party Congress indicates a return to quasi-normalcy, American efforts to break the vicious circle of Sino-American misperceptions may inaugurate a new era of realism.

Given the history of American contact with China, such a phase would represent not historical continuity with pre-Communist China but the inauguration of a new historical era. Future relations can be based neither on contempt nor on benevolence. They can be expressed neither by random quotations from the works of Chairman Mao nor by unilateral American pronouncements. Instead, they must spring from a thorough re-evaluation of the recent past. Most important, they must seek to define new parameters of legitimate interests in East and Southeast Asia for both Washington and Peking.

CHAPTER FIVE

Sino-Soviet Antagonisms

The history of Sino-Russian relations has a multitiered and ponderous structure. The recent and bitter search for a viable theory of international relations among socialist states is only the latest addition to a long series of encounters between two rival empires, too far-flung land powers whose very geopolitical positions were mutually annoying.

Just as Western incursions outweighed the traditional tribute system as a source of Chinese behavior, so Russia's colonial policy left a heritage that China has never forgotten. Drawn by the lure of gold, silver, furs, and arable land to the region of the Amur River (where the Sino-Russian frontier was still not delineated), Russian colonists sent emissaries to Peking in the hope of creating methods and institutions for the development of Sino-Russian relations. They wished to reach agreement not only on the demarcation of the border, but also on questions of trade, fugitives, local outlaws, and the collection of *yasak* or tribute from tribes inhabiting the disputed area.

What the emissaries encountered in Peking was an imperial court prepared to thwart the "hairy barbarians" from the north at every turn. The method employed was icy condescension. A delegation led by Ivashko Petlin in 1618, for example, was taken as a tribute mission, and in 1654 an emissary named Baikov was dismissed from the city for violating the elaborate and humiliating rituals of Chinese protocol. Meanwhile sporadic fighting temporarily halted the Russian wave.

In spite of their emphatic desire for peace on the border, the Chinese proved to be tough negotiators. The Treaty of Nerchinsk of 1689, China's first real treaty, was the result of two months of hard bargaining and compromise. After the Treaty of Kiakhta of 1727 the Russians sent only six official caravans because of the difficulties imposed by the arrangement. Both efforts nevertheless marked a conscious drive to establish an institutional bridge based on a certain degree of reciprocity which inaugurated a period of peaceful trade and lasted until the middle of the nineteenth century.[1]

The nature of these early Sino-Russian contacts and the shrewd nature of the Manchu response alters the stereotyped picture of China's diplomatic inexperience in the face of nineteenth-century imperialist pressure. Particularly under Emperor K'ang-hsi, China developed a vigorous trade policy which counteracts the assumption that she scorned the goods of other countries. Her institutional experience with Russia negates the view that she was incapable of anything but a tribute relationship. Instead, the fate of early Russian emissaries suggests that rigid insistence on ceremonial submission was a defensive maneuver designed to frustrate outsiders and to postpone the time for concessions. Judging from the record, this tactic was at least partially successful.

The appointment of N. N. Muraviev-Amurskii as Governor-General of Eastern Siberia, combined with the discoveries of the explorer Nevelskoy, put an end to the era of Sino-Russian harmony and threw China on the defensive. Pursuing a policy of vigorous expansionism, Muraviev took advantage of losses suffered during the T'aip'ing Rebellion to move into Manchuria. Meanwhile, the Opium Wars gave Russia the chance to wrest more concessions, including a most-favored nation clause and final title to Eastern Siberia. In 1896, fresh from defeat at Japanese hands, China concluded a treaty of alliance with Russia which included permission to build the Trans-Siberian Railway.[2]

1. For further details on the early history of Sino-Russian contact, see Michel N. Pavlovsky, *Chinese-Russian Relations* (New York: Philosophical Library, 1949), Chapters I and II.

2. For a detailed analysis, see Andrew Malozemoff, *Russian Far Eastern Policy, 1881–1904* (Berkeley: University of California Press, 1958).

To Chinese statesmen, the lesson seemed clear. Whenever China was weakened by internal disturbances or external pressures, Russia moved in to grab her share of the booty. Her greed for territory, which by 1900 included Shantung Peninsula and Port Arthur, apparently knew no bounds. Her promotion of an independent Manchuria seemed aimed at encouraging China's territorial fragmentation. At least an ocean separated China from the West, but Russia's long frontier generated constant anxiety. Only a Russian leadership completely divorced from this heritage of expansionism could even begin to win China's confidence.

For a while it seemed as if Lenin's revolutionary group might meet this qualification. In fact, the first soundwaves of the Great October Socialist Revolution made less of an impression than the publication and denunciation of Russia's secret wartime treaties. Although an early article by Li Ta-chao hailed the significance of the Russian Revolution, preoccupation with the anti-foreign stage of China's introspective revolution relegated class struggle to the background. At this point the spearhead of bitterness was still aimed at foreigners. Those who realized the need to transform Chinese society still thought in terms of education rather than class warfare. This phase of the introspective revolution still focused on national survival rather than on the liberation of the masses.

More than any other period, the years 1918 to 1924 was the Soviet Union's first and last chance for enduring friendship with China. Offering help and advice to both the Kuomintang and the newly founded Communist Party, the Russians seemed militantly hostile to all forms of imperialism. Chicherin, who had succeeded Trotsky as Commissar for Foreign Relations, even offered the return of the Chinese Eastern Railway as a sign of good will. Pledging support for the Chinese Revolution, the Russians upheld China's cause against the West.

Yet the Soviets soon thought better of discarding the legacy of tsarist concessions. Within a year of the Revolution signs of backtracking had already appeared. The Karakhan Proposals of 1919, for example, pledged friendship with China but deleted the offer to return the Railway. Support for Sun Yat-sen's Canton government was confined to declaratory statements. After establishing a Communist government in Mongolia, Moscow recognized China's sovereignty but insisted on an agreement which forbade Chinese entry. The "provisional" headquarters set up in Manchuria to supervise the Railway was dominated by Russians and assumed an increasingly permanent character. The record of Chinese grievances grew longer.

Disillusionment soon spread to the camp of the Chinese Communists. By strengthening the Kuomintang along Bolshevik lines and by ordering the Communists to enter the well-known united front of 1924–27, Stalin effectively turned the Communist Party into a sacrificial lamb. Based on an underestimation of Chiang Kai-shek, and rigidified in part by the Stalin-Trotsky dispute, this policy culminated in the Canton Massacre of 1927.

To the young Mao Tse-tung, the lesson of this debacle was painfully clear. In spite of their success at home, the Soviets were not infallible on matters concerning China. Neither their revolutionary seniority nor their efforts to place a patent on Marxism could justify orders from Moscow any longer. Looking for inspiration from abroad would have to be modified. Henceforth, Mao's anti-Western Westernism would limit itself mainly to permitting the importation of technology. Ideology, including the application of Marxism-Leninism to Chinese circumstances, would now come from China herself. Just as World War I discredited the West as a model for partisans of "science and democracy," so Stalin's disastrous policies gradually alienated Chinese Communist leaders and forced them to turn inward.

From this point of view the development of Mao's somewhat unorthodox ideas on peasant revolution signified a turning-point not only for China's revolution but for the future course of Sino-Soviet relations as well. From the still alien vocabulary of class struggle, Mao turned increasingly toward a vocabulary of Chineseness. Marxism-Leninism began to acquire greater appeal as it shed the stigma of foreign origin and became nationalized to suit Chinese conditions. In short, the new product had to be packaged attractively before it found a mass market.

Mao's discovery and exploitation of the concept of the Chinese "people" signified that Soviet efforts to foster proletarian internationalism at China's expense were doomed to failure. Thanks to Mao, nationalism and revolution were on their way to becoming synonymous. Almost by definition, class enemies became national traitors. Using actual political behavior rather than economic status as a criterion for judgment, the new formula linked the emotional appeal of nationalism to the bitterness of class struggle.

In this case, the contrast with the Soviet Union bears strong influence on Sino-Soviet relations. As a symbol of unity, the notion of the Chinese "people" differed from the equivalent Soviet rallying cry, the concept of "nation." Because the definition of the "people" is always subject to change, it is more revolutionary than the Russian word "nation." Particularly during World War II, for example, the Soviet emphasis on "nation" implied the essential unity of all elements within the borders of the USSR. Accordingly, this effort to unite the Russian people against the Germans was marked by a decrescendo of revolutionary measures. The Chinese solution set up no such contrast.

Mao's doubled-edged weapon meant that the familiar Comintern dilemma of the 1930's—choosing between nationalism without class struggle and class struggle without nationalism—did not apply to China. The most radical experiments in communization were in fact coupled with the most fervent nationalism vis-à-vis the Taiwan Straits crisis of 1958. By the same token, nationalistic hostility to the Soviet Union took the form of ideological contempt for right-wing deviations. The current bombast against Soviet "revisionism" is a fundamental component of a massive effort to unleash domestic tensions. In this sense the Cultural Revolution is the grand climax of Mao's ideological invention.

Another consequence of the Maoist style for Sino-Soviet relations springs from the populist element in Chinese Communist thought. Whereas Lenin despised the *narodniki* and preferred tight discipline, organization, and mass manipulation, both Li Ta-chao and Mao retained their early populist orientation. Combined with the vital need for good relations with the peasantry during the long years of guerrilla warfare, this trend has endowed Chinese Communism with a bucolic tinge. At least in the minds of its leaders, the Chinese Communist Party has a broad mass character which theoretically takes into account the needs of each individual Chinese.

It is precisely this real or imagined humanistic aspect which Chinese leaders feel is lacking in the Soviet Union. At least a portion of the Chinese leadership sees the need to look after the spiritual and emotional wants of the Chinese people as well as the physical and technological needs of the state. In "Serve the People," written in 1944 and recently reprinted, Mao wrote that "the Chinese people are suffering" and that "we have . . . the sufferings of the great majority at heart." The death of anyone in the Communist ranks, whether soldier or cook, called for a proper funeral ceremony and a memorial meeting.[3]

Whether the Chinese Communists practice what they preach is, of course, open to question. Yet Mao believes that 95 percent of them try, at least by comparison with the Soviets. This conviction finds expression in a populist distrust of the machinations of Soviet leaders. Anti-Soviet features of the Cultural Revolution include charges that the Soviet leadership is divorced from the people and that they seek only to augment their own power. From this point of view, revisionism signifies estrangement from the revolutionary essence of the masses. The latest fruit of this evil weed is said to be "social imperialism," that is, socialism in words but imperialism in deeds.[4] While applied to the case of Czechoslovakia, this could also refer to Rumania, Albania, and even China herself.

Curiously, the Chinese accusation that Soviet leaders are divorced from the people has an exact counterpart in Moscow's return volleys. Soviet theoreticians now charge Mao with bypassing the working class altogether.[5] In translated form, however, this criticism means simply that Mao has pushed aside the Chinese Communist Party. Such is actually the case, for the Cultural Revolution has been marked by a ground swell of devastating attacks on the Party by non-Party organizations and unofficial groups. Yet Mao initiated this attack precisely because he felt that the Party no longer represented the people. His attitude revealed a breathtaking admission that the Party can sometimes

3. Mao Tse-tung, "Serve the People," September 8, 1944, reprinted in *Peking Review*, Vol. 11, No. 36, September 6, 1968, p. 5.

4. "Social Imperialism," *Peking Review*, Vol. 11, No. 36, September 6, 1968, p. 12.

5. See, for example, T. Timofeyev, "Scientific Socialism and Petty Bourgeois Ideology," *Reprints from the Soviet Press*, Vol. III, No. 10, December 1, 1966.

be wrong. Quite correctly, Soviet leaders interpret this phenomenon as a severe threat to Party rule at home.

China's response to the Soviet charge uncovers an unusual facet of Chinese Communist thinking. In China, the working class or industrial proletariat has not been granted the role of supreme leadership either symbolically or theoretically. Although the ideal of a four-class united front consisting of the peasantry, the proletariat, the petty bourgeoisie, and the national bourgeoisie has been replaced by a supposedly proletarian cultural revolution, the term "working class" has acquired a new meaning. It is apparently defined not as the industrial labor force but as the entire collection of revolutionary working people in China. In the remarkable words of Yao Wen-yuan, whose attack on Wu Han fired the opening rounds of the Cultural Revolution:

Our Party is the vanguard of the proletariat. The proletarian headquarters headed by Chairman Mao and with Vice-Chairman Lin Piao as its deputy leader represents in a concentrated way the interests of the working class, the poor and lower-middle peasants, and the masses of labouring people; it is the only center of leadership for the whole Party, the whole army, the whole nation, and the masses of revolutionary people. Chairman Mao's proletarian revolutionary line and all his instructions reflect the pressing demand of the working class and of the hundreds of millions of revolutionary people.[6]

In the eyes of Soviet ideologues, this frame of mind seems contradictory. The vanguard of the proletariat, the Party, is clearly subordinate to Mao's group, which is nevertheless defined as the "proletarian headquarters." Furthermore, Lenin was already stretching Marxism to its logical limits when he claimed that the intellectuals could represent the proletariat; how the Maoists can embody "in a concentrated way" the interests of *all* the classes worthy of revolutionary notice is puzzling.

Although Marxism calls for a proletarian dictatorship, Chinese leaders shied away from the term before the Cultural Revolution. Bound by the ideological need for proletarian leadership as China

6. Yao Wen-yuan, "The Working Class Must Exercise Leadership in Everything," *Peking Review*, Vol. 11, No. 35, August 10, 1968, pp. 3–4.

moves toward Communism, however, they have tried to solve the dilemma by broadening the meaning and content of the working class. Only in this way can they reconcile a reasonable degree of ideological purity with efforts to unite several classes at once. At the same time, their effort fully conforms to Mao's equation between national unity and revolution. In short, the very notions that infuriate Soviet leaders are products of long-standing Maoist concepts.

Given this fundamental difference in attitude, compounded by historical rivalry and suspicion, the very existence of the Sino-Soviet alliance, however limited in duration, was far more surprising than the eruption of the Sino-Soviet dispute. Even during the years of supposed harmony, divisions remained beneath the surface. Although the final Communist victory was followed by the importation of the Stalinist model of economic development, Mao remained critical of Stalin's leadership methods.[7] Even the age-old border dispute remained unresolved, and the Chinese have retroactively accused the Soviets of carrying out subversive activities in frontier areas.[8] Such was the nature of the strains that surrounded the two Sino-Soviet agreements of 1950 and 1954.

The Sino-Soviet Treaty of Assistance of 1950 was apparently so difficult to negotiate that Mao spent an unusually long time in Moscow at a time when many domestic problems remained unresolved. As long as Chiang Kai-shek had continued to wield power on the mainland, Mao was willing to forgive Soviet aid to the Kuomintang on the grounds of realism, expediency, and fear of the Japanese. Yet once the Communists were in power, Mao saw no reason to continue the old pattern of concessions, joint stock companies, and the like. The actual Soviet terms must have come as a rude shock.

In final form the agreement of 1950 provided for Chinese recognition of the independence of Mongolia. Joint Sino-Soviet admin-

7. Such criticism of Stalin's leadership methods apparently arose in the 1930's. See John E. Rue, *Mao Tse-tung in Opposition* (Stanford: Hoover Institute on War, Revolution, and Peace, 1966).

8. For recent evidence of this tension, see China's letter to the CPSU of February 29, 1964, in *Peking Review*, Vol. VII, No. 19, May 8, 1964, pp. 12–18. This document charged that the Sino-Soviet boundary was a "legacy from the past."

istration was to continue in Manchuria, albeit in modified form. Both Port Arthur and the Changchung Railway were still to be used jointly, although Dairen was to return to China. All of these provisions undoubtedly represented Chinese concessions, probably in return for aid. Yet the actual amount of Soviet credits—$300 million—was notably small. What was even more galling was that the Soviets charged 1 per cent interest.

Seeking to soften the terms of this agreement, Chou En-lai went to Moscow in 1952. The resulting Soviet concessions, which were granted before Stalin's death, included the return of the rights and property of the Changchung Railway to China without recompensation. Yet on the pretext of the threat of American troops in Japan, a new understanding provided for a delay in the withdrawal of Soviet troops from Manchuria. This move, probably a *quid pro quo* for the railway, demonstrated the type of hard bargaining that continued to characterize the loudly proclaimed Sino-Soviet "alliance." Even more significant, however, were the things that were *not* mentioned during Chou's visit, notably an increase in Soviet aid.

The series of new agreements that followed the death of Stalin in 1953 made some improvements. The Soviets agreed to build a total of 156 industrial establishments in China, and by 1956 this total had swelled to 211. New and extensive trade protocols were signed, while the credits granted in 1950 were extended for a longer period of time. Moscow also agreed to complete troop withdrawal by 1955 and to return the joint stock companies to the Chinese. A joint technological commission was created in the name of scientific cooperation, and hints of assistance in the development of nuclear weaponry may have been made at this time.

Significantly, the improvement in China's bargaining position was granted before de-Stalinization had taken place. Khrushchev's drive for leadership almost undoubtedly included a plan to win Mao's approval in return for concessions. After all, next to Stalin, Mao could well consider himself the leading figure in the Communist world. Sensing the need for at least the token forms of equality, Khrushchev and Bulganin joined Chinese leaders in a declaration promising that the two governments would "consult and coordinate" on common problems. The Soviets also endorsed the Five Principles of Peaceful Coexistence, which the Chinese considered to be a genuine contribution to international relations.

China's new status of equality with the Soviet Union was soon put to the test, with shattering consequences. At the Twentieth Congress of the CPSU in February 1956, Khrushchev himself dropped the bombshell. The famous "secret speech," which attacked Stalin and set off a wave of repercussions in the Communist camp, came as news to the Chinese. Although this speech was probably a watershed not only in Sino-Soviet relations but in the entire cohesion of the Bloc, it was launched without prior consultation with Peking. Whatever hopes Mao may have nurtured with respect to Stalin's successors were severely damaged.

The "secret speech" coincided with Peking's recognition that the Stalinist models of administration and economic development did not suit Chinese circumstances. The first important hint that China's Soviet-inspired economic strategy was no longer practicable for China came with Lu Ting-yi's well-known speech of May 1956 on the Hundred Flowers. Adopting a new tone, Lu declared that learning from the USSR must not be "doctrinaire and mechanical" and that the Soviet experience must be adapted to concrete Chinese conditions.[9] Three weeks later, Li Fu-ch'un, a Vice Premier and Chairman of the State Planning Commission, put unprecedented emphasis on light industry and for the first time placed it on a par with heavy industry.[10]

By September 1956, at China's Eighth Party Congress, Chou En-lai's report announced that China was "quite different" from the Soviet Union. The country was now said to require a "reasonable" rate of economic growth on a "comparatively balanced" basis.[11] Although the Second Five-Year Plan continued to stress

9. Lu Ting-yi "Let All Flowers Bloom Together, Let Diverse Schools of Thought Contend," May 26, 1956, *Jen-min Jih-pao* (*People's Daily*), June 13, 1956, translated in *Current Background*, No. 406, August 15, 1956, p. 17.

10. Li Fu-ch'un, "The Situation Relating to the Implementation of the First Five-Year Plan," Report to the Third Session of the First National People's Congress on June 18, 1956, translated in *Current Background*, No. 393, June 28, 1956, p. 5.

11. Chou En-lai, "Report on the Second Five-Year Plan," September 16, 1956, *New China News Agency*, September 20, 1956, reprinted in *Current Background*, No. 413, October 5, 1956, pp. 5–10.

heavy industry, it differed significantly from its predecessor and thus from the Soviet blueprint for rapid industrialization of the 1930's. In short, the rebuff which Mao received at the CPSU's Twentieth Congress coincided with disillusionment for Soviet methods at home.

The reason why the events of the Sino-Soviet honeymoon have been discussed in such detail is that they illustrate the fundamental strains in Sino-Soviet relations. Like faithful allies, Chinese leaders tested the Soviet model and found it unsatisfactory. From then on they turned increasingly to their own experience in formulating programs to suit China's overwhelmingly agricultural, labor-intensive conditions. In this sense, the Great Leap Forward was a specifically Chinese formula for economic development. Party cadres worked hard to achieve mass mobilization in the service of small-scale, decentralized, and labor-intensive industrial projects. When viewed from Moscow, where Marxist-Leninist truths and Soviet experience were seen as synonymous, these efforts amounted to wild-eyed heresy. Accordingly, Chinese leaders had to justify them in ideological terms.

Significantly, China's case for the defense rested on Mao's ideas, fortified with a dash of Lenin, rather than on Stalin's pronouncements. Specifically, the problems that resulted from making massive efforts in both industry and agriculture were expressed in terms of Mao's theory of contradictions. While industry and agriculture were said to be interdependent, they were also contradictory. Under socialism, however, these contradictions were nonantagonistic because of the alliance between the peasantry and the industrial proletariat. Thus the shift away from Stalin's capital-intensive orientation toward heavy industry to the simultaneous development of heavy industry, light industry, and agriculture was justified in the name of revolutionary dialectics and the interaction of opposites.[12]

The general failure of the Great Leap Forward did not induce Chinese leaders to return to the Soviet fold. Instead they raised the level of capital investment in agriculture and pronounced it to be the "foundation" of China's economic growth. The years

12. Hsu Li-chun, "The Relations Between Industry and Agriculture, and Heavy and Light Industry," *Peking Review*, Vol. II, No. 20, May 19, 1959.

following 1960 have reflected a new emphasis on quality, inter-sectoral balance, scientific and technical innovation, and agri-cultural realities. In 1965, for example, Chou En-lai announced that China's order of priority was agriculture, light industry, and heavy industry, in that order, and that industrial growth would not exceed the pace of agricultural development.[13] Despite the thunder of the Cultural Revolution, efforts have been made to keep damage to the economy at the minimum.[14] Political frenzy continues to be accompanied by economic moderation.

In short, even apart from ideology, a combination of circum-stances has tended to perpetuate Sino-Soviet antagonisms. The suspicion generated by the vigorous expansionism pursued under the tsars was fed by Stalin's tactics in Manchuria. Bitter memo-ries of the Moscow-directed united front of 1924–27 were not eased when Chiang Kai-shek continued to receive aid and comfort from Soviet sources. The Bolshevik revolutionary experience, seiz-ing power first in the cities and only later in the countryside, led the Chinese Communists to disastrous defeats in 1929 and 1930. Mao's own struggle for supremacy within the Chinese Commu-nist Party in the 1930's was opposed by a group of Soviet protégés newly returned from Moscow, notably Wang Ming. Recent at-tempts to link Mao's enemies with Soviet machinations probably date back to this period.

For a brief period after the Communist victory and again after Stalin's death, Chinese leaders appeared to be giving the Soviets another chance. Yet the paucity of Soviet aid and the continu-ation of old-style imperialist measures revived old fears. More-over, the Korean War persuaded Mao that Moscow's division of labor added up to giving orders from the Soviet Union and imple-menting them with cannon fodder from China. While the Soviets

13. Chou En-lai, "Premier Chou En-lai Reports on Work of Gov-ernment," *Hung-ch'i* (*Red Flag*), No. 1, January 6, 1965.

14. Only a month after the Eleventh Plenum of August 1966, for example, Red Guards were ordered not to attack factories or com-munes or to disrupt production in any way. Unlike the *hsia fang* cadres of the Great Leap, Red Guards were never sent to engage in agricultural production. For further discussion, see Dwight H. Perkins, "Economic Growth in China and the Cultural Revolution (1960–April 1967)," *China Quarterly*, No. 30, April–June 1967.

would reap the fruit, China would suffer the loss. Although the agreements of 1953 and 1954 may have softened Chinese resentment, Khrushchev drove the last nail in the coffin of Sino-Soviet friendship when he snubbed the Chinese at the Twentieth Congress.

At first sight, to take such severe offense at Soviet policies seems unrealistic in view of China's international position. Yet Mao knew the difference between a love pat and a genuine slap in the face. Once again, the formal pretense of equality was far more important than the content of Sino-Soviet arrangements. If the Soviets had consulted with the Chinese as equals instead of as subordinates, some of these grievances might have been eased. The Chinese might even have been willing to permit the Soviets to use their railways and ports if the Soviets had not insisted on doing so from the start.

This summary of China's complaints does not mean, of course, that the quarrel was entirely one sided. To the Soviets, the Chinese posed a number of irritations. After all, from the standpoint of *Realpolitik* China had no reason to expect even the pretense of equality. Both economically and militarily she was then weaker than the Soviet Union. Furthermore, Mao's claim to be the senior ranking Communist leader could not have made much of a dent in Moscow.

What was even worse was China's rejection of the Soviet model, a step that Moscow saw as a threat to Soviet supremacy in Eastern Europe. At least for a while, China's experiments in agriculture encouraged other Bloc leaders who were unwilling to conform to the Soviet mold, notably the Poles. The break with Soviet tradition which the Great Leap Forward represented was thus doubly dangerous, threatening economic growth in China and damaging Soviet prestige in Eastern Europe.

Finally, from the Soviet point of view, Peking wanted to pursue risky policies under the cover of the Soviets' nuclear umbrella. When the news of the Soviet ICBM was topped by the announcement of the world's first satellite, it was Mao who wanted to exploit these achievements to the full. His famous slogan about the East wind prevailing over the West wind met with little enthusiasm in Moscow. When the Chinese tried to harness this alleged superiority to recapture Taiwan, Soviet leaders did not brandish the threat of nuclear weapons until the crisis was virtually over. The restoration of Taiwan to the mainland was simply not worth the risk.

At the same time, the Soviets began to suspect the Chinese of undercutting their influence in the Third World and of pursuing a policy of subtle racism. As early as 1949, while the Soviet attitude remained wavering, Chinese commentaries sought to establish the Chinese path as a model for all underdeveloped countries. At the Conference of Trade Unions of the Countries of Asia and Oceania in 1949, for example, Liu Shao-ch'i urged all colonial and semicolonial countries to follow China's example.[15]

While a Cominform editorial of January 1950 indicated that the Soviets had approved the Maoist strategy for the Third World,[16] the Kremlin was nevertheless unwilling to relinquish any authority over the Communist movement. Even while endorsing the Chinese victory as a model for other underdeveloped areas, the Soviets refused to attribute any originality to the Chinese path. In April 1950, for example, another Cominform editorial declared firmly that the international significance of the "Russian model" for all peoples had become clear. If socialism had found favorable soil on the banks of the Volga and the Dnieper, then it would also flourish beside such rivers as the Ganges.[17]

In spite of this rebuke, the Chinese refused to become junior partners of the Kremlin's policy-makers and ideologues. Even when Peking was still hoping for more aid from Moscow, China's attitude toward the Third World remained independent. While the Soviets vacillated between a "right" strategy, a Zhdanov-style "left" strategy, and endorsement of the Maoist model, the Chinese consistently advocated their own approach for Third World revolutions after 1951. Although the general failure of armed revolts prompted both countries to take a new look at Afro-Asian

15. Liu Shao-ch'i, "Speech by Liu Shao-ch'i," *Pravda*, January 4, 1950, translated in *Soviet Press Translations*, Vol. V, No. 6, March 15, 1950.

16. Editorial, "Mighty Advance of the National Liberation Movement in the Colonial and Dependent Countries," *For a Lasting Peace*, No. 4, January 27, 1950, p. 1.

17. Editorial, "May Day—The Day of Solidarity of Working People of the World, Day of Fraternity of the Workers of all Lands," *For a Lasting Peace*, No. 17, April 28, 1950, p. 1.

countries, China took the lead. While Soviet commentaries on the internal policies of the neutral nations remained critical even after Stalin's death, the Chinese were quick to adjust to the long-term existence of neutralism and to make the most of its anti-imperialist aspects. Peking also seemed willing to overlook such domestic practices as the widespread suppression of local Communists, a trend which the Soviet Union found more disquieting. All these trends tended to promote Peking's influence in the Third World at the expense of Moscow.

China's efforts in this direction came to a climax at the Bandung Conference of Afro-Asian states, held in Indonesia in the spring of 1955. No one could have accurately foreseen to what extent Chou En-lai's diplomatic skill could win so many friends for China from among the neutrals. Seeing that the mood of the Conference was one of general moderation,[18] Chou adapted himself to it with remarkable ease. Although the use of military force toward Quemoy and Matsu and even toward Formosa was a burning question at the time, no mention of such a possibility appeared in his speeches.[19]

One of Chou's greatest triumphs was achieving a strong bond of friendship with much of the Arab world, long a Soviet stronghold, and with Nasser in particular. Chou's vigorous anti-Israeli moves soon won diplomatic recognition from Egypt, Syria, Saudi Arabia, and Yemen. In addition, in moves aimed at winning the support of moderate or right-wing states his position was even more moderate than that of Nehru. In various proposals for putting an end to colonialism, for example, Nehru demanded that the liberation of all colonial areas should take place immediately, while Chou was willing to allow the colonial powers an additional fifteen years.[20] Ironically China also seemed to make an

18. The best Western coverage of the Bandung Conference can be found in *Le Monde* from April 17 to 27, 1955. For comments on the moderation of the gathering, see Robert Guillain, "M. Nehru Prône la Modération à la Conference de Bandoeng," *Le Monde*, April 20, 1955, p. 2.

19. Chou En-lai's major speeches are printed in George McT. Kahin, *The Asian-African Conference* (Ithaca: Cornell University Press, 1956), pp. 52–63.

20. "A Bandoeng M. Chou En-lai Propose un Sursis de Quinze Ans au Colonialisme," *Le Monde*, April 23, 1955, p. 2.

effort to bridge the widening gap between India and the Western-aligned states in the interests of unity.[21] Taken as a whole, China's impact on Bandung created the impression that there existed a common front between Communists and neutrals.[22]

Viewed from Moscow, these maneuvers aroused great suspicion. To Kremlin policy-makers China appeared to be unduly opportunistic. Her moves seemed aimed at founding an Afro-Asian club from which both the Soviet Union and the United States would be excluded. Although Moscow has repeatedly claimed that the Soviet Union is an Asian power by virtue of both territory and population, this argument makes little headway in the Third World. Even in the early stages, China's refusal to promote Soviet admission to the Afro-Asian circle has led the Soviets to press mounting charges of racism against Peking. On balance, however, Chinese leaders have stopped short of racism, arguing instead that the Soviet Union's dominant cultural and political heritage is European.

In short, still leaving ideology aside, another category has been added to the list of Sino-Soviet antagonisms: rivalry. Significantly, competition for the allegiance of nonaligned nations was in full swing *before* the ideological dispute came into the open. If China's hostility toward the United States was based partly on misperceptions and partly on her resentment of the Western world order as a whole, her bitterness toward the Soviet Union sprang from specific, tangible, and down-to-earth grievances.

It is often hard for Westerners to understand why ideological disputes can spark such spectacular emotional fireworks. This puzzlement, based on an inability to perceive the essence of ideological issues, has led to the view that Communists are not in touch with reality. Wrapped up in theory, they are thought to be unaware of the "real" nature of man or the "real" problems facing their political struggle. This view is incorrect. Curiously, it manages to coexist with its opposite, namely, the idea that Communists are grasping opportunists who are quick to take advantage of any weakness in the political fabric.

21. Kahin, *The Asian-African Conference*, p. 25.

22. This opinion is supported by Richard Lowenthal in "China," in Zbigniew Brzezinski, ed., *Africa and the Communist World* (Stanford: Stanford University Press, 1963), p. 151.

Understanding the dynamism of ideological debates requires an analysis of the part which ideology plays in Communist politics. First and foremost, it is the only medium of communication for any kind of public exchange. This means that all complaints, however picayune, must be surrounded by an ideological cloak. For this reason it is precisely those who are most concerned with practical problems who will throw themselves most fiercely into the fray. The Lenin-Roy debate, for example, revolved around the specific problem of exactly what Communists in underdeveloped areas should do. In many cases, ideology provides the ammunition for a power struggle, such as the Stalin-Trotsky dispute in the Soviet Union or the Mao-Liu confrontation in China.

This conclusion does not mean that ideology has no life force of its own. On the contrary, ideology usually turns into a pattern of communication which is more or less permanent. It sets limits on the variety and scope of available alternatives, and it tends to fall back on fixed assumptions. The secret documents captured from the Chinese province of Fukien, for example, reveal that private discussions rely upon the same terminology as public pronouncements. Nevertheless, ideological wrestling matches almost always refer to immediate issues. Only if their underlying frame of reference is kept in mind can the animosity surrounding verbal quibbling be understood.

In the Sino-Soviet case, ideology is almost the sole vehicle through which antagonisms can be expressed. Furthermore, since it seeks to replace the moral code of religion and traditional philosophy, it must confer a legitimizing influence upon the argument at stake. Disguising the hard core of national interests is not enough. It must also glorify these interests and project them onto a universal plane. Such has been the nature of the Sino-Soviet quarrel.

For a while after Khrushchev's speech at the Twentieth Congress, Chinese leaders appeared willing to compromise. From February to April 1956, the subject of de-Stalinization was virtually ignored. Finally two long articles[23] analyzing the Stalin era

23. Editorial Department of *Jen-min Jih-pao*, "On the Historical Experience of the Dictatorship of the Proletariat" (Peking: Foreign Languages Press, 1961), pp. 3–6. See further Editorial Department of

tried to limit the attack so that it would not be extended to Communist rule in general and to Mao's leadership in particular. Omitting Mao's name completely, they seemed to urge Khrushchev to admit that Stalinist "deviations" might reappear and that corrective leadership measures were needed. As noted above, leadership was an area in which the Chinese always considered themselves superior to the Soviets.

Another issue that made its appearance at this time was nuclear weaponry. Apparently to secure Chinese support at the forthcoming Moscow Conference, the Soviets signed a treaty in October 1957 promising nuclear assistance to China. According to a Chinese charge which Moscow has never specifically denied, the Soviets unilaterally abrogated this agreement several years later. From the Kremlin's point of view, the trick succeeded in winning China's support.

In retrospect the Soviet decision to hold a conference of ruling Communist parties was a bold one. Whereas the Stalinist system of intra-Bloc relations was admittedly a thing of the past, the events of Hungary showed that there were obvious limits on permissible behavior. Short of the Hungarian example, however, the exact nature and extent of satellite autonomy were not at all clear. Moreover, the Twentieth Congress had raised a host of ideological questions relating not only to the meaning of "separate paths to socialism" but also to Communist tactics outside of the Bloc. Finally, reactions to the successful development of both the ICBM and Sputnik were bound to differ as to their application to East-West relations. In short, there was little reason to expect that complete unanimity would prevail.

The actual November Declaration produced by the Moscow Conference of 1957 represented a compromise on many of the important points. Resulting from hard bargaining on all sides, the Declaration must be seen as a partial failure for Moscow. While it endorsed the concept of the several paths to socialism of the Twentieth Congress, as well as the main outlines of the Soviet world view, it failed to re-establish the ideological authority and political hegemony of the Kremlin. Although it referred to

Jen-min Jih-pao, "More on the Historical Experience of the Dictatorship of the Proletariat" (Peking: Foreign Languages Press, 1961), pp. 47–49.

"the socialist camp headed by the Soviet Union," this phrase supported by Mao was specifically designed to antagonize the Yugoslavs rather than to return to the past.[24]

Nevertheless, if later accounts are credible, the Chinese remained unhappy with the Soviet position. In their first comment on the Soviet "Open Letter" of July 1963, for example, they asserted that they only consented to the Moscow Declaration out of consideration for Khrushchev's domestic difficulties. Well aware that Khrushchev's supremacy remained precarious even after the ouster of both the so-called "Anti-Party Group" and Marshal Zhukov, they realized that the legitimacy of Khrushchev's ideological platform at the Twentieth Congress would be considerably enhanced by the unanimous endorsement of other Communist capitals and especially of Peking. They conceded, therefore, to the "expressed wish" of the leaders of the CPSU that the formulation should show some connection with the Twentieth Congress. Quite bitterly, the Chinese commentary remarked that once the declaration was signed, "the Soviet leaders . . . thought they had solved their internal problems and 'stabilized' their own position and could therefore step up their policy of 'being friendly to enemies and tough with friends.' "[25]

In 1957 and 1958, the Kremlin had looked askance at such Chinese policies as the Hundred Flowers campaign, the antirightist drive, and the Great Leap Forward. At the Lushan Plenum of August 1959, Mao apparently put down a secret revolt led by Minister of Defense P'eng Teh-huai, who allegedly enjoyed Soviet backing. This case brought to mind a similar charge connected with the dismissal and subseqeunt suicide of Kao Kang in 1954. Either actively or passively, Moscow clearly promoted Mao's downfall. Finally in the fall of 1959 the Soviet failure to

24. "Communiqué on Conference of Representatives of Communist and Workers' Parties of Socialist Countries," *Pravda*, November 22, 1957, p. 1, translated in *Current Digest of the Soviet Press*, Vol. IX, No. 47, January 1, 1958.

25. "The Origin and Development of the Differences Between the Leadership of the CPSU and Ourselves," Comment on the Open Letter of the Central Committee of the CPSU by the Editorial Departments of *Renmin Ribao* and *Hongqi, Peking Review*, Vol. VI, No. 37, September 16, 1963, pp. 11–12.

support China in the border clash with India was the last straw. These developments have caused one scholar to label the summer of 1959 as the "point of no return." [26]

Casting courtesy to the winds, Peking's publication of "Long Live Leninism" in April 1960 brought the ideological controversy into the open. This step was accompanied by the first overt evidence of Chinese factionalism. At a meeting of the World Federation of Trade Unions in Peking in June 1960, China made the first clear effort to detach other Communist parties from Soviet control. At the same time, at the Rumanian Party Congress Khrushchev exchanged public arguments with P'eng Chen. When Moscow sought to overthrow the Albanian leadership shortly thereafter, the Sino-Albanian alliance was sealed. Tirana's territorial and political disputes with the "revisionist" Yugoslavs added yet another ideological overtone to the canvas.

The next confrontation took place at the Conference of 81 Communist Parties in November 1960. On balance, the communiqué issued by this group represented a Soviet victory, but it included certain concessions to the Chinese point of view. In the open polemics that followed, each side stressed its contribution to the document. Many of the Dutch, the Norwegians, the Rumanians, the Cubans, the Poles, and the Hungarians, remained unhappy with this conglomeration of Chinese and Soviet attitudes.[27]

The brief lull that followed the Moscow Conference was abruptly terminated at the Twenty-Second CPSU Congress in October 1961 when Khrushchev publicly attacked the Albanians. This was a period of criticism by proxy, in which Albania served as a scapegoat for China and Yugoslavia for the Soviet Union. The spectacle of the immense and powerful Soviet Union attacking tiny Albania had its parallel in China's abusive tirades against far-off Yugoslavia. Recognizing the true nature of the attack, therefore, Chou En-lai rose to Albania's defense and publicly criticized such unfraternal behavior.

26. William E. Griffith, *The Sino-Soviet Rift* (Cambridge: The M.I.T. Press, 1964).

27. For further discussion, see Leopold Labedz, "The End of an Epoch," in Labedz, ed., *International Communism After Khrushchev* (Cambridge: The M.I.T. Press, 1965).

At the time, Chinese demands included the suspension of public polemics, multilateral talks on the basis of equality, the normalization of Soviet-Albanian relations, and adherence to the Declaration of the Conference of 81 Communist Parties, which still listed revisionism rather than dogmatism as the main danger. Briefly, the Soviets agreed to the need to end the polemics, which they accused the Chinese of starting, but they wished to revise the Declaration to brand dogmatism as most dangerous to international Communism. Yet these apparently superficial issues stood for deeper quarrels which declarations alone could not heal.

At the heart of this antagonism was the familiar Chinese suspicion, which had now matured into a certainty, that the Soviets were seeking to deny China her proper stakes in the game of international politics. Inside the Bloc, the Kremlin wished to rule with a firm hand, thus excluding Peking from the process of decision-making and from the benefits of prestige. Outside the Bloc, the Chinese suspected Moscow of making private deals with Washington at their expense. To Peking the formula for peaceful coexistence is another way of saying that the Soviet Union and the United States will carve up the world and rule it together.

Chinese leaders could point with some justification to certain examples which seemed to verify their point of view. In both the Taiwan crises of 1954 and 1958, the Soviets had failed to back them up. In the Sino-Indian border dispute, Moscow supported India, a crime which amounted to backing a non-Communist country against a Communist one. As if this violation of decency were not enough, the Kremlin turned around and threatened nuclear weapons on behalf of Cuba, whose leader was still an ideological Johnny-come-lately. Furthermore, Moscow's failure to consult with Chinese leaders on such world-wide issues as Berlin convinced them that their suspicions were accurate. The unilateral abrogation of the agreement to provide nuclear assistance was merely further proof that the Soviets wished to keep China dependent. For all these reasons, China's relationship with the Soviet Union has often been compared to that of France with the United States.

The dispute became clear in the summer of 1963 when a Sino-Soviet meeting in Moscow was deluged with a stream of documents issued by each side. By this time there was no point in concealing the charges. The Soviet letter of July 14, for example, revealed that the Chinese were now actively intervening to promote secessionist Communist parties instead of passively supporting dissident anti-Party factions.

The Chinese responded by bringing the border dispute into the open, claiming that the Soviets were subverting various minority groups living along the Sino-Soviet border. A notable incident of this sort had taken place in the spring of 1962, when Kazakhs and Uzbekhs fled across the frontier from Sinkiang. On the whole, however, the Chinese prefer to remain silent on cases of this sort, fearing that they damage their image of popularity at home. Chinese spokesmen further accused the Soviets of bullying other Communist parties, violating the spirit of the declarations of 1956 and 1960, and undercutting the national liberation movement. They also chose this moment to release the details surrounding the collapse of Moscow's offer of nuclear assistance. As if in defiance, the Soviets began a series of East-West test ban negotiations while the meeting was still in progress. The effort to reach agreement was doomed.

Curiously this confrontation was followed by a major reversal of Sino-Soviet tactics. In the past Chinese leaders had demanded multilateral talks based on equality, while the Soviets had preferred bilateral negotiations. By the fall of 1963, however, these imperatives had switched sides. Soviet leaders, now realizing the impossibility of forcing the Chinese to back down in the face of private pressure, urged a public gathering. They hoped that such a tribunal would condemn China to political isolation or extract from her a public apology. The Chinese, fearing that Khrushchev was preparing for a formal split, preferred formal unity.

Peking's attitude toward formal excommunication from the Communist Bloc bears striking resemblance to China's official position regarding the United Nations. In both cases China is in a small minority. Both groups refuse to grant her the influence which her leaders feel she deserves. Both seem to be trying to turn back the political clock and to withhold recognition of her new status as a nuclear power. Yet rather than nursing her wounds in the company of an insignificant splinter group, she prefers to keep the door open. Although her minority attitude would not change, her leaders rule out membership in the United Nations only so long as Taiwan continues to be seated.

Similarly, Peking has worked feverishly to avoid formal excommunication from the Bloc while continuing to promote factional activities. The Chinese leadership calculates that influence from a fringe position is better than no influence at all. Pursuing factional activities within Parties previously united in their loyalty to Moscow naturally depends on maintaining contact with those Parties in the first place. Implacable hatred in theory does not rule out pragmatism in practice. In fact a report by Mikhail Suslov made in February 1964 revealed that Peking's splitting tactics were making some headway even among the ranks of Soviet personnel.[28]

The publication of Suslov's report in April 1964 marked the opening of the second round of efforts to mobilize organizational machinery against Peking. Yet this new thrust soon ground to a halt, thanks mainly to opposition from other Communist Parties. Opponents of the plan, led by the Rumanian and Italian Parties, were not necessarily pro-Chinese. On the whole, they took a dim view of both China's domestic programs and her ideological platform. Yet on the question of tight organizational control from Moscow, they sided wholeheartedly with Peking. Togliatti's "Yalta Memorandum" of September 1964, for example, criticized Moscow's handling of the Chinese challenge and placed strong emphasis on the autonomy of each Communist Party. Insisting on "unity in diversity," Togliatti expressed "strong reservations" on the question of a conference to expel or to censure Peking.[29]

Another indication of the weaknesses of Moscow's position was the so-called Rumanian "Declaration of Independence" of April 26, 1964. At Rumania's request, the publication of Suslov's report had been delayed for two months in an effort to end the polemics. Finally, at an enlarged plenum of the Central Committee, Rumanian leaders continued their defiance of the Soviet Union in

28. Suslov's speech, entitled "Struggle of the CPSU for the Unity of the World Communist Movement," is published in Griffith, *Sino-Soviet Relations, 1964–1965* (Cambridge: The M.I.T. Press, 1967), pp. 204–269.

29. Togliatti's memorandum, published in *L'Unita* on September 4, 1964, is printed in Griffith, *Sino-Soviet Relations*, pp. 373–383.

the form of a statement on the international Communist movement. In this case, opposition did not take the form of objections
to an East-West détente or to peaceful coexistence. Instead, the
statement rejected Soviet efforts to integrate the Bloc as a tightly
knit economic whole based on a division of labor established by
Moscow. Under this plan, Rumania would have supplied the
Bloc mainly with agricultural goods and raw materials, thus
thwarting her plans for industrialization.

Asserting that socialist industrialization was the only road to
national economic growth, the statement denied that there could
be anything like "father" and "son" Parties. It also insisted that
no Party had the right to call for a change in the leadership of
another Party, a statement that added up to a defense of Albania
and therefore of Peking.[30] Combined with the Togliatti memorandum, it provided a platform for anti-Soviet resistance. Moscow's failure to contain Peking had now escalated into unexpected
proportions. The schism had opened up a Pandora's box of grievances and quarrels.

Support of China's stance on the organizational issue was
prompted by various motives. Perhaps the most important one
was the fear that whatever machinery Moscow employed against
Peking could also be used against other dissidents. To a greater
or lesser degree, opponents of the move to excommunicate China
had all failed to toe the Soviet line in some area or another.
Poland, for example, while dependent on Moscow for the maintenance of the Oder-Neisse frontier with Germany, had stalled
on the collectivization of agriculture.[31] Diversity is thus in Gomulka's interest. Tito's position is similar. Within the Bloc,
the only countries which lent staunch support to Moscow's position were East Germany, Bulgaria, and Novotny's Czechoslovakia. Even Hungary's support was lukewarm, while Rumania,

30. "Statement on the Stand of the Rumanian Workers' Party Concerning the Problems of the International Communist and Working-
Class Movement," published in Griffith, *Sino-Soviet Relations*, pp.
269–296.

31. Gomulka's attitude seems to be that the Polish Communist
Party can maintain a dictatorship without terror only if it avoids the
class struggle. See Hansjakob Stehle, *The Independent Satellite* (New
York: Frederick A. Praeger, 1965), Ch. 2.

Cuba, North Vietnam, and North Korea took the side of the Italians. This rough division remains today.

For a few short weeks, Khrushchev's downfall in October 1964 seemed to spell an end to Soviet efforts. A November speech by Brezhnev, however, put an end to such speculation by maintaining the previous Soviet line.[32] In response, a *People's Daily* editorial published the next day renewed the attack, upholding Chinese arguments on revolutionary violence, factionalism, revisionism as the main danger, and the need for stronger moves against American imperialism. The case for factionalism was fortified by a pronouncement by Chou Yang. Backed by the philosopher Ai Ssu-ch'i, Chou's thesis, known as "one into two," claimed that "contradictions" existing behind a façade of unity and harmony had to be resolutely exposed. Two opposing forces would then split, leading to victory for revolutionary purity.

Originally, Chou's thesis referred primarily to domestic politics. In contrast to the theme of four class unity characteristic of the 1950's, the new line introduced a call for class struggle.[33] Yet while signaling a new Maoist offensive at home, the argument could also be applied to the Sino-Soviet confrontation. If the cohesion of the Bloc under Moscow's leadership was merely a disguise for contradictions between revolutionary and revisionist forces, then it was China's sacred duty to expose them. Invoking frequent examples of Lenin's refusal to compromise, this unique logic placed factionalism on a higher plane than unity.

The full strength of the movement to block China's excommunication was revealed by the Moscow conference of nineteen Communist Parties, held in March 1965. The gathering was supposed to be a preparatory meeting for a full assembly of Communist Parties. Although the participants agreed in principle on the need to meet, they postponed the actual convocation indefinitely. Significantly, they failed to name dogmatism as the

32. L. I. Brezhnev, "47th Anniversary of the Great October Socialist Revolution," November 6, 1964, *Pravda* and *Izvestia*, November 7, 1964, translated in *Current Digest of the Soviet Press*, Vol. XVI, No. 43, November 18, 1964, pp. 3–9.

33. For the domestic application of this line, see Ai Ssu-ch'i, "In Refutation of Comrade Yang Hsien-chen's 'Composite Economic Base Theory,'" *Jen-min Jih-pao* (*People's Daily*), November 1, 1964.

main danger to the international Communist movement. The meeting was drained of its anti-Chinese potential before it ever began. In fact, the Soviet failure to mobilize an international condemnation of China continues to the present day.

Yet even in China this trend did not pass unchallenged. Just as sympathy for China's position found partisans within the CPSU itself, so a deep division split Chinese leaders on the question of relations with the Soviet Union. A close comparison of the speeches of Lo Jui-ch'ing and Lin Piao, for example, made on the same day, reveals two separate sets of ideas. Lin's speech was the famous call for "people's war." It placed overwhelming emphasis on "self-reliance" as opposed to both better relations with the Soviet Union and extensive aid to national liberation movements abroad, while Lo's speech only paid lip service to self-reliance. Lin dwelt on a long and glowing eulogy of Mao, while Lo was clearly less enthusiastic. Lin reasserted the primacy of guerrilla warfare, political training, and the importance of high morale, while Lo stressed technical expertise and the need for modern weapons development. To drive home the point, Lo even reminded his audience of the importance of aid from "friendly countries," obviously the Soviet Union.[34]

At first sight it is difficult to explain Lo's speech and subsequent downfall on grounds of policy. As a supposedly bona fide guerrilla he was appointed to uproot the same views, expressed by P'eng Teh-huai in 1959, that he is now accused of holding. Nevertheless, it is perfectly possible that he actually did give "first consideration to military affairs" instead of "putting politics in command." [35] Perhaps for similar reasons, the Tenth Plenum of the Central Committee of September 1962 had already dismissed Huang K'o-ch'eng and T'an Cheng, both of whom had been associated with Lo in the 1959 shake-up. Hoping to strengthen China's military arsenal, these men must have looked with longing upon

34. Lin Piao, "Long Live the Victory of People's War!" and Lo Jui-ch'ing, "The People Defeated Japanese Fascism," *Peking Review*, Vol. VIII, No. 36, September 3, 1965, pp. 9–39.

35. This view is shared by Ellis Joffe in "China in Mid–1966: 'Cultural Revolution' or Struggle for Power?" *China Quarterly*, No. 27, July–September 1966, p. 129.

the prospect of Soviet aid in return for ideological concessions. They may even have conferred secretly with Soviet agents.

Finding sympathy for a Sino-Soviet rapprochement at such a high level may be one of the reasons why Mao felt compelled to launch the Cultural Revolution. Once again, domestic enemies have been labeled national traitors. Specifically the group surrounding Liu Shao-ch'i are said to have collaborated with Soviet revisionism. This time, however, the charge may be more than just tactical, for it is hard to imagine that certain Chinese leaders might not be tempted by the fruits of a major accommodation with the Soviet Union.

Needless to say, Soviet commentators have poured scorn on the Cultural Revolution. A recent analysis, for example, holds that Mao's group is trying to establish a "military-bureaucratic dictatorship." Lacking a definite class foundation, they are forced to rely on the guns of the Army and on Mao's personality cult. Their slogan of "self-reliance" is actually an effort to separate the national liberation movement from world socialism. By splitting anti-imperialist forces, they are aiding imperialism.[36] This bombardment goes beyond earlier criticisms in that it paints Mao as an isolated fanatic rather than as a mere representative of petty bourgeois nationalism.[37]

As indicated above, the Soviets see the Cultural Revolution as a severe threat to the supremacy of Party rule. In this sense, their attitude recalls the Chinese reaction to Khrushchev's de-Stalinization speech at the Twentieth Congress. Yet while the Chinese agreed that the Party could sometimes err, the Soviets refuse to admit this possibility. They criticize Mao precisely because he has bypassed the regular Party establishment and even exposed it to direct attacks from non-Party groups. Whether in Czechoslovakia or China, Moscow cannot tolerate a direct assault on absolute Party control for fear of domestic and foreign reverberations.

36. N. Kapchenko, "The 'Cultural Revolution' and the Mao Group's Foreign Policy," *International Affairs*, No. 2, February 1968, pp. 15–21.

37. T. Timofeyev, "Scientific Socialism and Petty Bourgeois Ideology," *loc. cit.*

Soviet policy-makers also realize that any successful deviation from the classic Soviet path will encourage other rebels to prolong their defiance of Moscow. Although both de-Stalinization and the pattern of modern politics probably made polycentrism inevitable, China's behavior dramatized, publicized, and accelerated this trend. To preserve whatever influence remains, Moscow must therefore describe China in the most irrational terms possible. Just as the Great Leap Forward was dismissed as a death-blow to agricultural progress, so the Cultural Revolution is said to spring from the personal egotism and xenophobic delusions of Chairman Mao. Judging from certain American press reports, Moscow's opinions sometimes seem to be accepted at face value.

Another reason why the Kremlin throws verbal grenades at the Cultural Revolution is that Soviet leaders despise mass politics *à la chinoise*. They prefer the efficiency of a standing committee meeting to a mass rally in Tien An Men Square. They favor the machinations of the secret police over the dunce-cap tactics of the Red Guards. They realize that failure to provide for mass participation in the political process may lead to apathy and withdrawal, but they fear that efforts in this direction would get out of hand. Judged by the standards of tight control, of course, they are right. Seen from the perspective of national *élan*, however, they may be wrong. So far, only the Soviet space triumphs seem to have succeeded in arousing fervent public enthusiasm. In the long run, the Maoist policy of mass mobilization may succeed in forestalling the cynicism and discontent of China's non-Communist elite as well as the passivity of her population at large. If it fails, of course, the danger of anarchy cannot be overlooked.

Nevertheless, Chinese leaders appear to be straining every nerve to minimize the disruption of the Cultural Revolution. Aside from protecting the economy, they began to rein in the Red Guards almost as soon as they were given their role. In the last two or three weeks of September 1966, a number of measures were taken to limit excesses. Physical force was now prohibited at all cost, even though this ban has not always been respected. The organization of the Red Guards was significantly tightened as the formation of committees to supervise their activities was accelerated. New and more disciplined "Red Guards Corps" employed high-ranking PLA (People's Liberation Army) military district commanders and political commissars as instructors. After Chou En-lai criticized the Harbin Red Guards, a truce was temporarily established with provincial Party organizations. Henceforth, purges were to be directed from Peking and assisted from the streets rather than the other way around.

In October and November 1966 new tactics appeared in the form of wall posters denouncing prominent individuals rather than entire committees. Although schools were to remain closed, organized mass rallies declined in number. As the winter approached, Peking's food supply and transportation system became seriously overburdened. Numerous devices were invented to send the Red Guards elsewhere, such as miniature re-creations of the famous "Long March" of the 1930's.

Throughout 1967 three trends emerged that seemed to spell the end of the Cultural Revolution, at least as it was originally conceived. The first was a further clamp-down on the Red Guards. Instead of being the bearers and instructors of Mao's thought, young intellectuals and students were now commanded to "integrate themselves" with workers and peasants and to "learn modestly" from them as their "willing pupils." [38] Red Guards were warned not to attack Party cadres indiscriminately, but to take into account their merits as well as their errors.[39] At the same time, Mao's essay on correcting "mistaken ideas," written in 1929, was reissued as a timely attack against "putschism," disregard for organizational discipline, the use of violence, absolute egalitarianism, "ultra-democracy," anarchism, and other deviations that clearly applied to the Red Guards.[40]

Reflecting this shift, the slogans of 1967 now called for a thorough attack on the "selfishness" of Maoist groups as well as the "revisionism" of their bourgeois opponents. After August and September, the call to fight revisionism was even relegated

38. "Cadres Should Go Among the Masses," *Peking Review,* Vol. X, No. 48, November 24, 1967, p. 7.

39. "Cadres Must Be Treated Correctly," *Peking Review,* Vol. X, No. 10, March 3, 1967, pp. 6–8.

40. Mao Tse-tung, "On Correcting Mistaken Ideas in the Party," December 1929, reprinted in *Peking Review,* Vol. X, No. 6, February 3, 1967.

to a secondary position.[41] This change was coupled with a drive to promote production and to woo back humiliated lower level cadres who were needed in the spring and autumn harvests.[42]

The second trend was a vigorous counter offensive by the Liu-Teng faction. In January and February 1967, the Maoist press reported "new counter-attacks of the bourgeois reactionary line" in Chinghai, Fukien, and Inner Mongolia. For unspecified reasons, a much publicized "Shanghai People's Commune," modeled on the Paris Commune, had to close down in less than three weeks. Meanwhile, a wave of "economism" developed among workers and peasants which was interpreted as another sign of Liu's resurgence.[43]

Finally, anti-Mao elements in the Army, possibly backed by Lo Jui-ch'ing, P'eng Teh-huai, and the Liu-Teng faction, posed a serious threat to the Mao-Lin leadership. Although the details are still unclear, the Wuhan Military allegedly rebelled against Mao in the summer of 1967. In this incident two emergency envoys from Peking were "kidnapped, beaten, and humiliated" by local military leaders.[44] In the reaction that followed, the commander and political commissar of the region were replaced by men loyal to Lin Piao. Judging from Peking's vehement reaction, the "life-and-death" struggle used to describe P'eng Teh-huai's alleged revolt in 1959 is not yet over.

Nevertheless, Soviet leaders should not place too much hope in military opposition to Mao's leadership. The exact extent

41. See, for example, Lin Piao, "Comrade Lin Piao's Speech," *Peking Review*, Vol. X, No. 41, October 6, 1967, p. 10.

42. Chou En-lai, "Premier Chou En-lai's Speech," *Peking Review*, Vol. X, No. 41, October 6, 1967, p. 12. See also "Cadres Are Being 'Boldly Liberated' and Employed to Save Production," *China News Summary*, No. 195, November 9, 1967, p. 1.

43. See "Oppose Economism and Smash the Latest Counter-Attack by the Bourgeois Reactionary Line," *Peking Review*, Vol. X, No. 4, January 20, 1967.

44. Li Hsin-kung, "Settle Accounts with P'eng Teh-huai for His Heinous Crimes of Usurping Army Leadership and Opposing the Party," *Peking Review*, Vol. X, No. 36, September 1, 1967, pp. 12–14. This sudden barrage against a man purged eight years earlier suggests that other rebellions were expected.

of military discontent is impossible to ascertain, but it should not be exaggerated. Traditional units within the PLA could hardly be expected to approve of the near anarchy of the more virulent phases of the Red Guard movement. Their opposition may not be specifically to Mao and Lin but to the Cultural Revolution in general, which now appears to be dying or even dead.

Just as the slogans of the Great Leap Forward continued to be propagated long after economic upheavals had ended, so the Cultural Revolution seems to be fading away in spite of the persistence of revolutionary vocabulary. A recent slogan of the Red Guards—"make revolution through reopening classes" —is an illustration of this trend.[45] New directives on educational policy castigate the attitudes of "those short-sighted intellectuals who see only their small mountain-strongholds" and subordinate student activism to leadership by adult workers.[46] The takeover of schools by peasant-soldier teams in the countryside and worker-soldier teams in the cities is frankly intended to keep the Red Guards in their place.[47] Just as Mao looked down on the "fair-weather friends of revolution" in the 1920's and 1930's, so he seems to have only limited use for students in the 1960's. Thus far, however, the Soviets have not recognized the new trend.[48]

Besides the ups and downs of mass mobilization, Soviet leaders share the Western view that the Cultural Revolution is harmful to China's long-term economic growth. While political upheaval must have inflicted a certain amount of damage, the long-term consequences of the Cultural Revolution are a subject of controversy. One analysis even holds that Maoism and its policies are tools in the service of economic development.[49] Specifically,

45. "Students Warned Against 'Internal Struggle,'" *China News Items from the Press*, No. 177, July 6, 1967, p. 2.

46. Yao Wen-yuan, "The Working Class Must Exercise Leadership in Everything," *Peking Review*, Vol. XI, No. 35, August 30, 1968, p. 5.

47. See the analysis by Tillman Durdin in the *New York Times*, September 17, 1968, p. 10.

48. See, for example, "This Summer in Kwangtung," *New Times*, No. 34, August 28, 1968, pp. 19–20.

49. Rensselaer W. Lee, III, "The *Hsia Fang* System: Marxism and

Mao fears that the momentum for industrial development generated in past years may be halted by inertia, localism, and tradition. Accordingly, such measures as forcing the elite to participate in physical labor are to be understood not as nostalgia for the past but as crucial formulae for guaranteeing the effective use of the elite as an instrument of modernization.

Pursuing this analysis, the cultivation of selfless collectivism, a keynote of the Cultural Revolution, may thus be seen as an investment. In order to combat elitist values and bureaucratic styles of work that lower morale and hinder production, the Party has attempted to develop a social consciousness that is conducive to economic development. To counteract the waste of human resources caused by an overstaffed administrative network, the Maoist leadership has transferred cadres to the countryside. To develop self-sacrifice on the part of the masses and to prevent their alienation from the leadership, Mao continues to insist on the "mass line" style of work. There can be little doubt that these methods have been at least partly successful.[50]

In short, Soviet objections to the Cultural Revolution differ widely as to their validity. Each must be judged on its own merits. From the standpoint of China's domestic economy, Soviet charges are open to question. On the issue of what Moscow calls "bureaucratic militarism," China's record is fairly clean. While it is too early to discern whether Lin's efforts to keep the Army under political control have been successful, accusations of bureaucratism are out of place. The main brunt of the Cultural Revolution has been directed precisely against established bureaucracies, namely, the Party and the Government. Bureau-

Modernization," *China Quarterly*, No. 28, October–December 1966. Lee argues that Weberian models of routinized and structurally differentiated institutions may not be applicable to China's modernization.

50. Others who support this view include Michel Oksenberg in "China: Forcing the Revolution to a New Stage," *Asian Survey*, Vol. VII, No. 1, January 1967, p. 13; Lee, "The *Hsia Fang* System," p. 56; and A. Doak Barnett, "Social Stratification and Aspects of Personnel Management in the Chinese Communist Bureaucracy," *China Quarterly*, No. 28, October–December 1966, p. 26.

cratic patterns of the past have been at least partially toppled, and administration at present is still too fluid and too uncertain to permit their resurgence.

Yet other Soviet charges ring true. A personality cult has indeed arisen in China. Although Mao is throwing the full weight of his personal prestige into the battle to secure Lin's inheritance, the line between shrewd political tactics and personal egoism is indistinct at best. Furthermore Mao's style of leadership certainly does threaten the basis of Party rule. If Chinese leaders carry out their announced plan to re-establish Party leadership on a reconstituted basis, they may meet with opposition. Elsewhere, dissident groups are wondering whether similar attacks on their own Communist Parties may not be in order. Moscow's leaders have good reason to worry.

Most accurate of all are those charges accusing Mao of anti-Soviet activities and "petty-bourgeois" nationalism. Just as Peking condemns Moscow for subordinating revolutionary movements to cooperation with Washington, so China may be guilty of yielding to a burning drive to thwart the Soviet Union at every step at the expense of Communist solidarity. Peking's shrill concern for territorial integrity vis-à-vis both the Soviet Union and the United States is indeed a feature of nationalism. By the same criterion, however, no country has yet moved beyond this stage. It is merely that China's position as a challenger of the status quo forces her to articulate her demands more loudly and more bitterly than others.

From a pragmatic point of view, Chinese leaders have little reason to do otherwise. After all, the danger from an American attack is relatively slight. Even if the Vietnam War did spill over into China, however, there is little guarantee that the Russian bear will come lumbering to the rescue. In fact, Soviet policy-makers are more likely to sit back with folded arms and contemplate the destruction of the Chinese nuisance. Nor are economic arguments sufficiently compelling to force a compromise. Even during the interlude of good relations between the two countries, aid from Moscow was notoriously small. Finally, the contrast between the relative unity of Bloc politics in the 1950's and the rampant polycentrism of the 1960's suggests that now is not the time for compromise. Similarly, the erosion of bipolarity has given China an unprecedented opportunity to cultivate what her leaders consider to be a *sine qua non* of great power status: a sphere of influence.

In some ways the renewal of Sino-Soviet antagonisms resembles a return to the old game of historical rivalry. To Peking, the Soviets are still the crude and hairy barbarians from the northern steppes. To Moscow, the Chinese still maintain proud and un-yielding mannerisms.[51] Yet beneath this superficial resemblance, the similarity breaks down. A major difference from the past is that China's search for influence is not regional but world-wide. The Chinese no longer want the rest of the world to come to them. Indeed, they will go anywhere their resources and their imagination permit. They do not seek a new form of tribute system, nor do they wish to withdraw to the company of satellites. Instead of isolated superiority they want participatory equality with the great powers. They want full membership in the club of status quo powers.

Another difference is that the Sino-Soviet dispute reflects not the culturism of the Ch'ing court but the nationalism of its successors. China is quick to adopt a foreign invention that will serve her economic development. Although Chinese technicians may adjust foreign innovations to suit Chinese circumstances, they do so not because of any unwillingness to import an idea but because they wish to facilitate the specifically modern task of rapid economic growth. Unlike Japan, however, China will not permit any foreign troops on her soil. As long as she lacks the recognition and influence which she feels is due, she will not cooperate with any efforts to subdue her. Until she achieves great power status in both theory and practice, she will reject a junior partnership with any country.

This attitude does not mean that contemporary Chinese leaders have no conception of equality in international relations. They are not handicapped by a traditional tendency to think only in hierarchical terms. If what they want does not sound like equality, neither do the present-day actions of members in the Western

51. A full treatment of this point of view can be found in Mark Mancall, "The Persistence of Tradition in Chinese Foreign Policy," *The Annals*, Vol. 349, September 1963.

state system. The corridors of the United Nations are not populated by free and equal representatives but by a system which is as hierarchical in its own way as China's traditional tribute system. In the eyes of Mao and his colleagues, the world is run by two wealthy and opinionated stockholders. Together with a few moderately well-to-do dowagers and their minions, they hold a majority of the shares. To Peking, this scenario is out of date.

☆ CHAPTER SIX

China's Search for National Boundaries

The problem of boundaries is essentially a problem of the age of nationalism. A nation-state insists on territorial impermeability. It thus insists on the exact delimitation of its boundaries. It justifies its territorial claims on the basis of historical continuity, racial homogeneity, customary law, and, if possible, treaties and agreements.

The problem of non-Western boundaries, as with many in central and eastern Europe, is that they were drawn up on the basis of conquest, diplomatic convenience, and bargaining by the imperialist powers. The Congress of Berlin, for example, carved up large portions of Africa and distributed them like so many portions of beef. Yet, in itself this fact is not a sufficient reason for denigrating or changing boundaries. In world history there is hardly a single boundary which was not a product of conquest and violence at one time or another.

Before the era of the nation-state, boundaries were neither clearly delimited nor based on any territorial or racial premises. They were dependent on the ability of the central authority to control, administer, and police. For most periods in history, from the point of view of the central authority, outlying areas enjoyed military control at best and partial autonomy at worst. Emperors were far more concerned with maintaining their administration with the help of their slender resources and their narrow power base than with quibbling over boundaries. Frontiers were only attended to in the case of attack, either from dissident tribes or from rival empires. The policy applied to frontier areas was a strategy of denial, which sought to preserve them from foreign conquest, rather than a strategy of integration.

In modern terminology traditional empires, indifferent to the headache of exact delimitation, used border territories as buffer areas. Usually these lands were sparsely populated and communication to and from the capital was very difficult. Frontier violations were not always discovered, so that immediate reactions were out of the question. Strictly speaking, such areas should be known as frontiers rather than boundaries. This useful distinction between frontier and boundary was first made by Sir Henry McMahon in 1935.[1]

The search for rigid and delimited boundaries, the move to transform frontiers into border provinces, and the attempt to integrate them with the rest of the nation only began with the first stage of the nation-state. A very characteristic example is the search for natural frontiers by Louis XIV. A similar situation prevailed throughout nineteenth-century America. These years witnessed an age of American expansionism in search of national boundaries. In this sense, the Mexican-American War of 1846–1848 was a boundary war. The search for national boundaries, natural or unnatual, can thus take many forms. The most common, however, is war. The purchases of Alaska and Louisiana are exceptions that prove the rule.

The principle of national self-determination, propounded by Wilson and proclaimed by most Western powers to be a legitimizing device for national boundaries, has not usually worked in practice. If it had, most national minorities would have their own nation-states. There is hardly a single nation-state which does not have the problem of a national minority. Almost every minority, nursing some complaint, displays some secessionist tendencies. The Scots in the United Kingdom, the French in Canada, and the Kazaks in the Soviet Union and China all provide examples.

The degree to which these tendencies mushroom into a national problem, thus attracting gratuitous international attention, depends partly on foreign interest in the country in question.

1. Alastair Lamb, *The China-India Border: The Origins of the Disputed Boundaries* (London: Oxford University Press, 1964), p. 14.

Yet to a greater extent, it depends on the degree of integration which has taken place between the minority inhabitants of frontier areas and the rest of the nation. The question here is not of assimilation, but of integration. While attempts at assimilation have generally failed, attempts at integration have partly succeeded. The United States serves as the prime example of the failure of total assimilation and the success of partial integration. This balance, combined with the degree of territorial dispersion, helped to determine the proportions of the problem.

China's search for national boundaries started long before the Communist victory. This search coincided with the transition from the era of culturism to the era of nationalism. The last decades of Imperial China witnessed the beginning of this transformation. Not only did China start to modernize her foreign relations, but she increasingly sought to reassert control over her frontier areas as well. The actual nature and political complexion of the government in Peking are only of marginal importance to this general trend. Imperial, Republican, or Communist China would all have done the same thing.

China had begun the irreversible process of thinking in terms of a nation and talking in terms of national sovereignty and territorial impermeability. As far as Chinese frontiers were concerned, the value of the tribute system was more theoretical than practical. Regardless of the emphasis on tributary relationships with the frontier areas which marked nineteenth-century Chinese documents, the tribute system would have been unrealistic. The era of the nation-state affected not only China but her neighbors as well. Tributary relationships could not have settled the problem of national boundaries.

China shares her boundary problem with an impressively large number of countries. Her land frontier stretches from Vietnam and Korea to Soviet Inner Asia. In this respect the closest parallel is Brazil. Another complicating feature of China's boundary problems is that most of them arise with countries who are also in search of national boundaries. The only exception is possibly the Soviet Union.

Soviet nationalism differs from that of Asian nations, including China, in that the USSR is an industrially advanced country with a fairly high degree of national integration. After years of organizational and educational work among non-Russian minority groups, the Kremlin has succeeded in integrating the border areas into some kind of national society. Asian nations, however, have hitherto been unable to assert such a national identity. The loyalty of their migrant border populations is often in doubt. These countries are still transitional in the sense that national allegiance is still in the making.

From Korea to India, China's boundaries are shared with transitional national societies. with the exception of Outer Mongolia and Nepal there are no real buffer states between China and her two main rivals, India and the Soviet Union. Sikkim and Bhutan, being Indian protectorates, ultimately refer to the confrontation between China and India.

Added to political problems are questions of national security, strategic realities, and the topographical wilderness of Central Asia. China has embarked not only on a search for territory, but on a quest for economic resources as well. Two examples are the oil of Sinkiang and the gold and uranium of western Tibet. National honor and legal hairsplitting are not the only concerns at stake.[2] On all of these points, factual historical evidence is by no means the primary issue.[3]

In any realistic discussion of the Sino-Indian border problem, or for that matter any other similar controversy, it must be remembered that such nations are in the process of discovering and establishing themselves. Analysis must also take into account the need for security and raw materials. Mixed in with these priorities are confused historical records and assorted legal claims. Questions of ideology, nationalism, Cold War tensions, the interests of the superpowers, and, last but not least, tendencies toward universal moralism further complicate and inflame the issue.

2. Margaret W. Fisher, Leo E. Rose, and Robert A. Huttenback, *Himalayan Battleground: Sino-Indian Rivalry in Ladakh* (New York: Praeger, 1963), pp. 5–6.

3. The Rt. Hon. Kenneth T. Younger in Alastair Lamb, *The China-India Border: The Origins of the Disputed Boundaries* (London: Oxford University Press, 1964), p. vii.

To seek a logical or rational solution to these problems is of little practical use, for perceptions of logic and reason depend on an antagonist's point of view. Only two main methods remain. One is negotiations on the basis of compromise, and the other is a trial of strength. The first has been chosen by the smaller states surrounding China, notably Burma, Nepal, Pakistan, and Afghanistan. The second has been adopted by states which are themselves contenders for power and influence. Their leaders feel that there is something at stake which might be lost through negotiations. The state most prominent in this category at present is India. The Soviet Union may be next, for signs of a trial of strength are already mounting.

Contrary to general opinion, the difference between these two groups of states does not lie in China's reasonable approach toward one and her hostility to the other. The logic of conflict is built into the very structure of the international scenario. China and India are both great powers-to-be in search of national boundaries. The argument that Chinese Communism is inherently antagonistic falls flat when applied elsewhere. Since 1960 China has reached boundary agreements with Nepal, Burma, Pakistan, Afghanistan, and Outer Mongolia. Boundaries with North Korea and North Vietnam were established previously. To understand the two major problems remaining in the second category depends partly on an analysis of the settlement of those in the first. Most relevant in this respect is the case of China and Burma.

The Sino-Burmese boundary, although comparatively peaceful, still witnessed frequent border violations and armed incursions. The most important Chinese violation occurred in July 1956.[4] Even during the course of the subsequent negotiations, Peking admitted that clashes occurred.[5] In a revealing statement, the Chinese maintained that the renegotiation of the boundary was needed not so much to adjust territory as to solve a "problem

4. Harold C. Hinton, *China's Relations with Burma and Vietnam: A Brief Survey* (New York: International Secretariat, Institute of Pacific Relations, 1958), p. 56.

5. See Chou En-lai's speech at a state banquet in his honor given in Rangoon by Burmese Prime Minister U Nu on April 16, 1960, in *Peking Review*, Vol. III, No. 16, April 19, 1960, p. 16.

left over from history." They stressed that the negotiators had taken into account "both the historical background and the existing reality." [6]

This reference to history meant not only that the former Sino-Burmese boundary was drawn up by the imperialists, but also that said powers had not included the practical needs of either China or Burma. In a speech in Rangoon in April 1960, Chou En-lai stressed this practical aspect. Improvement had taken place because China returned the Meng-Mao triangular area in return for Burmese adjustments of the so-called "1941 line." [7] This arrangement is discussed below. The tone of the remarks, however, indicated that actual territorial exchange was less important than the spirit of the agreement. Even if the changes were only minor, negotiations on the basis of equality and mutual benefit were preferable to boundaries imposed by the guns of imperialism. Once again, China's perception of modern history was central to its acts.

The publicity devoted to the Sino-Burmese agreement was almost undoubtedly a broad hint to India regarding her northwestern boundary with China. If Peking could return some territory to Burma, the logic ran, then India could do the same in the Aksai-chin area. In this case practical considerations rested on the Chinese side, for they needed the road in question for the control and defense of Tibet, and India was supposed to take this fact into account. Similarly, Chinese spokesmen emphasized that China had given up her right to participate in the mining enterprises at Lufang in Burma. This message was probably aimed at the Soviet Union. By implication, the Chinese were better than the Soviets because they did not believe in violating national sovereignty by clinging to warmed-over imperialist rights in another nation's territory.

The Chinese continued to use the case of the Sino-Burmese boundary settlement for two further purposes. First, Peking wished to announce to the world in general and to India in

6. Editorial, "A Good Example of Peaceful Coexistence Among Asian Countries," *Jen-min Jih-pao* (*People's Daily*), August 3, 1960, *Peking Review*, Vol. III, No. 32, August 9, 1960, p. 13.

7. Speech of Chou En-lai on April 16, 1960, *op. cit.*

particular that border disputes could be solved through peaceful negotiations. Chinese commentators implied that in the course of such talks China would take practical considerations into account. This hint was another way of saying that the transfer of territory would have to be aimed at making the boundary more rational, at least from the Chinese point of view.

Second, Chinese leaders held up the Sino-Burmese agreement as an ideal to be followed by all countries which had boundary problems with China. They stressed that this settlement was territorially beneficial to Burma and that it was reached between two countries with different social and political systems.

Unlike the Sino-Burmese arrangement, the frequently cited Sino-Indian agreement of 1954 was not a border settlement. Confining itself only to trade and a statement on the relations of the two nations to each other, it laid down the famous Five Principles or Panch Shila. These were mutual respect for each other's territorial integrity and sovereignty, mutual non-aggression, mutual non-interference in each other's affairs, equality and mutual benefit, and peaceful co-existence. These platitudinous phrases were hailed as the basis of international law for China's relations with non-Communist countries. They became a model for similar agreements with other Afro-Asian nations.

In other words the Sino-Burmese Treaty served the same diplomatic purposes as the Sino-Indian agreement of 1954 on Tibet and the Bandung Conference. As far as China was concerned, all three were based on the Five Principles of Peaceful Coexistence, and all three bore important testimony to China's desire to enter into freely negotiated treaties and to live in peace.

The Sino-Burmese agreement specifically emphasized that in the Meng-Mao area Burma had built a highway. It pointed out that this highway linked the Shan and Kachin states of Burma to the rest of the country. This road thus constituted an important communications artery which entitled Rangoon to take over this area as a part of Burmese territory. In return, the Burmese government handed over to China the territory under the jurisdiction of the Panhung and Panlao tribes. This territory lay west of the 1941 line, which had divided the two tribes into areas of Burmese and Chinese jurisdiction. China considered this step to be beneficial to both countries.[8] The hint to India urging a similar exchange is too strong and too obvious to be missed.

The Sino-Burmese settlement did not totally discard historical factors. Both sides agreed that the entire northern section of the boundary had never been properly defined. They held that the villages of Hpimaw, Gawlum, and Kangfang, occupied by British troops between 1905 and 1911, should be returned to China. They also insisted that the 1897 treaty, which had given the Meng-Mao area in perpetual lease to British Burma, should be abrogated. The emphasis here was again on dissociation from the era of imperialism and an almost fanatical obsession with formal equality. Once this break with imperialism was solemnized, the Chinese handed the area over to Burma on the basis of practical considerations and communication needs.

To the Chinese, making a point about equality is thus more important than historical or treaty considerations. They were not prepared to accept the 1897 treaty because it talked of perpetual lease and therefore of unequal treatment. Even though the net result was the same, they insisted that it should be abrogated and that a new treaty should be negotiated in its place. The Meng-Mao area still belongs to Burma, but possession is now justified by the Sino-Burmese agreement of 1961 rather than by the British treaty of 1897. With both the Meng-Mao area and the Lufang mines, Peking's spokesmen scrupulously reiterated their desire to avoid perpetuating the unequal nature of the 1897 treaty. Instead, they wished neither to take advantage of nor to yield advantage to any country.

Whether it is a nineteenth-century view of sovereignty or an insistence on equality characteristic of Chinese nationalism which complicates China's border settlements is hard to say. Historians noting China's insistence on the abrogation of unequal treaties with the West have rarely, if ever, extended the same analogy to China's borders in south and central Asia. The Chinese have extended it themselves and have been quite consistent in so doing.

8. Editorial, "A New Example of Solidarity and Friendship Among Asian Countries," *Jen-min Jih-pao* (*People's Daily*), in *Peking Review*, Vol. III, No. 5, February 2, 1960, p. 10.

From this point of view, there is no difference between the Nationalist and Communist Chinese governments. Both have insisted in the past on the abrogation of all unequal treaties and the negotiation of new ones, and both will continue to do so in the future. Peking may not have realized the full diplomatic cost of this obsession. Any discussion of unequal treaties must be broadened from China's maritime frontier or treaty ports to include the entire scope of her frontiers. A culturistic China could tolerate such treaties on both maritime and land frontiers, while a nationalistic China can endure neither.

The boundary dispute which adds up to one of China's major diplomatic problems, and which in the short run represents China's biggest diplomatic gamble, is the Sino-Indian boundary. The key to unlocking this dilemma is, of course, Tibet. If Chinese control of Tibet had not become such a major issue, the Sino-Indian conflict would have been minimized. Between 1950 and 1958, the dispute would have been either underplayed or kept within peaceful limits. Sometimes it appears that the Sino-Indian border is secondary and that the primary issue is the control of Tibet.

The question of Chinese sovereignty over Tibet is one which has always baffled the historical analyst and thwarted any definitive historical conclusion. Always a difficult geographical area, Tibet was traditionally seen more as a buffer state than as an inherent component of the Chinese empire. In the traditional state system, sovereignty was not and should not be interpreted in terms of direct administrative control. Instead, it depended on indirect control and proclamations of allegiance or independence, which varied with the capabilities of the central authority.

This definition applies not only to the Chinese side of the border, but also to the Indian subcontinent. The ambitions of the rulers of Ladakh, Kashmir, and Sinkiang are thus wound up in a historical maze. Throughout considerable periods of history, the weakness of central authority permitted a considerable degree of freedom for ambitious local rulers to pursue their own dynastic interests.

The legitimacy of sovereignty, whether in Kashmir, Ladakh, Hunza, Tibet, or Nepal, thus depends not so much on historical rights of existence as on the power of the central authority on both sides of the Himalayas to extend and enforce their control. In this sense, Tibet has the same right to exist as Ladakh or Kashmir. Historical claims of one side can thus be balanced by counter-claims of the other. The historical picture is simply too murky to permit clear-cut conclusions.

With the rise of British power in India, it was impossible for any of these border kingdoms not to feel the weight of the new central authority which now ruled the Indian subcontinent. This new force was partially offset at the end of the nineteenth century, when Anglo-Russian rivalry led to a forward policy by both powers. Indeterminate buffer zones in an inaccessible region of the world were now exposed to conflicting pressures rather than to a single authority. It was in the British interest to maintain not the independence and sovereignty of Tibet but rather an autonomous Tibet which the British could manipulate. Kashmir and Ladakh were similar cases.

In addition to the complications of British policy, the issue of Tibet is clouded by a long history of interaction with China. From the sixth to the ninth century A.D., ambitious Tibetan rulers waged sporadic conflicts with China from Szechuan to Turkestan.[9] In the tenth century, Ladakh emerged as an independent state with its own ambitions regarding the establishment of an independent empire. The Sino-Indian boundary problem, therefore, is not limited to the Indian government on the one hand and the Communist government acting as a successor to the British and the Manchus on the other. Its solution also involves trying to straighten out the various treaties concluded from 1000 A.D. to 1914 between Tibet and Ladakh, Tibet and China, and Tibet and India. The difficulty with all of them is that they were not drawn up between nation-states and that they thus provided for frontiers rather than for precise boundary lines. The treaty between Tibet and Ladakh of 1684, for example, failed to define a clear boundary between the two areas. Both China and India admit this fact. Both have used historical records to support their cases and have

9. For a detailed account of historical background of this area, see Margaret W. Fisher, Leo E. Rose, Robert A. Huttenback, *Himalayan Battleground: Sino-Indian Rivalry in Ladakh, op. cit.* and Alastair Lamb, *The China-India Border: The Origins of the Disputed Boundaries, op. cit.*

discarded them when they do not. Both sides thus make a selective use of history.

Neither in 1954 nor in subsequent years have the Chinese ever claimed Tibetan jurisdiction and therefore Chinese control over Ladakh. Although the 1954 arrangements with India spoke of the "Tibetan region of China," the problem of Ladakh was omitted. The Chinese merely say that the boundary between Tibet and Ladakh should be redrawn. They realize that tribute missions from Ladakh to Tibet do not indicate Ladakh's submission to Tibet. Instead, Ladakh was following a normal diplomatic method of conducting international relations between preindustrial societies. Opening the door to this kind of historical claim would unleash a host of historical problems which Peking prefers to avoid.

From time to time the Chinese have tried to keep both Ladakhis and Tibetans from extending their influence into Chinese Turkestan, now known as Sinkiang. By the same token, they have tried to enforce their suzerainty over Tibet. Between 1718 and 1720, the Chinese tried to halt the extension of the sovereignty of Dsungar Mongols to Tibet and to replace it with their own control. Ladakh ceased to pose its own threat in 1840, when it was taken over by the Dogra rulers of Kashmir.

It was at this time that the Dogras started to follow a forward policy in western Tibet. Their actions aroused British interest because of the prospect of a Dogra-Nepalese alliance and the possible loss of the wool trade. The Dogra-Tibetan War of 1840–41 finally ended all Ladakhi pretensions to western Tibet. It also revealed that the Tibetans considered themselves to be under some kind of Chinese suzerainty. In fact, Lhasa even called upon the Chinese and received their help. In 1847, in the face of increasing Chinese noncooperation, the British unilaterally marked the boundaries between the Dogra kingdom and Tibet. It is this unilateral boundary which the Indian side now claims.

As the Chinese moved from culturism to cultural nationalism, they grew increasingly aware that a nation-state could not tolerate unequal treaties and unilateral boundary settlements. Yet two problems inhibited them from taking any actions at first. One was uncertainty as to how far they should go in pressing their claims. The second was the very limited stock of power and resources available for coping with internal and external threats. In the face of more serious problems, boundary demarcation had to wait.

Yet the Chinese did what they could. In 1877 they reconquered Chinese Turkestan from the Mongols. During the last decade of the nineteenth century, they resisted British expansionism in the northwest frontier area, particularly in the region of Aksai-chin. As soon as China entered the Republican era, she claimed Tibet as a province of China. Under these circumstances Yuan Shih-k'ai's government agreed to border talks to settle the boundaries of Tibet with British India at Simla in 1913 and 1914. At these meetings the Chinese Minister for Foreign Affairs accepted a separation between the Dalai Lama's political and religious authority. His sovereignty was not to extend all through the Himalayas wherever religious tribute was paid to him. This agreement excluded any Tibetan or Chinese claims to such areas as Ladakh, Nepal, Sikkim, and Bhutan. Neither in theory nor in practice has the Chinese Communist government proclaimed any sovereignty over these areas.

The 1914 Simla Conference did not decide upon the Ladakh-Tibetan border. In fact, the question was not even discussed. Only in 1959 did the Chinese Communists raise the issue for the first time. Their claims were founded more on territorial considerations than similar ones made by Tibet in 1917, 1929, and 1947. Religious hegemony has never been a criterion to Peking.

In both 1914 and 1951 Chinese sovereignty over Tibet was recognized by the British government in India and its successor and, in the latter case, by the Tibetans themselves. In October 1950, Peking had emphasized that Tibet must accept Chinese sovereignty. To enforce this demand, the Chinese insisted that a Tibetan delegation should visit Peking. At the time, the only government seriously interested in Tibet's autonomy was India. In order to go to Peking the Tibetans passed through Delhi and tried to delay the resumption of their journey as long as they could. Meanwhile India tried to suggest to China that Peking should not take a harsh line in the reassertion of its sovereignty over Tibet. Among the arguments used was the opinion that bloodshed in Tibet would hurt Peking's chances of being admitted to the United Nations.[10]

10. Editorial, "There Must Be No Interference with the Liberation of Tibet by the PLA," *Jen-min Jih-pao*, Nov. 17, 1950, CB, No. 31,

As with other cases, including Taiwan, the Chinese maintained that Tibet was a matter of domestic jurisdiction. As far as they were concerned, the establishment of their national boundaries was more important than admission to an international debating club. Actually India saw the two cases in a different light. In the diplomatic correspondence between India and China in 1950, New Delhi never really questioned Chinese sovereignty over Tibet. The question was one of tactics. India's diplomatic argument was therefore weakened, because once sovereignty was accepted, domestic jurisdiction came to the fore. Once this step was taken, nothing could be done. The Tibetans had no choice but to resume their journey to Peking and to formalize their wayward historical relationship with China. After some hesitation, the Tibetan Assembly finally ratified the resulting Sino-Tibetan agreement on November 19, 1951. This agreement is not a treaty under the terms of international law. China's claim to sovereignty over Tibet obviously rules out an international framework. Instead the document is comparable to agreements made between white settlers and the American Indians, between the Indian government and the Nagas, or between the Iraqi governments and the Kurds.

Yet the Sino-Indian border problem does not stop here. Besides the question of sovereignty over Tibet, two important thorns remained. One was the question of residual British rights in Tibet, which the Indian government had inherited. The second was the demarcation of Tibetan boundaries along India's eastern, central, and northwestern frontiers.

Until 1950 the Indians enjoyed a mission in Lhasa. According to the Sino-Indian agreement of September 15, 1952, this mission was converted to the status of a consulate general. In return the Indian government agreed to the establishment of a Chinese consulate general in Bombay. The very fact that the status of the Indian mission was changed and a Chinese consulate general established suggests that the Indian government had given im-

November 27, 1950, pp. 8–9; and "China Reaffirms Her Position in Tibet in a Reply to India" (NCNA), Peking, Nov. 16, 1950, CB, No. 31, Nov. 27, 1950; and "Reply of the CPG of the PRC on October 30, 1950, to the Memorandum and Note of the Indian Government on the Question of Tibet," Oct. 30, 1950, CB, No. 31, Nov. 27, 1950, pp. 4–5.

plicit recognition to China's sovereignty over Tibet. The question of Tibetan autonomy, which formed such a large part of the Simla agreement of 1914, was ignored. Regardless of historical or legal arguments, the political fact remains that once China's sovereignty over Tibet was recognized, whatever autonomy the Tibetans may have enjoyed from then on depended not on international pressures but on China's consent. Peking can no more tolerate interference in Tibet than the United States can in Alaska.

The first Chinese steps to integrate Tibet into the Chinese nation were slow and hesitant. From 1950 to 1958, Chinese leaders held that the integration of all minority areas, particularly Tibet, would have to drag behind the pace of the rest of the country. Implementation of the land reform act of 1950, for example, was postponed in minority areas because they could not keep up with China's modernizing revolution. Accordingly, upper classes in Tibet were to be given as much time as possible to recognize political reality and to embrace revolution. In fact, various radical programs, including the socialization of agriculture and economic life, were not extended to Tibet until after the Tibetan revolt of 1959. In this specific sense at least a minimal degree of Tibetan autonomy survived the first decade of Communist rule.

The Sino-Indian agreement of 1954, which finalized the withdrawal of Indian rights from Tibet, had dealt indirectly with the Indian-Tibetan boundary. Between 1955 and 1958 a considerable number of border violations ensued, the first erupting in June 1955, within two months of the Bandung Conference. Even between 1955 and 1958, the Sino-Indian boundary dispute was still a low-key affair. It was only after the Tibetan Revolt of 1959 [11]

11. For Chinese reactions to the 1959 Tibetan Revolt see "Exchange of Letters" between Dalai Lama and General Tan Kuan-san, acting representative of the Central People's Government and Political Commissar of the Tibet Military Area Command, March 10 to March 16, 1959, *Peking Review*, Vol. II, No. 13, March 31, 1959, pp. 10–11; "Proclamation of the Tibet Military Area Command of the Chinese P.L.A." March 20, 1959, *Peking Review*, Vol. II, No. 13, March 31, 1959; "Communiqué on the Rebellion in Tibet," Hsinhua News Agency, March 28, 1959, *Peking Review*, Vol. II, No. 13, March 31, 1959, pp. 6–9; "Order of the State Council of the PRC," March 28, 1959, *Peking Review*, Vol. II, No. 13, March 31, 1959, p. 6; "Put

that the dispute assumed a new dimension and therefore qualitatively a new character.

During the course of the Tibetan revolt, the problem of Ladakhi nationals living in Tibet arose for the first time. Until 1959, there had never been a dispute regarding nationality, problems of the border, and buffer areas. In that year, Ladakhi residents of Tibet were maltreated by the local Communist authorities. This maltreatment was protested by the government of India. The Chinese, who had taken the initial position that Ladakhis of Tibet were Chinese nationals, retreated to a new position. They now argued that these people were in Tibet illegally. Detained by the Chinese from 1959 to 1961, they were finally allowed to return to India.

Between 1955 and 1958, the Chinese Communists built a road from Sinkiang to Lhasa. This road passed through Aksai-chin. The British had occupied this piece of territory on the northwestern frontier in the days of their forward expansion. In 1898 they offered to return it to China in return for certain border adjustments in an adjoining area. Curiously enough, the Chinese rejected this offer in spite of its geographic importance.

The road through Aksai-chin is of great strategic value to China. Until 1966, when the first railway line was supposed to have been completed, it was the only major surface route to Tibet. It assumed added importance in connection with the nature of Chinese power in that area. China's initial inability to control the Tibetan revolt of 1959 underscored the need to build further connecting links. Since then, Tibet has remained more or less under Chinese military occupation. Beginning in 1962 China has also maintained an extra number of troops because of Sino-Indian tension. All of these considerations increase the strategic importance of both the Aksai-chin area and the road to Tibet.

It was under these circumstances that the first serious meeting on boundaries took place between India and China in April 1960.[12] At these talks Chou En-lai emphasized that a genuine

Down the Rebellion in Tibet Thoroughly," *Jen-min Jih-pao*, March 31, 1959, *Peking Review*, Vol. II, No. 14, April 7, 1959, pp. 6–8.

12. For the Indian case, see *India's Fight for Territorial Integrity*, Publications Division, Government of India, Delhi, 1963; *Prime Minister on Sino-Indian Relations*, Vol. 1: *In Parliament*, External Pub-

boundary dispute did exist between the two countries. Designating the present borderline as a line of actual control rather than as an actual boundary, he stressed the need for a clear demarcation. In the process of such delimitation, geographical considerations were to be taken into account. Pending the completion of this task, the lines of actual control were to remain as they were in order to avoid further boundary incidents.

Chou also made it very clear that the McMahon line was not acceptable to Peking. At the same time, however, the Chinese would respect it, would not cross it, and would make no territorial demands beyond it. While denying its legal validity, they were prepared to respect its practical value, pending a final settlement. Finally Chou hinted that China was prepared to accommodate India in the eastern sector provided that India did the same for China in the western sector.

On April 26, 1960, Nehru's press conference in New Delhi clarified the positions of the two sides. He admitted that Chou En-lai

---

licity Division: Ministry of External Affairs, Government of India, New Delhi, Mar. 17, 1959–April 3, 1961; *Prime Minister on Sino-Indian Relations*, Vol. II: *Press Conferences*, External Publicity Division: Ministry of External Affairs, Government of India, New Delhi, Mar. 6, 1959–Mar. 17, 1961; *Notes, Memoranda and Letters Exchanged and Agreements Signed Between the Governments of India and China 1954–1959*, White Paper, Ministry of External Affairs, Government of India; *Summary of the Report of the Officials of the Governments of India and the People's Republic of China on the Boundary Question*, Ministry of External Affairs, No. 32, Government of India; *Notes, Memoranda and Letters Exchanged Between the Governments of India and China, Sept.–Nov. 1959* and *A Note on the Historical Background of the Himalayan Frontier of India*, White Paper, No. II, Ministry of External Affairs, No. 2, Government of India; *Notes, Memoranda and Letters Exchanged Between the Governments of India and China, Nov. 1960–Nov. 1961*, White Paper, No. V, Ministry of External Affairs, No. 44, Government of India; *Notes, Memoranda, and Letters Exchanged Between the Governments of India and China, Nov. 1961–July 1962*, White Paper, No. VI, Ministry of External Affairs, Government of India, 1962; *Notes, Memoranda and Letters Exchanged Between the Governments of India and China, July 1962–Oct. 1962*, White Paper, No. VII, Ministry of External Affairs, No. 52, Government of India, Delhi, 1962.

was prepared to accept the McMahon line as a demarcation of actual control provided that India made a concession in return. Specifically, India was to agree to a border from that portion of Ladakh through which the Chinese strategic route to Tibet passed. Nehru's position was clear and unequivocal. He rejected outright any exchange of border territory. For all practical purposes, this is the central issue in the Sino-Indian dispute. It arose for the first time in 1959–60, not in 1955.

A comparative study of the Sino-Indian and Sino-Burmese efforts at boundary settlements underlines the importance of the central point. Burma agreed to China's border proposal; India did not. On her part, Burma consented because the arrangement was favorable to her. The Chinese agreed to an unfavorable settlement because of the diplomatic capital they could make of it. Obviously it could be used as a precedent for asking India to do the same for China. These calculations underscore the value the Chinese placed on the road to Tibet. For the purposes of gaining the required territory in Ladakh, Peking was prepared not only to embrace an unfavorable settlement with Burma, but also to accept the McMahon line with India.

The Indian side was not impressed by the Burmese precedent, nor was it prepared to exchange territory without being bothered by public opinion. India, on the other hand, faced all the obstacles of a democratic country. Beginning in 1958, as soon as the news of border incidents started to pour in, both opposition parties and the press started to exert pressure.

It was precisely to avoid this kind of tension that Nehru did not make the border violations public from 1955 to 1958. Once unleashed, nationalistic emotion is hard to control. In the same period India was also trying to seek her national frontiers. There was already considerable pressure on the Indian government to take over Goa and the rest of the Portuguese possessions in India. This action was finally taken in 1960.

Under these circumstances, even if Prime Minister Nehru had been willing to adopt a conciliatory position, he would have found it difficult. Moreover, the whole aftermath of the Tibetan revolt came as a shock and a surprise. All these actions and reactions meant that compromise on the question of the Sino-Indian boundary was almost out of the question.

From 1947 onward, an emotional pan-Asianism had pervaded
Indian attitudes. It was believed that problems like boundary disputes or territorial *irridenta* could never arise between Asian
countries in the first place. Even if they did, they could not lead
to armed clashes. The euphoria of India's emotional pan-Asianism
was combined with the certainty that the borders were demarcated, at least in terms of British India. These attitudes provided
the emotional and political stumbling blocks in the way of an
immediate reassessment of the Asian situation.

Instead of thinking in terms of political compromise, the Indian
reaction was typically nationalistic. Earlier, India had given way
on the most important issues, namely, the Chinese sovereignty
over Tibet and the elimination of Indian rights in the area. She
had done so on the grounds that she did not have sufficient power
to do otherwise. Now, however, New Delhi suddenly reversed its
position and decided against a compromise settlement of the
boundary question.

The Sino-Indian talks were shifted in June 1960 to Peking. At
this point, the Indians wanted a total settlement of the border
problems. From the Indian point of view, the final arrangement
was to include not only India's direct boundaries with China, but
also the boundaries of such Indian protectorates as Bhutan and
Sikkim. Peking objected to this wish because of the belief that a
final settlement had to await the solution of the Kashmir problem.
Naturally this view was not acceptable to India. Indian spokesmen
also pointed out that China's interpretation of the boundary was
always made at India's expense. The watershed criterion, which
both Indians and Chinese had accepted on principle, could not
be applied everywhere in this area because of the topography.

Both sides did agree that there was a customary boundary between Ladakh and Tibet. They could not decide the precise loca-
tion of this line. Their major point of disagreement, however,
concerned British imperialism. The Chinese insisted that both
maritime and land boundaries were imposed through unequal
treaties and were therefore invalid. To them, no anti-imperialist
nation could agree to the perpetuation of such settlements. On
this point China's obsession with sovereignty and its corollary, the
rejection of imperialism, came to the fore.

China thus insisted that unequal boundary settlements had to be revised in form if not in substance. This psychological argument was favorable to China's bargaining position, but it also reflected sincere conviction. A debate on this subject broke out between the two delegations at Peking, but results were inconclusive. The Chinese continued to insist that the question of British imperialism was relevant. The Indians refused to accept this logic.

The entire discussion of the boundary settlement and the mounting demands which China made on India between 1960 and 1962 can only be understood in view of China's need for a strong bargaining position. The Burmese precedent, publicized so loudly by the Chinese side, had not worked. China thus moved to create a new bargaining position. As proclaimed by Chou En-lai in April 1960, this new offer would have traded acceptance of the McMahon line in return for the acquisition of strategic interests in Tibet.

All through this debate the Indians missed the point by failing to realize the full extent of China's obsession with imperialism and unequal boundaries and misunderstanding the symbolic nature of China's position. Peking simply refused to accept the results of treaties imposed by imperialist powers. All of them would have to be renegotiated.

This misunderstanding arises from the nature of the two nationalisms. Chinese nationalism had shed the protective device of culturism, while its counterpart in India had not. In fact, Indian nationalism had become introverted. For a thousand years Indians had turned inward when faced with a foreign enemy or culture. From the Moslem conquest through the British occupation they responded with the same attitude. Indian nationalism, which is essentially Hindu, had retreated inward and ignored the occupying authority. It had never lost its ostrich-like mentality. India's concern with imperialism, therefore, was more negative than positive. It was natural that these two nationalisms should clash. Each failed to understand the other.

The international likes and dislikes of Indian nationalists have been governed by a process of selectivity which has made them swing rapidly from one extreme to the other. Such men have generally admired people and nations hostile to Britain and this was the case with India's friendship with the Soviet Union and China. From 1911 to 1941 Indian nationalism was pro-Soviet and pro-

Chinese. During World War II it was anti-Soviet and anti-Chinese. After the rise of Communist power in China, it again became pro-Chinese.

These vacillating preferences have not been based on India's true interests. Instead, they have followed the dictates of anti-Westernism. In this case the West was synonymous with Britain. In the Sino-Indian border dispute, this nationalism again swung toward an anti-Chinese stance. Neither before nor after 1959 did these extremist positions reflect India's true national interests. The negative content of Indian nationalism is largely responsible for this selectivity and vacillation.[13]

In 1954 India had signed a trade agreement with China. Unless renewal was effected by December 1961, it would automatically expire six months later. Chinese leaders, insisting that other diplomatic relations should continue in spite of the unsettled border situation, attempted to renegotiate this document. Such a gradualist attitude was rebuffed.

India, which had taken a gradualist position before 1961, had now swung to a totalistic and fundamentalist platform. As long as the border dispute remained unsolved she demanded restrictions on all relations with China. So perished the 1954 treaty. As a result China demanded that India's trade agencies in Tibet be withdrawn. Trade between Tibet and India, which had already been dwindling, became impossible to continue. By June 1962, therefore, Sino-Indian estrangement was complete.

Ever since 1955 India had been following a forward policy in the area of the Northeast Frontier Agency. In her efforts to establish administrative posts, she was attempting to substitute direct control for indirect rule. This policy was as natural for India as for China. Both sides were trying to consolidate their frontier areas so that they could control their respective sides of the McMahon line. Such activity hastened the likelihood of conflict, particularly since the Indian government's inability to seek a compromise solution rapidly degenerated into mass hysteria.

The border problem had now become intensely emotional. The

13. For further discussion of this negative and selective nationalism see, Nirad C. Chaudhuri, "Nationalism in India," *Survey*, No. 67, April 1968, pp. 41–56.

negative and apolitical content of Indian nationalism had taken over. Slogans like "no settlement until vacation of aggression" started to dominate the scene. Actually, it is difficult to talk about aggression without knowing where one's boundaries are. For that reason many commentators and analysts have not considered the Sino-Indian clash to be a clear-cut case of aggression. Indian public opinion, however, side-stepped this logic completely.

As both sides rapidly prepared for a showdown, their forward military policies were stepped up until June 1962. It cannot be said that India was not prepared. Nehru himself had given assurances to the Indian parliament that all necessary military steps had been taken. He had even ordered India's commander-in-chief to repel Chinese moves.

India's subsequent defeat, therefore, was due not so much to a lack of military preparation as to a complete misunderstanding of China's military strategy. Indian officers were unable to graduate from the military teachings derived from Sandhurst in the 1930's. They had no experience to speak of, even with respect to World War II. Although a large Indian contingent had contributed to the Allied cause, Indian officers at the general staff level could be counted on the fingers of both hands.

To make matters worse, India's pan-Asiatic euphoria had prevented her from sending any military observers to the Korean War. Although Indian soldiers had fought in two world wars, Indian officers had fought only with Pakistan in 1947 and 1948. The officer corps of India and Pakistan were evenly matched in their ignorance and inexperience. The officer corps of India and China could not be compared. After all, there is some truth in the Maoist saying that men are more important than weapons. Among other things, India's defeat in 1962, like Egypt's defeats from 1948 to 1967, arose from the inability of her officer corps.

War is a more serious business than military uniforms and attending dinners in officers' mess halls. Even with inferior weapons, India could have put on a better performance if her officers had understood Chinese methods of warfare. After all, the Chinese Fourth Route Army had won victories in the face of superior Japanese and American weapons. The Chinese also took advantage of Korea, where they learned and practiced the essence of conventional warfare for the first time on any large scale. It was this lesson that they applied to India with such devastating results.

The Chinese applied to India in October 1962 what Schelling has described as the diplomacy of violence.[14] To support their diplomatic aims they applied force. Their purpose was to undermine India's influence in Asia and to force her to negotiate a boundary settlement on Chinese terms. They used only enough force to show that they were not impressed with India's forward policy in the area. The duration and nature of the Chinese pullback indicate an adroit combination of force and diplomacy. Nevertheless, the Chinese failed to reach their objective. India refused to go to the negotiating table from a position of weakness.

Only two choices are open in international relations. One is negotiating before using force, or matching forces to create a stalemate. The other is the total destruction of the enemy's power and the imposition of unconditional surrender. If the Chinese thought that the border problems could be solved by the limited use of force, they committed a serious but common mistake. If they wished to weaken India's influence in Asia, however, they at least partially succeeded.

The Indians also found that nonalignment, being a universal ideology, could work against them. In this case it was applied to India. Afro-Asian nations, urging a negotiated settlement, did not want to take sides. They correctly perceived that neither side should be antagonized and that each could claim some share of the truth. They were genuinely unsure about the merits of the case. It is easy to dismiss their hesitation as due to their being impressed by China's power. Yet there was also an element of dismay at the dissolution of the emotional united front between poor nations which had existed shakily ever since Bandung.

The Chinese did not achieve their aim of bringing India to the negotiating table by the limited use of force. Yet they could not use more force. In spite of the Cuban crisis, both the Soviet Union and the United States supported India. As in the Taiwan crisis, the Chinese again discovered that they could not depend on the Soviet Union. In fact, they found that they could not rely on

14. Thomas C. Schelling, *Arms and Influence* (New Haven and London: Yale University Press, 1966), especially, pp. 1–34.

Moscow even when the Soviets themselves were in direct conflict with Washington. The Sino-Indian crisis taught them the familiar lesson that Soviet national interest was far stronger than proletarian internationalism.

The Sino-Indian boundary conflict of 1962 was a watershed in China's policy toward both the Third World and the Soviet Union. The Chinese had incorrectly interpreted their experience with India. Like many other powers, China had underestimated the force of nationalism. As in 1927, the Chinese Communist Party had made another mistake in the international arena. Like Kashmir, the Sino-Indian boundary dispute had become too emotional to be solved by negotiation.

The other boundary which has caused great concern to both Moscow and Peking is the Sino-Russian boundary. China shares with the Soviet Union and Mongolia what is probably the longest land boundary in the world. Its total length is approximately 5500 miles. It includes about 2000 miles on the far eastern frontier, 1500 miles with Mongolia, and another 2000 miles with Sinkiang and inner Asia. The Chinese have listed over 5000 violations of this boundary.

Each section of the boundary differs with respect to its population content and to its degree of modernization. In recent years the Soviets have been trying not only to populate these areas but also to integrate and modernize them through new means of communication. Russian expansionism along this boundary did not stop with the Treaty of Aigun of 1858, which demarcated the Sino-Russian far eastern boundary along the Amur River. In fact, the first step taken by the Soviets after the triumph of the Bolshevik Revolution was support for the formation of a people's revolutionary party in Outer Mongolia in 1918.

In March 1921 the Soviet government announced the establishment of a provisional government in exile on Russian territory in Kiakhta. To take over Outer Mongolia, however, they had to wait until the Red Army had established Soviet control throughout Siberia in 1922. Taking advantage of the Japanese withdrawal, the Soviets then took over the Chinese Far Eastern Railway. In 1936 Moscow formed a defensive alliance with Outer Mongolia. By this time the Soviets had started to move into Sinkiang.

As early as 1924 a Soviet agreement with the local government had established consulates throughout Sinkiang. In 1930, the Soviets completed the Turkestan-Siberian Railway, a step which further helped them to take over Sinkiang's foreign trade. It was at this time that the Dungans revolted in Sinkiang. The local governor, Sheng Shih-ts'ai, had to enlist Soviet military support to quell the revolt. In return, without consulting Peking, he granted them a monopoly of the export trade in Sinkiang's raw materials. For all practical purposes, Sinkiang was completely in the Soviet sphere of influence between 1932 and 1943.[15]

In the Sino-Soviet treaty of 1945, the Soviet Union made a trade with the Nationalist government. Moscow recognized Chinese sovereignty over Manchuria and Sinkiang, with the exceptions of Port Arthur and Dairen. On the Chinese side, Chiang Kai-shek had to agree to recognize the sovereignty of the Mongolian People's Republic if a Mongol plebescite supported independence. Not surprisingly, on October 20, 1945, the plebescite supported independence with almost a 100 per cent "yes" vote. In line with the results and with the Sino-Soviet treaty, the Chinese government recognized the independence of the Mongolian People's Republic in January 1946. The Chinese Communists have never tried to question this settlement.

According to the same treaty of 1945, the Soviets were supposed to remain in Manchuria until either 1952 or the signing of a peace treaty with Japan, whichever came later. In 1950 another Sino-Soviet treaty decided on the formation of joint Sino-Soviet enterprises in Sinkiang, which were supposed to last until 1980. Both the cases of Manchuria and Sinkiang, however, were revised by 1955, and the Soviets finally left these areas.

The Chinese have never publicly questioned the Sino-Soviet treaty of 1945. As far as Soviet interests in China were concerned, the terms of the 1950 treaty did not differ significantly from those of 1945. The Soviets wanted a buffer state in Outer Mongolia, and they got one. This step reduced the Sino-Soviet boundary by at least 2000 miles. With the Sino-Mongolian Treaty Agreement of 1962, the Chinese renegotiated and formalized this demarcation.

15. For a detailed account of Soviet relations with Sinkiang between 1933 and 1949, see Allen S. Whiting and General Sheng Shih-ts'ai, *Sinkiang: Pawn or Pivot?* (East Lansing: Michigan State University Press, 1958).

In the same manner, the question of Chinese sovereignty over Sinkiang, Inner Mongolia, and Manchuria has not been questioned by Moscow. By 1954 and 1955, therefore, the Chinese had finally won from India and the Soviet Union recognition of their full sovereignty over all their frontier areas from Tibet to Manchuria, although the border problems had not been resolved.

Before the Sino-Soviet dispute erupted into the open, there was no public indication that the Communist Chinese wanted to win back the territories that tsarist Russia had taken over from China in the regions of the Amur River and the lower Ili Valley. At the time, no great irridentist conflict had emerged between the two countries. The problem of Outer Mongolia had already been solved. In this respect it is interesting to compare the Indian and Soviet cases. In both instances border problems were raised only after diplomatic relations had deteriorated because of some other reason. Specifically, the first public revelation that the Chinese had been trying to renegotiate the boundary for the previous ten years came only in February 1964.

At this time the Chinese held that pending a settlement of the boundary, both sides should maintain the status quo. They then accused the Soviet Union of refusing to do so and of creating subversive activities along Chinese frontier areas. They also admitted that tens of thousands of Chinese citizens from minority areas, most of them presumably from Sinkiang, had been "coerced into going to the Soviet Union." [16]

In this case the Chinese were probably referring to the disturbances in Sinkiang of 1958 and 1959. In 1958, during its nation-wide rectification campaign, the Chinese government purged certain people from posts in Sinkiang. Among other things, these people were accused of making an unfavorable comparison between Chinese administration in Sinkiang and Soviet administration on the other side of the border. Minority troubles in both Sinkiang and Tibet also came to the fore in 1958 and 1959. In both areas there was an exodus of local minority groups to a neighboring state.

These simultaneous disturbances may have resulted from the general tightening of Chinese politics initiated by the anti-rightist

16. "Letter of the Central Committee of the CCP of February 29, 1964, to the Central Committee of the CPSU," *Peking Review*, Vol. VII, No. 19, May 8, 1964, pp. 12–18.

campaign of 1957 and the Great Leap Forward. They may also have been purely coincidental. A third possibility is that the Soviets may have taken advantage of the Tibetan disturbance to stir up trouble in Sinkiang. One hint is that in both Sinkiang and Tibet, Peking had pursued a milder policy than in the rest of the country. From a broad perspective, minority unrest seems to stem from the first impact of modernization. By making them transitional, modernizing efforts made these areas more acutely aware of the distinctions between Han and non-Han nationalities.

It may also be true that in constitutional terms, the Soviet minority policy may be more appealing to China's national groups. Soviet minority policy is institutionally federative in character, while the Chinese is unitary. Furthermore, ever since 1953 the Chinese had tried to move large numbers of Han peoples into minority areas. This great influx of Han Chinese into Sinkiang and Tibet may well have exacerbated national minority resentment.

Between 1955 and 1960 there were few hints indicating that the Sino-Soviet boundary could erupt into an important problem.[17] To some extent China's irridentist claims regarding the Sino-Soviet boundaries were linked to two developments. One was Soviet support for India in the Sino-Indian clash of 1962. The other was Khrushchev's taunting of December 12, 1962, when he said that the Chinese were only verbally harsh on imperialism. On this occasion, Khrushchev praised India over China. While the Indians had taken over Goa, the Chinese were still tolerating Hong Kong and Macao. It was not Khrushchev's intention to goad China into a conflict with the British or the Portuguese, because he also made the point that he understood the reasons for China's restraint. He was merely telling them that his retreat from the Cuban crisis did not amount to submission to imperialism but to conformity with the rules of international politics.

In an article in *People's Daily* on March 8, 1963, the Chinese hit back. This article reminded the Soviets that Hong Kong and

17. Allen S. Whiting, "Sinkiang and the Sino-Soviet Relations," *The China Quarterly*, No. 3, July–Sept. 1960. Here Whiting still thought that Sinkiang was not on the conflict side of the balance sheet of Sino-Soviet relations. He was also of the opinion that China had shown no irridentist hopes of recovering lost territories in the Ili Valley.

Macao were not the only problems left over from unequal treaties. There were still nine unequal treaties with the Soviet Union which the Chinese would be happy to raise. The Chinese continued to make the point that the actual readjustment of territory was less important than renegotiation itself. In February 1964 talks directed at this end were started in Peking. Chinese spokesmen held that although the treaties relating to the Sino-Russian boundary were unequal, the Chinese government was nevertheless "willing to respect them" and would take them as the basis for a "reasonable" settlement of the Sino-Soviet boundary.[18]

China's search for national boundaries is not so much concerned with territorial readjustment per se as with an assertion of China's new status. Even on this question China has waited until other aspects of her relations with India and the Soviet Union compelled her to bring the boundary dispute to the level of open hostility. In neither case did the boundary cause antagonism by itself; it was rather the effect of certain other basic needs. In the case of India the quarrel stemmed from the necessity of securing control of Tibet. In the case of the Soviet Union, more basic antagonisms were reflected in the boundary dispute. In both cases China as an independent nation, whether Communist or Nationalist, would probably have insisted on renegotiation. Without other complicating influences, however, such renegotiation would not have led to such serious conflicts.

China's tactics in the settlement of these boundaries, particularly in the case of the Sino-Indian border, are open to serious question. China is certainly not unique in using force to settle boundary problems. Instead, what is in question is the connection between these tactics and China's overall diplomatic gains as well as her specific aims in India. It is true that China wanted to expose India's weakness and to jeopardize her economic development by forcing her to rearrange her economic priorities. The conflict did succeed in seriously undermining India's position as a neutralist power. Nevertheless, these achievements were side effects. As reflected in Chinese press statements from 1962 onward,

18. "Letter of the Central Committee of the CCP of February 29, 1964, to the Central Committee of the CPSU," *Peking Review*, Vol. VII, No. 19, May 8, 1964, pp. 12–13.

China's main aim was to force India to go to the negotiating table and to accept a barter arrangement. This settlement was made along Burmese terms, with a major exception: this time the trade would be *unfavorable* to India's strategic position. It was toward this end that China employed the diplomacy of violence and failed.

CHAPTER SEVEN

China, the Third World, and the Politics of Weakness

One of the most challenging areas of Communist China's foreign policy is the Third World. Two broad topics are particularly pressing. One concerns Chinese attitudes toward Afro-Asian leaders and the various degrees of neutrality which they adopt. The other is centered on the national liberation movement in general and on "people's war" in particular. In shaping opinions on both of these questions, Chinese Communist leaders draw heavily on both their own domestic experience and international priorities. In fact, there are definite links between Peking's attitude toward neutrality, appraisals of national bourgeois leaders, economic advice to the Third World, the Communist reconstruction of China's revolutionary history, Mao's military doctrines, the Sino-Soviet dispute, and China's national security.

Up to the early 1960's, Chinese press comments on the Third World were dominated by day-to-day reports of missions, delegations, and cultural exchanges. Few substantial, theoretical discussions appeared. This scarcity of substantive material was continually acute in the case of Africa; until the end of 1963 the five articles which appeared in *World Notes*, a fortnightly published in Peking, included such subjects as a description of the zoo in Uganda. Moreover, it was only in 1962 that Peking established the China Asia-Africa Society. Although organizations like the Afro-Asian Solidarity Committee of China (1956), the Sino-African Friendship Association (1960), and friendship associations with certain individual nations existed prior to 1962, the role of the

China Asia-Africa Society was different. Not limited chiefly to propaganda and cultural exchanges, its aim was to provide an increasing number of country experts and to give a general boost to Afro-Asian studies in China.

Several trends have been responsible for the upswing in the degree of interest which Chinese commentaries have devoted to the Third World in the mid-sixties. First and foremost is the rapid escalation of the war in Vietnam. This political and military headache has dramatized and intensified long-standing Chinese attitudes toward guerrilla warfare. No matter how esoteric, every major Chinese pronouncement on everything from minute details of military strategy to broad characteristics of the national liberation movement carries an ultimate message on Vietnam.

Another major trend has been both the Soviet and the American disillusionment with the Third World. Convinced that massive efforts were producing few and untrustworthy results, both superpowers have cut back their aid programs and toned down their optimism. Although Peking's level of sophistication remains low, particularly with respect to Africa, Chinese leaders share the Soviet and American attitude; despite their rhetoric they have few expectations. Nevertheless they have taken advantage of the general lull in Soviet-American competition to use the Third World as an offensive tool. Their policy is primarily an instrument directed at the United States and the Soviet Union rather than at the realities of the small and scattered revolutionary movements dispersed throughout the area. Their aim is to keep the two superpowers off balance without becoming dependent on the success of any particular guerrilla band.

The history of recent Chinese attitudes toward Afro-Asian neutrality is closely bound up with Mao's experience with the national bourgeoisie. To understand this relationship requires a look at the Chinese concept of the "people" and the role assigned to the national bourgeoisie. The profound mistrust which Chinese leaders have shown toward Afro-Asian leaders is a natural offspring of this concept.

For the Chinese, the term "people" includes all those who approve of or are prepared to work for the objective of socialism irrespective of their social or class origins. At the core of this group are the workers and the peasants, while the petty bourgeoisie and the national bourgeoisie are definitely marginal. Being the least reliable and most expendable members of the united front, these so-called "marginal people" must eventually undergo socialist re-education before they can be fully incorporated into the "people." Recent contemptuous discussions of China's intellectuals, assigned by definition to the petty bourgeoisie, suggest that this analysis is surviving the shockwaves of the Cultural Revolution.

Mao was one of the first Communist theoreticians to place detailed emphasis on the bourgeoisie in the colonies. As early as 1935 he distinguished between the national bourgeoisie and the "comprador bourgeoisie." Unlike the comprador bourgeoisie, which had economic connections with imperialism and was therefore pro-imperialist, the national bourgeoisie was anti-imperialist. At the same time, however, the national bourgeoisie feared the revolutionary activity of the proletariat, a fact which accounted for its vacillation and unreliability.[1] According to Mao, therefore, such middle-of-the-road forces could serve as allies only against imperialism and not against feudalism.[2]

As the Chinese Communist Party neared power, Mao further expounded on the role which the Communists wanted the Chinese national bourgeoisie to play. Maintaining that the new democratic revolution did not aim at wiping out capitalism altogether, he equated the upper petty bourgeoisie with the national bourgeoisie and defined them as small industrialists and merchants employing workers or assistants. Independent craftsmen and traders were also included in this group.[3]

In 1948 Liu Shao-ch'i repeated Mao's argument that to a cer-

1. See Mao Tse-tung, "On the Tactics of Fighting Japanese Imperialism," December 27, 1935, *Selected Works of Mao Tse-tung* (5 vols., New York: International Publishers, 1954–64), Vol. I, p. 158. See also "The Chinese Revolution and the Chinese Communist Party," *ibid.*, Vol. III, pp. 89–90, and "On New Democracy," *ibid.*, Vol. III, p. 117.

2. See Mao Tse-tung, "Questions of Tactics in the Present Anti-Japanese United Front," *Selected Works*, Vol. III, pp. 195–197.

3. See Mao Tse-tung, "The Present Situation and Our Tasks," *Selected Works*, Vol. V, p. 168. Mao here was speaking to party members and was specifically referring to the Chinese national bourgeoisie. This speech was delivered on December 25, 1947.

tain extent, the national bourgeoisie in the developing areas could play a useful role in the revolutionary process; as examples, he cited the roles of the American bourgeoisie in the War of Independence, the French bourgeoisie in the French Revolution, and the Italian bourgeoisie in Italian unification. While advocating strict exclusion of the big bourgeoisie, the bureaucratic capitalists, and the comprador bourgeoisie, Liu called for an alliance with the national bourgeoisie.[4] Finally, throughout 1948 and 1949 Mao Tse-tung continually emphasized the broad nature of the united front, the importance of the national bourgeoisie for socialist construction, and the policy that capitalism was to be regulated and not destroyed.[5]

A look at all of these various attempts to define the national bourgeoisie reveals that neither economic origins nor social class determined its content. In fact, membership in the national bourgeoisie could be drawn from any nonrevolutionary class, since the all-important criterion was anti-imperialism. For this reason, the national bourgeoisie cannot be considered as a class in the orthodox Marxist sense.

Quite clearly, Mao was not the first to overlook the determinist aspect of social origin or economic function. A pure determinist, seeing the inexorable laws of history as the sole source of progress, would passively await the general collapse of capitalism. Similarly, he would deny that proletarian consciousness could ever be achieved by individuals coming from a nonproletarian background. Even the intelligentsia, defined as members of the petty bourgeoisie could not break their bourgeois fetters. Fortunately for the Chinese Communist movement, Mao's vision was not restricted by these ideological blinders.

Faced with the tactical problem of organizing and leading the Russian proletariat to victory, Lenin had been forced to justify the role of the nominally petty bourgeois intellectuals by calling them the "vanguard" of the proletariat. Similarly, Liu Shao-ch'i argued

4. Liu Shao-ch'i, *Internationalism and Nationalism* (Peking: Foreign Languages Press, Undated), pp. 4–10.

5. See Mao Tse-tung, "Speech at a Conference of Cadres in the Shensi-Suiyuan Liberated Area," April 1, 1948. *Selected Works*, Vol. V, p. 235; and "On the People's Democratic Dictatorship," June 30, 1949, *Selected Works*, Vol. V, p. 421.

that in underdeveloped areas the Communist party could not help but draw upon nonproletarian classes for its membership and that social origins were irrelevant to becoming a good Communist.[6] Although the Cultural Revolution has revealed that it is harder to overcome one's background than Mao had previously thought, this attitude still survives, at least in modified form.

In the first few years after 1949, Chinese Communist analyses of the national bourgeoisie were made only in the context of the united front. Having just won an astounding victory over their own "flabby" national bourgeoisie, the leadership repeatedly stated that the Chinese national bourgeoisie could not be relied upon to complete the democratic revolution. Unless they were kept under the leadership of the Communist Party, they were liable to go over to the imperialists. At best, they were to be won over as allies; at worst, they were to be neutralized.[7]

In applying this view to other countries, the Chinese maintained that in the colonies and semicolonies, the national bourgeoisie had few or no ties with imperialism.[8] At the same time, they called for

6. See Liu Shao-ch'i, *On the Party*, Report delivered on May 14, 1945, pp. 10 and 18; and Editorial, "China's Revolution and the Struggle Against Colonialism," *People's China*, Vol. II, No. 4, February 16, 1950, p. 5.

7. See Liu Shao-ch'i, *Internationalism and Nationalism*, pp. 3–5; and Mao Tse-tung, "On the Question of the National Bourgeoisie and the Enlightened Gentry," Inner Party Directive Drafted by Mao Tse-tung for the Central Committee of the Communist Party of China, March 1, 1948, *Selected Works*, Vol. V, pp. 207–209. See also "A Circular on the Situation," Inner Party Circular for the Central Committee of the Chinese Communist Party by Mao Tse-tung, March 20, 1948, *Selected Works*, Vol. V, p. 221; "Manifesto of the Lao Dong Party to the Vietnam People's National Congress," *New China News Agency* (NCNA), Peking, March 25, 1951, trans. in *Survey of the China Mainland Press* (SCMP), No. 88, March 25–27, 1951, p. 42; and "Programme of Vietnam Lao Dong Party," NCNA, Peking, March 26, 1951, translated in SCMP, No. 88, March 25–27, 1951, pp. 44–45.

8. See Lu Ting-yi, "The World Significance of the Chinese Revolution," *People's China*, Vol. IV, No. 1, July 1, 1951; Mao Tse-tung, *New Democratic Constitutionalism*, February 20, 1940 (Peking: Foreign Languages Press, 1960), p. 3; Mao, "The Present Situation and

armed struggle against those national bourgeois leaders who had already gained what they called "formal independence" through a "deal" with the imperialists.[9] Although Peking made no definitive theoretical distinction between the ruling and the nonruling national bourgeoisie, it seems that only the latter, under the hegemony of the Communist Party, was assigned a positive role. Up to this point, therefore, China's international attitudes were still based on the domestic united front strategy.[10]

Nor did the Chinese take seriously the proclaimed neutrality of the new states. To Mao, true neutrality was impossible; in his famous phrase, all nations eventually had to "lean to one side" (*i-pien tao*). In terms of the leadership, the neutralist national bourgeoisie had either to become part of what the Chinese called the "people" or to lean to the side of imperialism.[11] To adopt a kind of neutrality which would have satisfied Peking, these leaders would have had to accept the domestic hegemony of local

Our Tasks," December 25, 1947, *Selected Works*, Vol. V, pp. 167–68; Liu Shao-ch'i, "Speech at the Conference of Trade Unions of Asia and Oceania," *For a Lasting Peace*, No. 33 (60), December 30, 1949, p. 2; and Miao Chu-huang, "The Vacillation of the National Capital Class as Shown in China's Modern Revolutionary History," *Hsueh Hsi (Study)*, March 18, 1952, trans. in *Soviet Press Translations*, Vol. VII, No. 12, June 15, 1952, p. 280.

9. See, for example, "Achievement of Philippine People's Armed Forces in Nine-Year Struggle," *NCNA*, March 29, 1951, *SCMP*, No. 89, March 28–29, 1951, p. 17.

10. Chalmers Johnson has called this path the "strategy of poverty." He points out that the applicability of China's domestic model to the Third World stems from the political and military weakness that links wartime China with contemporary Africa and Asia. For this reason, he thinks, the Chinese Communists interpret their own revolution almost exclusively in terms of strength and military insights. See Chalmers Johnson, "The Third Generation of Guerrilla Warfare," *Asian Survey*, Vol. VIII, No. 6, June 1968, pp. 436–441.

11. See Mao Tse-tung, "On the People's Democratic Dictatorship," June 30, 1949, reproduced in the United States Department of State, *United States Relations with China* (Washington: Government Printing Office, 1949), pp. 723–724. This edition is used here, as later editions have modified Mao Tse-tung's original statements on neutralism.

Communist parties and the international leadership of the Socialist camp. On the whole, China's adherence to this view of neutrality remained relatively constant even while corresponding Soviet attitudes underwent several basic changes.

As late as April 1952 the Chinese leader Ch'en Po-ta was still telling the Soviet Union that in time the Chinese Communist Party would expose the reactionary nonsense of nonalignment, the "so-called 'third path'" of the national bourgeoisie.[12] In the previous year, however, the beginnings of a change in Peking's attitude could be detected. In particular, the Chinese gave wholehearted support to the Wafd government of Egypt in its struggle against Great Britain and to the Iranian Government's plan to nationalize foreign oil companies.[13] This posture was all the more remarkable in view of the fact that the Soviets were simultaneously publishing articles written by the Communist Party of Iran which denounced the nationalization measure as a trick aimed at winning over the landlords, the bourgeoisie, and American oil magnates against the British.[14]

By October 1952 this new and more favorable attitude toward the leadership of the Third World had found more general expression.[15] It is hard to state conclusively whether this change was independently derived or whether it was a part of the new Soviet

12. See Ch'en Po-ta, "Problems of the Chinese Revolution," *Pravda*, April 23, 1952, pp. 2–4.

13. See Shao Ya-min, "The Egyptian People Struggle for Independence and Liberation," *Jen-min Jih-pao*, Nov. 16, 1951, *Current Background (CB)*, No. 195, July 25, 1952; and Saifudin, "The Just Struggle of the Iranian People," *People's China*, August 1, 1951, *CB*, No. 195, July 25, 1952.

14. See, for example, Tudeh, "Concerning Oil Nationalization in Iran," *For a Lasting Peace*, No. 33, August 17, 1951, p. 4.

15. See editorial, "Still Greater Unity to Conquer the Menace of War and Defense of Peace," On the Occasion of the Asian and Pacific Peace Conference in Peking, *Jen-min Jih-pao*, NCNA, Peking, October 2, 1952, translated in *SCMP*, No. 428, October 2–4, 1952, pp. 35–36; and Fu Ying, "Victory of the Foreign Policy of People's China," *Shih Chieh Chih Shih (World Knowledge)*, Peking, October 3, 1953, translated in *SCMP*, No. 680, October 31–November 2, 1953, p. 40.

shift toward peaceful coexistence, seen in Stalin's *Problems of Socialism in the USSR* and at the Nineteenth Congress of the CPSU. Since the Chinese never fully explained the application of peaceful coexistence to the Third World, it is difficult to know whether or not the phrase meant anything more than a declining emphasis on the use of armed force in those areas. Furthermore, the real nature of the change that had occurred in Chinese foreign policy was further obscured by a relative absence of theoretical pronouncements on the neutrality and leadership of the Third World from Peking from the end of 1952 until the early months of 1954.

By 1954 the new Chinese policy of recognizing the positive role of national bourgeois leaders of the Third World had become apparent. As a way of winning the friendship of these leaders, China started to identify its interests with those of Afro-Asian countries, using common experiences with imperialism as a common denominator.[16] In April 1954 the agreement with India over Tibet formulated the Five Principles, or Panch Shila, by which relations with the states ruled by neutralist national bourgeois leaders were to be conducted. In June of the same year a similar statement was announced with Burma.[17]

In his address to the First National People's Congress, which opened in Peking in September 1954, Chou En-lai emphasized these five principles and suggested that they be extended as the basis of China's relations with other Asian countries. Another concession to the ruling national bourgeoisie which appeared in this address was made in the form of a request to the overseas Chinese to abide by local laws and customs.[18] At the same time, Liu Shao-ch'i announced that the national bourgeoisie presented no problem

16. See, for example, Chu Jung-fu, "Foreign Relations of New China During the Past Five Years," *Shih Chieh Chih Shih* (*World Knowledge*), October 5, 1954, CB, No. 307, Dec. 6, 1954.

17. See Royal Institute of International Affairs, *Documents on International Affairs* (N.Y. and London: Oxford University Press, 1954), pp. 313 and 314 for Sino-Indian and Sino-Burmese declarations, respectively.

18. For the text of Chou En-lai's speech, see *New China News Agency*, September 24, 1954, pp. 4–12.

at home; according to him, the Chinese national bourgeoisie had accepted socialist transformation and in the transitional period had played an important role in national reconstruction.[19]

It is difficult to define with precision the reasons why Peking altered its pronouncements on the leadership and neutrality of the Third World so noticeably. To suggest a few, the general failure of Communist uprisings in Asia in the late 1940's and early 1950's, the occasional anti-Western actions and attitudes of which the neutrals proved themselves capable, the role of certain neutral nations in the Korean War, and open Soviet reluctance to continue to promote the Maoist strategy for revolutionary change[20] may all have played a part in influencing the evolution of Chinese foreign policy toward the Third World. At any rate, this new attitude, which found its most publicized expression at the Bandung Conference of Afro-Asian States in April 1955,[21] clearly differed from that which prevailed in the years when China seemed to present a threat to the newly independent countries.

During the period 1954 to 1957 a new description of the national bourgeoisie appeared. While theorists continued to assert that the bureaucratic-capitalist bourgeoisie had ties both with the comprador bourgeoisie and with imperialism, the national bourgeoisie was now supposed to constitute an oppressed group. At home, its oppressors were said to be the bureaucratic capitalists.[22] At the same time, however, the role of the national bourgeoisie in-

19. See Liu Shao-ch'i, "Report of the Draft Constitution of the People's Republic of China," Delivered at the First Session of the First National People's Congress of the People's Republic of China, September 15, 1954 in *Documents of the First National People's Congress of the People's Republic of China* (Peking: Foreign Languages Press, 1955), pp. 31–32.

20. Proof of this reluctance can be found in an important conference held in Moscow at the end of 1951; see "On the Character and Attributes of People's Democracy in the Orient," *Journal of the USSR Academy of Sciences (Izvestia* IX, No. 1, January–February 1952), pp. 80–87, in *Current Digest of the Soviet Press,* Vol. IV, No. 20, June 28, 1952, pp. 3–7 and 43.

21. See Chou En-lai's speech in George McT. Kahin, *The Asian-African Conference* (Ithaca: Cornell University Press, 1956).

22. Chin Chia-chu, "The Capitalists in People's China," *World News,* London, Vol. 2, No. 6, February 5, 1955.

side and outside of China was not completely accepted as either constructive or revolutionary. While it was contended that a united front with all international forces was necessary to build socialism,[23] it was also held that the imperialist influence on the newly independent countries was not yet completely eliminated.[24] Moreover, an article appeared in *Hsueh Hsi (Study)* which placed the contradictions between the working class and the national bourgeoisie in the antagonistic category.[25]

From negative evaluations like these, it seems that the proclaimed international united front against imperialism, to be established by the socialist nations and the leadership of the Third World, should not have been taken too seriously. In the first place, a key principle of the united front practiced in China was the leadership of the Chinese Communist Party, but Peking scrupulously avoided translating this feature into terms of the hegemony of the socialist bloc. In the second place, the very caution with which China evaluated the national bourgeoisie makes it unlikely that any meaningful alliance was contemplated at this time.

On the whole, the friendliness of the years 1954 to 1957 did not represent any real change in Chinese foreign policy as far as China's national interests were concerned. Foremost among these national interests was and is the elimination of American influence in Asia and Africa. "Neutrality" was strictly defined as the denial of military bases to the West and the rejection of all alliances directed against Peking. The "constructive" features ascribed to the neutrals during these years were intimately linked with the

23. See Chi Hung, "Notes on the Study of the International Relations Section of the Political Report of the Central Committee of the Chinese Communist Party to the Eighth Congress," *Shih Chieh Chih Shih*, No. 20, Oct. 20, translated in *Extracts from China Mainland Magazines (ECMM)*, No. 63, Dec. 31, 1956, p. 35.

24. Shih Chen, "A Year of Rapid Development of the National Independence Movement in Asia and Africa," *Shih Chieh Chih Shih*, No. 24, December 20, 1956, translated in *ECMM*, No. 68, February 4, 1957, p. 4.

25. Kuan Ta-ting, "The Current Handling of Contradictions Between the Working Class and the National Bourgeoisie," *Hsueh Hsi (Study)*, No. 12, June 18, 1956, translated in *ECMM*, No. 139, Aug. 18, 1958, p. 24.

goal of eliminating Western influence. Similarly, Peking's efforts to remove the mantle of Asian leadership from the shoulders of India were never abandoned. In fact, the border incidents against India were begun only two months after the Bandung Conference.

With these aims in mind Chinese commentators stressed that friendly relations between independent Afro-Asian countries and the socialist nations would seriously hurt colonialism.[26] Economic aid from Bloc countries was said to promote a more independent foreign policy. In this context the word "independent" could be translated as "leaning away from the West." Above all, economic aid was aimed at hurting imperialism and thwarting pro-imperialist leanings, not at permanently consolidating the legitimacy of the rule of the national bourgeoisie.[27] China's own experience with the national bourgeoisie in 1927 had been too painful to repeat. Once again, a major Chinese effort in the Third World found ultimate explanation in international exigencies, not in the realities of Afro-Asian economic growth.

By late 1957 a definite rejection of both domestic and international united fronts and the foreign national bourgeoisie had taken place. There are several views regarding this shift of policy. On the one hand, this new trend could have been linked to a change in the Chinese perception of the balance of forces between the socialist and the capitalist camps, a change which received impetus from Soviet missile developments and from the launching of the Sputnik satellite in October 1957. On the other hand, the results of the abortive Hundred Flowers Campaign may have led to the Chinese realization that the policy of "re-educating" the national bourgeoisie had failed. Acceptance of a similar failure of the

26. Shih Lu, "Important Achievements in the World Movement Against Colonialism," *Shih Chieh Chih Shih*, No. 2, January 20, 1956, translated in *ECMM*, No. 32, April 23, 1956, p. 12; see also Feng Chih-tan, "Development of Friendship and Co-operation between the Soviet Union and Asian Nations," *Shih Chieh Chih Shih*, No. 1, January 5, 1956, translated in *ECMM*, No. 30.

27. See Yan Po, "The Development of Economic Relations Between the Socialist Countries and the Asian-African Countries," *Shih Chieh Chih Shih*, No. 5, April 20, 1956, translated in *ECMM*, No. 43, July 16, 1956.

Bandung policy was also implicit in this foreign policy change. The new policy led to a revival of the earlier and more rigid view of the world, a view which denied the possibility of genuine neutrality.

In line with this change, the earlier revolutionary model was slowly revived, with the Chinese again viewing the East-West struggle as a class struggle. A natural corollary to this view was that any Afro-Asian nation which joined a Western military pact was directly aiding the international exploiters. Conversely, Chinese press reports made it clear that neutrality had become more or less equivalent to the denial of military bases to the West and to the adoption of a favorable attitude toward China—views which were obviously motivated by Chinese national security. By 1961 the only nations Peking listed as neutral countries in Asia and Africa were Burma, Indonesia, Cambodia, Guinea, Ghana, and the Republic of Mali.[28]

At this stage, attitudes toward the domestic bourgeoisie were closely linked with those toward the national bourgeois leadership of the neutral nations. As early as September 1957, General Secretary Teng Hsiao-p'ing of the Central Committee of the Chinese Communist Party considered that the elimination of the national bourgeoisie was a fundamental task of the socialist revolution. A few months later, Chou Yang held that bourgeois individualism and proletarian collectivism could never be reconciled and that the former was the greatest obstacle to socialist reconstruction.[29] On the international scene, the national bourgeoisie of the neutralist nations were declared to have turned

28. See Editorial, "What is Independence, What is 'Neutrality'?" *Kung-jen Jih-pao (Workers' Daily)*, Peking, July 9, 1961, translated in *Joint Publications Research Service (JPRS)*, No. 11590, 1961.

29. Teng Hsiao-p'ing, "Report on the Rectification Campaign," presented to the Third Enlarged Plenary Session of the Eighth Central Committee of the Chinese Communist Party on September 23, 1957, NCNA, Peking, October 19, 1957, translated in *Current Background*, No. 477, October 25, 1957, p. 4; Chou Yang (Vice-Director, Department of Propaganda of the Central Committee of the Chinese Communist Party), "A Great Debate on the Literary and Art Front," *Jen-min Jih-pao*, February 28, 1958, translated in *Current Background*, No. 498, March 14, 1958, p. 6.

reactionary, even though contradictions between them and the imperialists made them cherish peace and neutralism. At the same time, however, the intimate relations which these neutralists maintained with imperialists meant that they were "double-faced" and that they followed a policy of vacillation.[30] These developments reveal a "leftward" shift in China's national liberation strategy and, naturally, a more hostile view of the national bourgeoisie.[31] This attitude unveiled yet another interpretation of Mao's famous slogan: the fact that the East wind now prevailed over the West wind represented a new stage in the struggle against imperialism.[32]

The new line was accompanied by a further differentiation of the national bourgeoisie into left, middle, and right sections. Characteristically political in nature, this differentiation was based on attitudes toward imperialism.[33] It was increasingly emphasized that the policy toward the national bourgeoisie was that of "unity and struggle," that is, tactical cooperation but basic antagonism. In addition, perhaps, the most prolific writer on the subject of the united front, Li Wei-han, proclaimed that a united front from below of the "peoples" of the socialist and neutralist nations was to replace the rather loose and vague united front from above that marked the years 1954 to 1957.[34] The years after

30. Ying Yu, "Ten Years' Peaceful Foreign Policy," *Shih Chieh Chih Shih*, No. 19, October 5, 1959, translated in *ECMM*, No. 199, Feb. 8, 1960, pp. 5–6.

31. Yu Chao-li (pseudonym meaning "strength of millions"), "A New Upsurge of National Revolution," *Hung-ch'i (Red Flag)*, No. 5, translated in *Peking Review*, Vol. I, No. 38, November 18, 1958, p. 12.

32. It was in November 1957 that Mao, then in Moscow, first came forth with the famous slogan about the East and West winds; see *Jen-min Jih-pao*, November 20, 1957, in *Survey of the China Mainland Press*, No. 1662, p. 2.

33. Teng Li-ch'ien and Wu-Chiang, "Dialectics is the Algebra of the Revolution," *Hung-ch'i (Red Flag)*, Nos. 20–21, November 11, 1960, translated in *SCMM*, No. 237, November 28, 1960, p. 13.

34. See Li Wei-han, "The Characteristics of the Chinese People's Democratic United Front," *Hung-ch'i (Red Flag)*, No. 12, June 16, 1961, translated in *SCMM*, No. 268, July 3, 1961, pp. 10–11; also see Hsiao Shu and Yang Fu, "The Party's Policy is the Guarantee of Victory in the Revolution," *Hung-ch'i* translated in *Peking Review*,

1957 therefore witnessed an upsurge in what is called "people's diplomacy," namely, contacts between Peking and nongovernmental, unofficial groups in the Third World.

From 1959 on, more and more stress was placed on the concept of class struggle as an important component of the national liberation movement. In January 1960, for example, a Chinese journal of international affairs carried an article asserting that the class struggle in Asia and the Middle East was sharpening.[35] It was also emphasized that national liberation was not possible without bitter struggle and that this struggle could be waged only under the leadership of the proletariat.[36] Moreover, class struggle was said to be a protracted struggle, one that would continue for decades until the last vestiges of "bourgeois ideology" were completely destroyed. While this class struggle would take the form of armed struggle, the actual waging of such armed struggle would depend on the revolutionary potential and the concrete, objective conditions in each nation. For the attainment of national liberation, the broadest possible united front from below was recommended.[37]

This shift in favor of class struggle had the interesting side effect of putting the Chinese on the defensive regarding their earlier policies toward the national bourgeoisie. Liu Shao-ch'i, for example, came out in defense of this earlier policy by claiming

---

Vol. III, No. 52, December 27, 1960, pp. 22–23; and Lin Yi-chou, "The Peasant Question in the Democratic Revolution," *Hung-ch'i*, March 1, 1961, translated in *Peking Review*, Vol. IV, No. 13, March 31, 1961, p. 7.

35. Kuo Wen-yen, "Facing 1960: Relative Positions of East and West," *Kuo-chi Wen-t'i Yen-chiu (Studies in International Problems)*, No. 1, January 3, 1960, translated in *JPRS*, No. 6211, 1960.

36. Shih Tsu-chih, "The Fundamental Path for the Liberation Movement in the Colonial and Semi-Colonial Areas," *Kuo-chi Wen-t'i Yen-chiu (Studies in International Problems)*, No. 5, May 3, 1960, translated in *JPRS*, No. 6211, 1960.

37. Ch'i Tso-wen, "Rightists and the 'Almost' Theory," *Chieh-fang*, Shanghai, No. 23, Dec. 5, 1959, translated in *JPRS*, No. 6375; see also Editorial, "Mao Tse-tung's Ideas Are the Victorious Banner of the Great Revolution of the Chinese People," *Jen-min Jih-pao*, September 30, 1960, translated in *JPRS*, No. 6497, 1960.

that uniting with the national bourgeoisie in China was not the policy of class collaboration.[38] In view of the general failure both of the Great Leap Forward and of the "re-education" of the national bourgeoisie, the Chinese leadership must have felt that a dual attempt was necessary: on the one hand, disillusionment with the national bourgeoisie led to greater emphasis on class conflict, while on the other hand, the special position of the national bourgeoisie in China during the last decade was defended.[39] With all its apparent contradictions, this view probably represented Peking's acceptance of its failure to re-educate the "marginal people" into the "people." In other words, while "education" was overwhelmingly preferable to liquidation, the economic usefulness of the national bourgeoisie could not indefinitely obscure its political unreliability.

Chinese attitudes toward the Third World became even clearer after the Moscow Declaration of 1960 introduced the concept of the national democratic state. This innovation, which tried to legitimize the new role of the ruling national bourgeoisie was not accepted by the Chinese. Peking did not modify its criticism of either the Soviet interpretation of peaceful coexistence in the context of nuclear politics or the Soviet denial of the necessity of wars of national liberation.[40] The Chinese also managed to interpret the Moscow statement as sanctioning the struggle

38. Liu Shao-ch'i, "The Victory of Marxism-Leninism in China," *NCNA*, Peking, October 1, 1959, translated in *Current Background*, No. 595, Oct. 5, 1959, p. 7. It is clear that Liu was writing this article in defense of the Party's failure with the Great Leap Forward, the communes, and earlier efforts to re-educate the national bourgeoisie.

39. Chen P'o and Cheng Hui, "Lenin on Class Struggle in the Transition Period," *Hung-ch'i*, Nos. 23–24, December 5, 1962, translated in *SCMM*, No. 346, January 7, 1963, pp. 6–7. For defense of the earlier policy toward the national bourgeoisie, see Liu Shao-ch'i, "Speech at the 40th Anniversary Celebrations of the Chinese Communist Party," *China News Analysis*, No. 380, July 14, 1961, p. 5.

40. See Editorial, "Banner of Victory, Banner of Unity," *Jen-min Jih-pao*, December 7, 1960, translated in *Peking Review*, Vol. III, No. 49–50, December 13, 1960, p. 26; and Hsiao Shu and Yang Fu, "The Party's Policy is the Guarantee of Victory in the Revolution," *Hung-ch'i*, translated in *Peking Review*, Vol. III, No. 52, December 27, 1960, pp. 22–23.

against imperialism.[41] They further emphasized their earlier stand toward the national bourgeoisie, namely, "unity and struggle." [42] Cooperation in pursuing anti-imperialist measures was not to obscure the basic antagonism between the national bourgeoisie on the one hand and the worker-peasant alliance on the other.

The controversy between the Soviets and the Chinese also included Chinese charges that the Soviets were flirting with the national bourgeoisie and defending such flirtation with the argument that national bourgeois leaders foster neutralism and indirectly weaken imperialism.[43] In this respect, Sino-Soviet attitudes toward the Sino-Indian border crisis sprang from differences on the question of the national bourgeoisie, just as Sino-Soviet views of the Cuban crisis centered around the question of peaceful coexistence and nuclear escalation.

With the Sino-Indian border crisis, Sino-Soviet differences on the treatment of the national bourgeoisie and neutralism erupted into the open. It is possible that the Chinese, in a state of open conflict on this issue, hoped to be able to influence Soviet policy, especially in areas away from China's immediate geographical boundaries.[44] At the Afro-Asian People's Solidarity Conference at Moshi, Tanganyika, in February 1963, both the Sino-Soviet conflict over the Sino-Indian border dispute and Chinese attempts to exclude the Soviets from Afro-Asian front organizations became so obvious that they were harmful to the prestige of both the Soviets and the Chinese.[45]

41. See Editorial, "Wage a Common Struggle for the Solidarity and Victory of the International Workers' Movement," *Kung Jen Jih Pao* (*Workers' Daily*), January 1, 1961, translated in *Peking Review*, Vol. IV, No. 1, January 6, 1961, p. 21.

42. See Lin Yi Chou, "The Present Question in the Democratic Revolution," *Hung-ch'i*, March 1, 1961, translated in *Peking Review*, Vol. IV, No. 13, March 31, 1961, p. 7.

43. *Deutsche Zeitung*, September 30, 1960, quoted in D. S. Zagoria, "Sino-Soviet Friction in Under-developed Areas," *Problems of Communism*, Vol. X, No. 2, March–April, 1964.

44. See Herbert Dinerstein, "Rivalry in Underdeveloped Areas," *Problems of Communism*, Vol. X, No. 2, March–April, 1964.

45. See William E. Griffith, *The Sino-Soviet Rift* (Cambridge: The M.I.T. Press, 1964), pp. 124–125.

The exchange of letters between the Communist Party of the Soviet Union (CPSU) and the CCP in 1963 featured Chinese charges about the Soviets' un-Marxian attitude toward the ruling bourgeoisie and their treachery to the cause of the national liberation movement. Nevertheless, the Chinese stressed their equally un-Marxian determination to welcome anyone in the united front who was in favor of national liberation.[46] From this exchange of letters, it is difficult to see the difference in the Soviet and Chinese views of underdeveloped countries.

In their letter of March 30, 1963, for example, the Soviets echoed the Chinese preference for the uniting of all patriotic forces into a single united front of the working class, the peasantry, the national bourgeoisie, and the democratic intellectuals.[47] Similarly, in their polemical debate with the Soviets during 1963, the Chinese, as in the past, maintained that they were prepared to welcome anyone, including certain "kings, princes, and aristocrats," in the anti-imperialist united front, provided that such people were "patriotic." [48] This posture is similar to the united front policy adopted by the Chinese Communists during the years of anti-Japanese resistance and civil war. Both then and now,

46. See especially "CPSU Letter of March 30, 1963," reprinted in *Peking Review*, Vol. VI, No. 25, June 21, 1963, p. 43; Editorial Departments of *Jen-min Jih-pao* and *Hung-ch'i*, "Comment on the Open Letter of the CC of the CPSU (4), Apologists of Neo-colonialism," translated in *Peking Review*, Vol. VI, No. 43, October 25, 1963, pp. 7–13; and "Letter of the CCP to the CPSU, June 14, 1963, in Reply to March 30, 1963, Letter," translated in *Peking Review*, Vol. VI, No. 25, June 21, 1963, pp. 11–16.

47. See "The Letter from the CC of the CPSU to the CC of the CCP, March 30, 1963," *Pravda*, April 14, 1963, translated in *Peking Review*, Vol. VI, No. 25, June 21, 1963, p. 28.

48. See "A Proposal Concerning the General Line of the International Communist Movement—The Letter from the Central Committee of the CCP in Reply to the Letter from the Central Committee of the CPSU of March 30, 1963," June 14, 1963, *Jen-min Jih-pao*, June 17, 1963, translated in *Peking Review*, Vol. VI, No. 25, June 21, 1963, p. 10. The Chinese also emphasized in this letter that the state everywhere was based on class conflict, and that not to launch revolution after the subjective conditions were ripe was a "right" deviation. See pp. 12 and 18.

alliance with these groups depended upon their acceptance of Communist hegemony.

In their open letter of July 14, 1963, the Soviets replied by attacking the Chinese for allying with "princes and kings." [49] In other statements they accused the Chinese of trying to turn the USSR into an instrument of national liberation alone rather than of revolutionary change for the whole world. They argued that promotion of the national liberation movement was not the sole reason for their existence, as the Chinese seemed to demand. Yet in so doing they fell into the Chinese trap. Actually Peking did not want Soviet advisors scurrying from one revolutionary movement to another. Knowing that the priorities of Soviet foreign policy ruled out this possibility, they could safely goad Moscow into revealing what appeared to be an indifferent attitude toward the national liberation movement.

In his secret report of February 1964, the Soviet Party ideologue Mikhail Suslov continued to accuse the Chinese of promoting racism and of giving too much thought to the national liberation movement at the expense of the world socialist camp.[50] More recent Soviet diatribes are dominated by the charge of "splitting," that is, forming pro-Chinese splinter groups within revolutionary organizations which were previously pro-Soviet. They correctly interpret "self-reliance" to mean noncooperation with the Soviet Union. Insisting that the socialist system rather than the national liberation movement is the "main force" against American imperialism, they build up the importance of Soviet aid to the Chinese Communists and minimize China's aid to the Third World. While taunting China for tolerating Hong Kong and Macao on the one hand, they accuse her leaders of promoting ultraleftist policies on the other. They even blame Peking for the massacre of the Indonesian Communist Party. Actually, despite friendly relations with China, Aidit pursued quite a different strategy from the Maoist model.

49. See "Open Letter from the CC of the CPSU to Party Organization and All Communists of the Soviet Union," July 14, 1963," *Pravda*, July 14, 1963, translated in *Peking Review*, Vol. VI, No. 30, July 26, 1963, pp. 31 and 43.

50. Suslov's report is contained in William E. Griffith, *Sino-Soviet Relations, 1964–65* (Cambridge: The M.I.T. Press, 1966).

Ironically the Soviets even quote such American notables as John K. Fairbank, Alexander Eckstein, and Kenneth T. Young in asserting that Mao's foreign policy is the Middle Kingdom writ large, intent on expanding Chinese hegemony along traditional lines. They also agree with American commentators that China is ferocious in word but cautious in deed. They heap scorn on the Cultural Revolution, claiming that it actually helps American imperialism. Finally, and most important, they charge Peking with trying to sway Afro-Asian opinion against the Soviet Union.[51] This last accusation hits the analytical nail on the head.

Besides domestic experiences with the national bourgeoisie and the international priorities generated by the Sino-Soviet dispute, yet another influence shaping Peking's policy toward the Third World is China's domestic economic experience. Chinese advice to Africa and Asia is definitely linked to the various strategies or "general lines" of economic development on which Chinese leaders have pinned their hopes.

Perhaps the most important domestic lesson has been the overwhelming importance of agriculture, a theme which Chinese policy-makers were slow to realize but which they have often repeated to Afro-Asian audiences. Light industry has also received considerable attention, primarily because it requires a low level of capital investment but yields quick returns. Heavy industry is still seen as crucial, but its growth is now said to be limited by agricultural development. The growth of these attitudes in China is paralleled by their application to the Third World.

The evolution of these attitudes did not come easily to Chinese leaders. At first China relied on a heavy industry-oriented, capital-intensive plan of development which left agriculture and light industry to adjust themselves. In their zeal for industrialization the Chinese went even further than the Soviet Union's Five-Year Plan: 58.2 per cent of overall capital investment was devoted to industry, which considerably outweighed the Soviet Union's 49

51. See, for example, M. Kapitsa, "National Liberation and the Mao Group's Splitting Activity," *International Affairs*, No. 7, July 1968, pp. 11–16.

per cent, and of this total 88.8 per cent went to heavy industry.[52] In discussing their first Five-Year Plan of 1953–57, Chinese commentators made it plain that China wished to copy the Soviet experience. Heavy industry was said to be the "key" to this process.[53]

Even though the Soviet Union faced initial isolation while China supposedly did not, Chinese spokesmen were well aware of the limits of Soviet aid as early as 1953. As in the Soviet case, heavy industry was considered to be the stepping-stone to self-reliance. Writing in *People's Daily*, for example, Chi Yun glorified economic independence and asserted that reliance on other countries was "parasitic." Comments on the Third World corresponded to this view. India, for example, was declared to have a "colonial" economy because, in spite of many light industrial enterprises, capital goods were still imported from Britain.[54]

Disappointment with the results of the first Five-Year Plan was reflected in a new strategy of economic development. While not fully formulated until 1958, this strategy was aimed at maximizing the overwhelmingly agricultural, labor-intensive conditions prevalent in China. While building up a raw materials base for industry, the new Five-Year Plan was simultaneously directed at improving rural market conditions for light industrial goods as well as at solving the problem of food shortages in the cities. While heavy industry was by no means abandoned, the slogan

52. Yang Chien-pai, "A Comparative Analysis of China's First Five-Year Plan and the Soviet Union's First Five-Year Plan," *Tung Chi Kung Tso T'ung Hsun* (*Statistical Work Journal*), No. 8, August 1955, in *Survey of China Mainland Magazines* (*SCMM*), No. 10, October 18, 1955, p. 18. The same figures are also used by T. J. Hughes and D. E. T. Luard in *The Economic Development of Communist China, 1949–1960* (London: Oxford University Press, 1961), p. 41.

53. See, for example, "Why is Emphasis Laid on the Development of Heavy Industry?" *Hsueh-Hsi* (*Study*), No. 6, June 2, 1955, *SCMM*, No. 2, August 22, 1955, p. 11.

54. Chi Yun, "How China Proceeds with the Task of Industrialization," *Jen-min Jih-pao* (*People's Daily*), May 22, 1953, in *CB*, No. 272, January 5, 1954, pp. 11–12.

of the upcoming Great Leap Forward was "Simultaneous Development of Industry and Agriculture." China had ceased trying to copy the Soviet experience and was soon to put herself forward as a separate economic model for the Third World.

The shift away from a one-sided emphasis on heavy industry was accompanied by a more favorable attitude toward economic development in India. Previously condemned for having a "colonial" economy, India was now said to be adopting many "positive" measures to realize her second Five-Year Plan.[55] While Chinese leaders now had new respect for agricultural priorities even at the expense of heavy industry, they were probably also referring to such desirable political features as acceptance of Soviet aid and restrictions on Western capital. At this time Peking also launched a systematic and far-reaching drive toward economic cooperation with other Afro-Asian nations without regard for their domestic economic programs.[56] While these moves naturally harmonized with the new diplomatic attitudes expressed at Bandung, they also reflect a new appreciation of both agriculture and pragmatic economic measures.

Contrary to Chinese expectations, the low level of investment in agriculture, the overly ambitious scale of targets and quotas, the more drastic aspects of communization, and a series of natural calamities combined to undermine the Great Leap Forward. The period since 1960 has thus witnessed a third stage, one in which moderation and a high level of investment in agriculture are prominent features. In spite of the Cultural Revolution the economic guidelines of the Third Five-Year Plan for 1966–1970 have remained moderate. Even the claims regarding economic progress have been more sober. Whereas Chou En-lai asserted in 1956 that China would need fifteen years to achieve a modern industrial economy, one of the more recent figures has been twenty to thirty years.[57]

55. Ch'en Yi, "For a Common Economic Advance of All Asian-African Countries," *Peking Review*, No. 5, February 3, 1959.

56. See, for example, Ch'en Yi, "Asian-African Economic Conference," *Peking Review*, No. 6, February 10, 1959.

57. "Welcoming 1966—The First Year of China's Third Five-Year Plan," *Peking Review*, Vol. IX, No. 1, January 1, 1966, p. 5. For a clear analysis of this recent phase, see Jan S. Prybyla, "Commu-

Chou En-lai's first visit to Africa in late 1963 and early 1964 gave rise to new comments on economic developments in the Third World. Economically China's aims were to encourage economic cooperation and to promote the more moderate aspects of China's experience as a model for the Third World. When presenting this paradigm, Chou and others deliberately omitted such radical measures as intensive communization.[58]

On the one hand, Peking was anxious to impress upon African minds the speed and magnitude of China's industrial development. On the other, Chou had to avoid giving the impression that China had become just another industrial power devoid of sympathy for Africa's economic problems. According to the tenets of this logic, China was supposed to have a "developed" substructure and an "underdeveloped" superstructure or world view.[59] This contradiction still figures prominently in statements on the Third World.

Omitting any explanation of the basic shifts in economic strategy that had taken place in China, Chou declared that his country had always pursued the policy of "taking agriculture as the foundation and industry as the leading factor." According to the so-called "Eight Principles of Economic Aid," China's aid program would stress projects that required small investment but yielded quick results.[60] This emphasis on light industry again mirrored China's own recent experience, but it also conformed to the limitations of Chinese aid. In other words, the downgrading of heavy industry and the moderation which now characterized Chou's economic formulae corresponded both to domestic lessons and to the need to compete in the field of foreign aid.

---

nist China's Strategy of Economic Development, 1961–66," *Asian Survey*, Vol. VI, No. 10, October 1966.

58. This view contrasts with the statement of one prominent Western analyst, who suggests that China's collective farms and communes are intended to serve as lessons for the rest of Asia. See Roderick MacFarquhar, "The Chinese Model and the Underdeveloped World," *International Affairs* (London), Vol. 39, No. 3, July 1963, p. 372.

59. To learn how skillfully Chou handled this contradiction, see "Answers to Middle East News Agency Questions," *New China News Agency*, International Service in English, December 25, 1963.

60. Chou En-lai, "Revolutionary Prospects in Africa Excellent!" *Peking Review*, Vol. VII, No. 7, February 14, 1964, p. 8.

Discussions of the remaining eight principles of foreign aid stressed popular themes, such as the absence of political conditions, the extension of time limits for the repayment of loans, the training of local technicians, and the Third World's supposed ability to catch up with the economic level of the West in a short time. Chou reasoned that since China and Africa shared similar experiences and similar problems, China could understand African needs better than any wealthy country, presumably meaning both the West and the Soviet Union.

The theme of self-reliance, by no means new in Chinese pronouncements, received special emphasis during Chou's trip. As a means to political independence, self-reliance was defined as primary reliance on a country's own efforts, peoples, and resources. Foreign aid with conditions attached was strongly condemned, and China's own progress was said to have been achieved without help of this kind.[61] No mention was made of Soviet aid to China, which, although small in comparison to China's needs, was instrumental in establishing several small cornerstones of industrial development.

The implication that China's interests in Africa extended beyond economic cooperation found concrete expression at a meeting of FLN cadres in Algeria. On this occasion, Chou went furthest in stressing China's economic experience, but this time he also linked economic progress both to revolution and to socialism. Declaring that the Chinese had accumulated experience of their own, he added that "the truths of revolution cannot be monopolized." He instructed his audience to adhere to a broad united front, to carry on new struggles after the victory of the revolution, to carry out nation-wide rectification campaigns, and to provide correct leadership. He also stressed that Algeria had a "sacred duty" to help other countries to achieve revolution.[62] In other

61. Chou En-lai, "Premier Chou En-lai on the Growing Friendship Between the Chinese and African Peoples," *Peking Review*, Vol. VII, No. 1, January 3, 1964, p. 39.

62. Chou En-lai, "Premier Chou En-lai's Speech at Algerian Cadres' Meeting," *NCNA*, Algiers, December 26, 1963, in *SCMP*, No. 3130, January 2, 1964, pp. 26–29. Chou's stress on the relevance of China's experience apparently provoked some criticism. On the very next day,

words, Peking attached its own conditions to close relations with Algiers; in return for economic and political support, Algeria was clearly expected to promote and support national liberation movements elsewhere in Africa.

Chou's trip has been discussed in detail because it was a watershed in China's economic and political attitudes toward the Third World. It was followed by many systematic and thorough discussions of Afro-Asian economic problems. Peking was now more confident that even the details of China's economic policies could serve as an example to the Third World. Chinese spokesmen issued economic prescriptions for Africa and Asia with greater vigor and specificity than ever before.

More significantly, the year 1964 witnessed the start of direct attacks on Soviet foreign policy toward the Third World. At the much publicized meeting of the Afro-Asian People's Solidarity Council in March 1964, the Chinese delegate Kuo Chien accused the Soviet Union of "great-power chauvinism and national egoism" in giving aid. He charged that Soviet aid actually harmed the economic and political interests of the recipients. Politically, Moscow was accused of ignoring the struggle against imperialism.[63] In short, China's policy toward the Third World was now hopelessly entangled with undisguised and bitter rivalry with the Soviet Union.

Just as Chinese aid to Algeria was attached to certain political conditions, so an important article of 1964 extended this reminder of the mutual nature of Chinese aid to all countries. The basic obligations attached to Chinese aid were anti-imperialism, friendly relations with Peking, and, if possible, political support for na-

---

he declared modestly that China's experience could only serve as "a kind of reference" and that conditions in China and Algeria were not quite the same. See "Premier Chou En-lai Gives Press Conference in Algiers," NCNA, December 26, 1963, in SCMP, No. 3130, January 2, 1964, p. 30.

63. Kuo Chien, "Chinese Delegate Refutes Soviet Delegation's Slander," NCNA, March 28, 1964, in SCMP, No. 3190, April 2, 1964, p. 37; and Kuo Chien, "Chinese Afro-Asian Solidarity Leader Flays Imperialism, New and Old Colonialism at Algiers Meeting," NCNA, March 24, 1964, in SCMP, No. 3188, March 31, 1964, p. 31.

tional liberation movements elsewhere. By an interesting piece of logic, dispassionate and one-sided aid was said to be based on charity and on a lack of respect for Afro-Asian countries; in contrast, mutual aid conformed to the principles of political equality.[64]

Apparently sensing that the theme of self-reliance was encountering opposition in Africa and Asia, a long article in its behalf appeared in the fall of 1964. Reinforcing Chinese comments at various Afro-Asian economic seminars, this message again hammered on self-reliance. While a self-reliant economic policy admittedly yielded slow results at first, quick results were said to follow even in the case of small countries. Possessing its own revolutionary vitality, self-reliance would contribute to the formation of attitudes necessary for rapid economic growth. To add political fuel, the article quoted allegedly standard Western insults directed at the peoples of underdeveloped areas. After this naked appeal to nationalism, the author took the predictable step of assigning the opponents of self-reliance, notably the Soviet Union, to the camp of big-nation chauvinism and capitulation to imperialism.[65]

At the Afro-Asian Economic Seminar held in Algiers in February 1965, the lessons listed by the Chinese delegate included the abolition of privileges enjoyed by imperialists, the nationalization of foreign enterprises, land reform, taking agriculture as the basis for development, investment in productive enterprises, capital accumulation based on domestic stringency, and scientific and technical training. He also made a noteworthy concession to Afro-Asian opinion. In practice, Peking had encouraged friendly relations with many recipients of Western aid; in theory, however, such aid had always been considered to be both harmful and incapable of being offered on the basis of equality and mutual benefit. After failing to earn support for this view, the Chinese spokesman officially sanctioned what had always been tolerated in practice. As if to explain this shift, he revealed that China

64. Ai Ching-chu, "Some Problems of Economic and Technical Aid to Foreign Countries," *Jen-min Jih-pao* (*People's Daily*), May 27, 1964, in SCMP, No. 3237, June 12, 1964, p. 3.

65. Yung Lung-kuei, "Road of Developing the National Economy by Afro-Asian Countries Through Self-Reliance," *Ta Kung Pao*, August 26, 1964, in SCMP, No. 3303, September 23, 1964, pp. 3–9.

was still unable to embark on any substantial aid programs, a fact admitted in 1959 but publicly ignored since then.[66]

In ideological terms, Peking's conception of the economic development of the Third World called for pushing ahead the social and political revolution. Significantly, proletarian leadership was not considered to be a prerequisite for this development. Instead, a somewhat laissez-faire view of revolution held that quantitative changes would lead to qualitative ones.[67] If this statement can be taken at face value, Peking did not insist on a Communist-led, Maoist type revolution, at least in the initial stages.

Instead, Chinese leaders on the eve of the Cultural Revolution hoped that the very momentum of what they call a national democratic revolution of the Algerian or Cuban type would eventually carry a country toward socialism. It was not local Communist parties which were important to Peking but rather left-wing nationalists committed to anti-imperialism and to rapid socioeconomic change. Peking's relative indifference to the plight of local Communists conforms to this analysis. A broad social revolution was considered preferable to conspiratorial terrorist tactics. Chinese leaders were probably sincere in their conviction that national liberation movements are inevitable developments springing from the revolutionary potential of Afro-Asian nations.

Supporting this conclusion was a Chinese tendency to treat entire nations as proletarian or poor-peasant units. Afro-Asian nationalists representing their country rather than their class were placed on a level equal or even superior to Communist or left-wing movements in the West.

Like Moscow and Washington, Peking has recently expressed disappointment over the course of events in the Third World. Among the causes for their discouragement have been the fall of Ben Bella in June 1965, the indefinite postponement of the proposed second Bandung Conference, the disaster of Indonesia in

66. Nan Han-chen, "For the Economic Emancipation of Afro-Asian Peoples," February 23, 1965, *Peking Review*, Vol. VIII, No. 10, March 5, 1965, pp. 18–26. *Peking Review* printed the reference to China as a model for Africa and Asia in bold-face type.

67. Hsu Nai-chiung, "The Interrelation of Political and Economic Independence," *Peking Review*, Vol. IX, No. 5, January 28, 1966, p. 14.

September 1965, the fall of Nkrumah in the spring of 1966, and the rash of military coups in Africa. Although domestic preoccupation with the Cultural Revolution limits general comments, Chinese attitudes toward Burma, Vietnam, and other countries have dropped their earlier tolerance for left-wing nationalists. Genuine Maoist-type revolutions, complete with territorial bases, are the order of the day.

China's economic advice to the Third World is revealing. A number of themes spring from China's own domestic experience, namely, the importance of agriculture, self-reliance, and shared experiences. More numerous, however, are those economic perspectives which stem from political priorities rather than from domestic experience. Chief among these has been a desire to expel Western influence from Africa and Asia. In support of this aim, Peking has tolerated almost any domestic economic system, provided that a country's foreign policy was sufficiently anti-imperialist. The criterion was not the economic substructure but the international stance.

India is an example of the relation between economic tolerance and political approval; the Sino-Indian border dispute prompted Peking to denounce Indian socialism as fraudulent, but no attacks were made on such notions as "African socialism" and "Arab socialism." Similarly, Peking has preferred the so-called "revolutionary camp," a category which excludes the Soviet Union and all but the most revolutionary governments and national liberation movements as well. The Third World is becoming transitional, so that membership in this camp is likely to swell as the prospects for stability decline.

Besides appraisals of the national bourgeoisie and economic perspectives, China's attitude on people's war is absolutely fundamental to understanding her overall policy toward the Third World. As faith in all but the most radical governments has declined, emphasis on people's war has increased. Self-reliance, always a theme in China's pronouncements on other matters, has permeated this area as well. Once again, China's own experience has been elevated into a model.

As outlined by Lin Piao's famous article, six points are essential to the Maoist strategy of people's war. A fundamental feature is a broad united front consisting of all classes willing to coop-

erate in any way. Lin even points to the Sian Incident in which
the Chinese Communists helped to obtain the release of Chiang
Kai-shek from rebellious Manchurian troops. In fact, one of Peking's chief criticisms of the Vietcong is its preference for iso-
lationist, terrorist tactics instead of a broad united front. Esoteric
hints urge the Vietcong to court all potential allies, including the
Buddhists, the intellectuals, and the national bourgeoisie. If necessary, the Party should even take such steps as changing its name
and moderating its land policy.[68]

The second point is the leading role of the Party. The line to
be followed here is a thin one. Lin even suggests that the Lao
Dong Party of North Vietnam does not have firm control over
the National Liberation Front. Yet the Communists must avoid
alienating their allies within the united front. Occasional references to Wang Ming's "left" extremism and also to his "right"
opportunism point out the delicacy of this two-edged task.

Base areas are a third ingredient in the recipe for people's war.
These territorial islands, difficult to establish, should be self-
sufficient miniature states. Each one should provide its own
schools, industrial projects, and agricultural programs, to be run
by its own administration and its own taxes. Once again, Lin's
article carries weighty instructions to Vietnam. Even at the expense of shrinking the territorial area under Vietcong control, firm
base areas must be established and defended. The fluid nature
of Communist control should be abandoned. Within each base
area, policy should be moderate. The key themes should be anti-
imperialism and the united front.

The fourth component is an army founded on mass support,
aided by a peasantry loyal to both party and army. Success in
this direction depends on adopting the Maoist mass line, developing good relations with the masses, organizing a local militia, and
offering leniency to captured enemies. Mao's writings during the

68. For this topic and for the other components of people's war,
see Lin Piao, Long Live the Victory of People's War (Peking: Foreign
Languages Press, 1965). One of the few clear-headed and accurate
interpretations of this document is D. P. Mozingo and T. W. Robinson, "Lin Piao on 'People's War': China Takes a Second Look at
Vietnam" (Santa Monica: The RAND Corporation, Memorandum
RM-4814-PR, November 1965).

war against Japan and the civil war abound with such instruction, so Lin's advice is not new. What is surprising is the degree of dissatisfaction with Vietcong tactics that the article expresses. Clearly, Vietnamese Communists are being scolded for their failure to enlist the support of potential allies and for their inability to shake the peasants out of their political apathy.

Correct military tactics constitute the fifth ingredient—guerrilla warfare. Both Mao and Lin have devoted tremendous attention to the specific details of military success. Fighting must begin with guerrilla warfare, moving on to mobile warfare only when conditions are ripe. Failures of timing can lead to a leftist error—adventurism—or to a rightist one—opportunism. Guerrilla forces should avoid large-scale confrontations. At first they should be on the defensive and should content themselves with harassing the enemy. Only as the balance of power shifts in their favor can they begin a strategic offensive. Even then they must avoid pitched battles and must be quick to disperse and hide in the face of superior forces. Whenever possible they should isolate and annihilate small enemy units.

When applied to Vietnam, this advice on guerrilla warfare points up numerous Vietcong failures. Emphasizing "just" methods, Lin disparages terrorism. In his comments on avoiding frontal assaults, he suggests that the Vietcong are recklessly losing too many men. His strong insistence on the prerequisites for the shift to mobile warfare reveals that the Vietcong have taken this step too soon. In the face of massive American involvement, the Vietcong are simply pursuing the wrong strategy. Besides the Sino-Soviet dispute, this disapproval may be another reason why China is holding up shipments of Soviet aid.

Sixth on the list is self-reliance. As the RAND commentators point out, nothing in Lin's speech is really new. Citing China's own experience, Lin points out that no amount of aid can turn a spark into a prairie fire unless conditions are ripe. To begin with, the revolutionary movement must already be rumbling and its leaders must be trained in correct leadership methods, that is, in Maoism. In other words, Chinese leaders refuse to pour massive amounts of aid into the hands of any revolutionary group unless their advice is taken. Even if the insurgents are model students, however, aid may still be cut off because of China's domestic needs or international exigencies. China thus reserves the right to withhold aid even from movements which look to Peking for guidance. Just as self-reliance in the field of economic aid justified China's parsimony while undercutting Soviet influence, self-reliant military attitudes permit vociferous revolutionary haranguing without the danger of a Sino-American war.

The Chinese are quite clearly in a dilemma. Judging by Lin's article, they feel that the United States will try to stay in Vietnam and to turn the country into a colony. Given this prospect, the validity of the Maoist revolutionary model would be damaged even though the Vietcong are not following it correctly. In other words, the prestige of people's war would sink because of mistakes made in its application. Whether China likes it or not, the West views Vietnam as an application of the Chinese model. This misunderstanding stems from an inability to recognize other features of people's war besides guerrilla warfare. Moreover, judging both from Lin's article on people's war and from the wave of urban assaults, even that ingredient has been incorrectly handled.

Yet in the face of mounting criticism of China's lack of support for Vietnam and her obvious desire to avoid a confrontation with the United States, Chinese leaders cannot criticize Hanoi and the NLF too loudly. Unless Lin's advice is accepted, they have little choice but to remain passive and to continue to disguise their warnings. Like all middle-of-the-road positions, this one pleases nobody—except, perhaps, Washington. This dilemma places the future of the Mao-Lin Vietnam policy in grave danger. Nevertheless, Mao cannot afford to abandon it without appearing to discard the entire heritage of people's war in China. Since Chinese assessments of the Communist revolution devote so much attention to its military contribution, such a step would amount to withdrawing the Chinese model from the international production line.

To express this problem in different terms, the "lower risk policy of indirect confrontation" may protect China's territory while tarnishing her influence. Short-run physical safety may amount to a long-run loss of prestige. Many Afro-Asian nations have already expressed various degrees of contempt for the Cultural Revolution. Unless they fully understand Lin's criticism, the difficulties which they are witnessing in Vietnam may condemn China to political irrelevance. Ironically, steps leading back to China's isolation may result not from the "hard line" of 1957 but from its opposite in practice. No one can afford to ignore a tough China whose leaders mean business, but they can overlook a country whose verbal violence is not translated into action.

Were it not for their disillusionment, Chinese policy-makers might counteract this image by new diplomatic offensives in the Third World. As it is, many have been purged. Those who remain have limited themselves mainly to the "revolutionary camp." To make matters worse, many of these revolutionary movements are erupting in countries firmly backed by the United States. Leftist insurgencies are reportedly on the upsurge in Thailand, Laos, Cambodia, Burma, and, to a lesser extent, Malaysia,[69] four of whom can count on Western protection in the event of significant Chinese intervention or infiltration. In Africa, where an American response is less likely, revolutionary prospects have reached a new low. Maneuvers in Latin America, where chances of upheaval are better, are like trying to tiptoe into Washington's back yard.

In short, China's impact on the Third World continues to be stalemated. Unless the Maoist leadership is willing to take greater risks against the United States, the gap between theory and practice will remain. Even the theme of self-reliance does not rule out aid from China, not to mention political and diplomatic support, but even aid has slowed to a trickle. Both preoccupation with domestic economic growth and the confusion of the Cultural Revolution go a long way toward explaining this apparent paralysis. Nevertheless, China's present inaction also bears witness to the credibility of the American deterrent. To Peking only nuclear weapons and a comprehensive delivery system can free China from this political and military trap.

As for shared experiences with imperialism, Chinese arguments make little headway in the Third World. Even in Mao's language, China was not a colony but a semicolony with her own administrative personnel. Colonial activities were confined mainly to the coast. More significantly, the wide variety of material resources

69. Terence Smith, "Grim Report to SEATO Says Communist Insurgency Grows," *The New York Times*, September 11, 1968, p. 12.

available to China contrast sharply with the reliance on a single cash crop which characterizes Africa and parts of Asia. Other differences include China's enormous population, undoubtedly an asset in making an impact on international politics.

Seen as a whole, the past two decades of China's policy toward the Third World have been woven from a number of complex strands. These include domestic experiences with the national bourgeoisie, the dynamics of the Sino-Soviet dispute, the shifts and turns of various economic strategies, the formula for people's war, and the demands of China's international position. Relatively low on this list are the actual realities of Afro-Asian revolutions. The Third World has had to learn that it is primarily a tool to be used in a larger international context. Chinese leaders do not judge issues on their face value but in reference to their overall significance to China's struggle for power and influence.

Each of the stages of China's policy toward the Third World expresses a different set of perspectives drawn from these various strands. From 1949 through 1951, while Communist insurgencies were being waged in many parts of Asia, Chinese commentaries were critical of both the domestic measures and the international postures adopted by most Afro-Asian nations. Still hopeful of an increase in Soviet aid, they emphasized guerrilla warfare but kept self-reliance on a low key. Mindful of the debacle of 1927, they profoundly distrusted the national bourgeoisie of other countries.

The second stage, 1952 to 1957, differed sharply from the first. Quick to recognize the anti-Western potential of the newly independent nations, the Chinese, less bound by responsibility for local Communists, outstripped the Soviets in extending friendship to Afro-Asian governments. People's war was minimized accordingly. As Sino-Soviet friction mounted, Peking placed growing emphasis on China's affinity with the Third World at the expense of Moscow. Nationalist leaders were no longer branded as members of the national bourgeoisie but as progressive leaders of nondescript social origin. In this case, silence spoke louder than words. Bandung climaxed this tolerance.

The third stage, extending from 1957 to about 1966, witnessed a sharp upswing in Sino-Soviet competition. The desire to expel Western influence from Africa and Asia was almost subordinated to undisguised rivalry with Moscow. At the same time, wishing to take advantage of Sputnik and the Soviet ICBM, Peking risked a confrontation with the United States over Taiwan. Through a series of humiliating border clashes with India, China tried to win leadership of Asia for herself. Meanwhile, faced with the general failure of the Great Leap Forward, economic platforms at home and abroad were built squarely upon agriculture as the foundation for sound growth. This shift had the advantage of minimizing the importance of heavy industrial aid from both the Soviet Union and the West and of disguising the fact that China was incapable of extending such aid herself.

During this immediate period, Chinese leaders maintained friendly relations with a great variety of governments. In spite of their theoretical disapproval, they upheld good relations even with those countries which accepted American aid and which pursued capitalist or semicapitalist policies. Frequently citing Cuba and Algeria, they apparently hoped that the very momentum of national liberation would carry the social and political revolution to eventual victory regardless of specific nationalist regimes. In the meantime, they rapidly expanded their program of area studies and strained every nerve to expel the Western presence from Africa and Asia.

Within this general framework of tolerance, the Chinese did not wait for their maximal vision to materialize in the form of miniature Chinas. Instead they encouraged Afro-Asian leaders to carry out the nationalization of foreign enterprises and to bar the establishment of Western military bases. Stressing self-reliance, Peking unsuccessfully urged them to lessen or to halt their dependence on Western aid and, by implication, Soviet aid as well. Beyond these points, however, China's diplomatic attitudes toward economic questions remained flexible. On controversial questions of domestic politics, Chinese spokesmen usually remained silent. Vehement criticisms of Yugoslavia's policies, being directed largely at the Soviet Union, were not extended to far more blatantly capitalist policies adopted by Afro-Asian governments cordial to Peking.

China's relative benevolence was justified by a tendency to treat entire Afro-Asian nations as proletarian or poor-peasant units. Whereas the Soviet Union reserved the word "fraternal" to Communist nations, Chinese reports used such phrases as "fraternal peoples" and "revolutionary working peoples" to refer to nations of the Third World. By the same token, local Communist parties could even be sacrificed in the interests of maintaining good relations with an anti-imperialist government. As Geoffrey Hudson has pointed out, China's relative weakness, combined with long-standing pro-Soviet loyalties on the part of local Communists, gave China an advantage. Her freedom of action was greater than that enjoyed by Moscow.[70]

As Chinese politics took a radical turn, attitudes toward the Third World shifted accordingly. Mao could not escalate the class struggle at home while continuing to downgrade it in the Third World. Contributing to this radical trend was the same general disillusionment which caused aid cutbacks in both Moscow and Washington. The obstacles encountered by the socialist education campaign placed the progressive nature of Afro-Asian leaders in question. Contrary to Leninist and Maoist teachings, non revolutionary social backgrounds were hard to overcome. As Mao encountered open recalcitrance from his less revolutionary oppo nents, he must have realized that the spontaneous development of national liberation was a fiction. A laissez faire attitude had not succeeded in producing more Cubas and Algerias, let alone more Chinas.

These trends coincided with the sharp escalation of the war in Vietnam. As American bombers flew dangerously close to China's borders and pummeled her buffer state of North Vietnam, verbal frenzy mollified the frustrations of inaction. Meanwhile, the youthful fanaticism and idealism unleashed by the Cultural Revolution had a spill-over effect on Chinese inhabitants of Southeast Asia, particularly Burma and, in a somewhat different manner, Indonesia. The upsurge of overseas Chinese nationalism provided another excuse for channeling political support away from Asian governments.

On the whole, however, this political freeze was not matched by stepped-up support for local insurgents, at least overtly. The gap between theory and practice, already painfully embarrassing, may inhibit Chinese leaders from talking their way into a com-

70. Geoffrey Hudson, "The Chinese Model and the Developing Countries," in Werner Klatt, ed., *The Chinese Model* (Hong Kong: Hong Kong University Press, 1965), p. 209.

mitment they do not wish to keep. If the pendulum of Chinese politics swings in another direction, this combination of hostility and inaction can always be knocked aside.

Yet the diplomatic north wind still blowing from Peking does not necessarily indicate a preference for local Communists. In addition to the desire to avoid a general Sino-American confrontation, the Chinese are not placing bets on the dark horse of local Communism because of its inability to build up mass support. The recent republication of many of Mao's works dealing with the mass line is no coincidence. More than almost anyone else, Mao insists that a revolutionary movement must have mass character. This view, which contrasts sharply with the Soviet preference for conspiratorial tactics, is still another product of Mao's populist-style nationalism.

As a populist, Mao places great faith in the power of the people to work revolutionary miracles. He assumes that their revolutionary potential is merely lying dormant, waiting to be tapped by correct revolutionary leadership. As a nationalist, he downgrades class struggle on the assumption that imperialism still exists and that the broadest united front is necessary to defeat it. Even the class struggle proclaimed by the Cultural Revolution is only half-baked, for it has reverted to the call for unity among all members of the Chinese "people." Membership in the revolutionary camp still depends on attitude rather than on class origin or occupation. Just as the Vietcong is being admonished for failure to build a broad united front, so China will probably resume friendly overtures to Afro-Asian governments, albeit with reservations, now that the Cultural Revolution has faded. New ambassadors have already been dispatched.

Compared to the Soviet Union and the United States, China's experiences do have relevance for the Third World. Chinese formulas for economic development and revolutionary strategy were slowly and painfully worked out. The growth of Mao's forces from pitiful proportions to nation-wide victory was indeed an impressive feat. China's position as an underdeveloped country in transition and as a challenger of the international status quo is at least partially similar to the plight of Afro-Asian nations.

Nevertheless, this similarity, exploited for political headway, bears limited fruit. China's sophistication in area studies still lags far behind that of the Soviet Union. China's performance in Vietnam does not impress the leaders of the Third World. Furthermore, as long as the foreign aid programs of the two superpowers continue to function, China will have to be content with third place. At this point in Afro-Asian history, money is far more attractive than empathy. In the long run, Peking's leaders are probably wise to concentrate on building up domestic economic and military strength. China's current stress on the omnipotence of Mao's thought simply cannot dent the surface of nations enthralled by the omnipotence of machines.

CHAPTER EIGHT

Revolutionary Change and Foreign Policy: The Impact of the Cultural Revolution

Probably the greatest misunderstanding about the Great Proletarian Cultural Revolution is its Western title. It should rather be translated as "a full scale revolution to establish a working class culture." [1] This misapprehension led both to a serious underestimation of the original vision of the Cultural Revolution and to confusion regarding its content. Initially, to most analysts, the Cultural Revolution was aimed primarily at the arts and literature and should have stayed there. Its transformation into a power struggle, the argument runs, corrupted it from its original vision and seriously undermined the Chinese polity.

It was therefore natural that public, journalistic, and even academic opinions on the nature of the Cultural Revolution emphasized only the iconoclastic acts of the Red Guards. They were more concerned with Red Guard opinions about the color of the traffic lights, the style of living of the ambassadors, the length of cuffs, and similar stray incidents. While these are probably newsworthy events, they have little to do with the philosophical or the structural content of the Cultural Revolution.

No two opinions on the nature of the Cultural Revolution are alike. The Cultural Revolution has been generally regarded as

1. Neale Hunter, *Shanghai Journal* (New York: Frederick A. Praeger, 1969), p. 5. For an original and refreshing analysis of the Cultural Revolution see pp. 3–13.

either a power struggle or a manifestation of Maoist senility, reinforced by Mao's irrational longing for the so-called "Yenan syndrome," that is, for a simple, Spartan, egalitarian society. Yet the struggle sought not so much to revive the past as to adapt Yenanrooted leadership methods to new circumstances. Only by viewing the Cultural Revolution as an attempt to change the entire nature of the Chinese polity under contemporary conditions can we come to a clear understanding of its motives. Central to the many themes of the upheaval is a fundamental attempt to establish new conceptions of authority.

The Cultural Revolution attacked people in authority. Who were these people in authority? Pointing to men like Liu Shao-ch'i, Teng Hsiao-p'ing, Ch'en Yi, P'eng Chen, T'ao Chu and the like would be too simple. All these leaders represented a certain type of people in authority, but they were by no means a complete list. In fact, the list of survivors is as astounding as the list of victims. While the day-to-day political maneuvers surrounding the selection of targets remain hidden, a few general explanations can be hazarded.

Ever since the centralization and consolidation of the Chinese People's Republic in 1953-1954, certain changes had been taking place in Chinese society. Complex patterns of bureaucratic stratification based on the differentiation of rank and salary had replaced the near egalitarianism of guerrilla days. Status-oriented career aspirations had taken hold of a youthful population born too late to remember the Japanese invasion and the Civil War. Following the completion of land reform and the economic emasculation of the industrial bourgeoisie, memories of class exploitation were fading.

Nevertheless, it would be a mistake to conclude that all the victims of the Cultural Revolution were simply bureaucrats devoted to the status quo. Many or most of them believed themselves to be good revolutionaries. In fact, some of them might well have accused Mao of abandoning certain key elements of his own Yenan program, particularly those concerning inner-Party disputes and Party reform. A striking innovation of the Cultural Revolution is the treatment of inner-Party affairs in the same manner as "contradictions" between the people and the enemy. Analogies of curing the patient gave way to the language of rooting out class enemies. Self-reform within the Party was replaced by the large-scale unleashing of non-Party forces, most notably the Red Guards but more importantly the People's Liberation Army. The man who had placed such emphasis on Party leadership seemed to have abandoned his own creation.

Other important issues involved in the leadership dispute were economic strategy and relations with both the United States and the Soviet Union. As genuine patriots, a number of Chinese leaders appear to have disagreed with some (but by no means all) of Mao's ideas on these subjects. Some of them may have seen themselves as more orthodox in a Marxist-Leninist sense than Mao. The elevation of Mao's thought beyond Leninism, and the use of Mao's personal prestige to bolster his forces, could only feed the flames.

Beyond this handful of key issues lay the whole fabric of organizational politics. Again and again the top-ranking victims of the Cultural Revolution have been accused of building up "independent kingdoms," that is, watertight organizational networks practicing mutual advancement and mutual defense. Seemingly insignificant members of such groupings were the first to fall, not only because they served as scapegoats but also because the most important nuts were too tough to crack directly. Finally, of course, the tendency of conflicts to polarize opposing groups lumped together men of different political persuasions, a phenomenon which transcended issues altogether.

Given the apparent resistance to some of his ideas after 1959, Mao came to the conclusion that political and economic revolutions had not sufficed. What was required was a social and ideological revolution. Within a revolutionary framework his reasoning was correct: the elimination of the economic foundation of the feudal and bourgeois classes had not eliminated feudal and bourgeois ideas. Only a revolution in what Marx had called the superstructure—ideology and culture—could ensure a truly revolutionary future. In fact, the word "culture" (*wen-hua*) has a very broad meaning in China, referring to the entire realm of thought and consciousness as well as to the narrower realm of literature and art.

Yet this social revolution was to differ from its political and economic predecessors in one important respect: it was supposed to be nonviolent. It may come as a jarring surprise to most students of Chinese politics to hear the events of 1967 described as nonviolent. Although the focus of the revolution shifted to personalities and even to civil violence, the basic character and aims of the Cultural Revolution were concentrated on the nonviolent replacement or remolding of people in authority at all levels. Traditional Chinese Communist methods of criticism, self-criticism, and public humiliation were employed. Like all social movements, the agitation turned at times into civil violence. Yet this was the intention of neither the various idealist groups who promoted the Cultural Revolution nor the Maoist faction in Peking. It must be remembered that in spite of the most non-violent protestations, civil violence usually does occur in mass movements. Good examples include the Gandhian civil disobedience movement in India and Martin Luther King's civil rights movement in the United States.[2]

Another aim, also partially unrealized, was to cultivate a new type of leader. To the dismay of certain ultra-leftist student groups, the attack on men in authority did not signify that the Cultural Revolution intended to destroy all authority whatsoever. Instead, the movement was aimed not at authority but at a certain type of authority, not at leadership but at a certain type of leader. The goal was the cultivation of a new type of leader whose authority came from within himself rather than from his position in a bureaucracy. So it was that the seemingly authoritarian glorification of Mao's thought came to symbolize a revolt against a certain type of authority as well as the triumph of human perseverance over physical or economic difficulties, both of which represent to Mao another type of domination.

Given the legacy of backwardness and the need for sustained hard work, much of the content of Mao's thought is reminiscent of the many maxims and proverbs of eighteenth- and nineteenth-century America. Among the pages of Maoist slogans can be found the equivalents of "waste not, want not" and "if at first you don't succeed, try, try again." [3]

2. *Ibid.*, pp. 3–13.
3. For an interesting comparison of Gandhi and Benjamin Franklin along these lines, see Lloyd I. and Susanne H. Rudolph, *The Modernity of Tradition* (Chicago: University of Chicago Press, 1967), pp. 221–224.

Attempts to bring about this social revolution were neither hap-hazard nor totally spontaneous. Careful preparations had gone on for at least seven years. From the Lushan Plenum in 1959 to the beginning of the Cultural Revolution in the summer of 1966, education and the People's Liberation Army had already been affected. What is more important is the emergence and consolidation of radical groups during this period. At the time, these groups operated only marginally within the framework of the Communist Chinese polity. In the three-year period 1960 to 1962, young actors and their instructors in the Shanghai theaters had already fought a campaign against the mass production of poor plays. They also established their contact with Chiang Ch'ing, who had already become famous in such marginal groups for her efforts to transform Peking Opera. The East China District Action Drama Competition, held in Shanghai from December 25, 1963, to January 22, 1964, was probably one of the more successful examples of a breakthrough of radical groups leading towards a social revolution in dramatic circles. Since 1958, these people had been working at the Shanghai Theatrical Academy; after six years, with the help of Madame Mao they succeeded in establishing Maoist ideas in the theater.

A closer look at these ideas does not reveal power struggles or civil violence, but an attempt by the actors not to behave like actors in the sense we know them. They were supposed to behave like proletarian individualists, to be self-sufficient, self-reliant, and to perform all the tasks necessary for the production of a performance. This ideal was aimed at changing the social attitudes of actors and the role and use of drama in a socialist society.

Many people involved in such efforts felt, rightly or wrongly, that they were held back by people in authority at all levels. Such a social revolution was aimed at changing the remnants of traditional attitudes and at carrying forward the dynamic transformation of Chinese society. To certain leaders, the Russian form of modernization was no longer acceptable. To them, technology first had made Russia not significantly different from the capitalist West and from its symbol, the United States. Chinese attitudes toward a new kind of social revolution, therefore, fought on two fronts at the same time, namely, the traditional Peking Opera and Soviet revisionism. If China were to be a revolutionary society, then it must not follow the priorities of both the capitalist West and the technocratic Soviet Union.

A real social revolution must build new priorities. This is what the Maoist ideals practiced in the Yenan period started out to achieve, and this is what the consolidations of 1953 and 1961 and the realities of global politics eroded. To reestablish them in the context of a rapidly industrializing society was the primary objective of the marginal idealist groups which were supposed to be the spearhead of the Cultural Revolution. Such a social revolution, if successful, would have provided China with a new kind of system and made it a viable alternative to both Soviet and American Models. Such was the substance of the aim to establish a working class culture in China.

From January 1965 onwards, emerging groups in universities and art circles were generally regarded as radicals and troublemakers and effectively held in check by visiting work teams. This period of phony revolution lasted almost through the summer of 1966. Actually these groups were not radical, but were composed of young idealists. They were not demanding an end to Communism; neither were they seeking a liberalization of economic and political activities in the Western sense. They thus cannot be compared to the younger generation of Czechs. What they were demanding was that adult people in authority follow the Maoist ideals of a working-class culture. Wherever they looked around them, they found routinization of these ideals, excessive specialization, and other aspects of what Western social scientists would call technical "rationality." To the Maoist idealists, this rationality sounded like inertia and the end of an attempt to establish a revolutionary culture.

Most of the people who participated in this social revolution, whether Red Guards or younger members of the bureaucracy, whether in high schools or the Ministry of Foreign Affairs, were highly motivated idealists. Only a small percentage of them turned "radical" in the sense that they wished to extend or even redefine the ideals themselves. This change occurred in 1967, when they realized that even Mao was not prepared to follow his own logic in translating the ideals of this revolution into practice. By the end of 1967, it became clear to the most arduous participants that the social revolution had failed. It had not established a new culture or a revolutionary domestic or economic infrastructure. It had succeeded only in affecting the personnel and character of the Chinese polity. Such a failure led to the serious disillusionment of the ultra-idealists, or in Western parlance, ultra-leftists.

On October 11, 1967, one of the many ultra-idealist organizations was formed. It was called Sheng-wu-lien, short for "Hunan Provincial Proletarian Great Alliance Committee." This was only one of a number of such youth groups which had started to turn from idealistic to radical politics. This particular group has been selected here because of accessibility to its documents, as well as the detailed nature of its critical evaluation of the failure of the social revolution.

The members of the Sheng-wu-lien were opposed to the survival of "bureaucratic" cadres in the new revolutionary committees as well as to the domination of "capitalist roaders" within the People's Liberation Army. They had half-baked ideas about the reality of the Paris Commune, being more inclined toward a romantic conception than an intellectual understanding of it. The Commune meant to them a sort of direct and extensive democracy, with the power of recall of the bureaucracy vested in the people. Such a Commune was established for a short period in Shanghai in February 1967. Even these radicals were not absolutely sure why the Shanghai Commune was abandoned and particularly what Mao's role was in its abandonment. Their documents insist that the members of the Sheng-wu-lien wanted to take the slogan "all power to the masses" literally. This could have meant an end to a centralized and effective China.[4]

Even the members of such ultra-idealist groups were looking backwards into the pristine periods of revolutionary promise, like the Paris Commune of 1871 and the Russian Soviets of 1917. It is

4. For the documents of the Sheng-wu-lien, see, "The Program of the Sheng-wu-lien," *SCMP*, No. 4174, pp. 10–13; "Sheng-wu-lien's Resolutions on Several Problems in the Current Hunan Great Proletarian Cultural Revolution. Passed on December 21, 1967," *Union Research Service*, Hong Kong, Vol. 51, Nos. 5/6 April 19, 1968, pp. 72–78; "Whither China?", *SCMP*, No. 4190, pp. 1–18. For an analytical discussion of these documents see Klaus Mehnert, *Peking and the New Left: At Home and Abroad* (Berkeley: University of California, Center for Chinese Studies, June 1969), pp. 11–19.

surprising that they did not include the Yenan model. In this respect, they made a serious departure from the Maoists' syncretism of nationalism and Communism. Yet the official policy of the Cultural Revolution, as set forward in the Sixteen Points at the 11th Plenum of the Central Committee of the Chinese Communist Party, did refer to the Paris Commune in its Point Nine.[5] Describing the institution of electoral and bureaucratic changes similar to those of the Paris Commune, Point Nine held that:

It is necessary to institute a system of general elections, like that of the Paris Commune, for electing members to the cultural revolutionary groups and committees and delegates to the cultural revolutionary congresses. The lists of candidates should be put forward by the revolutionary masses after full discussion, and the elections should be held after the masses have discussed the lists over and over again.

The masses are entitled at any time to criticize members of the cultural revolutionary groups and committees and delegates elected to the cultural revolutionary congresses. If these members or delegates prove incompetent, they can be replaced through election or recalled by the masses after discussion.[6]

Such a far-reaching change had obviously not occurred, and hence the disillusionment of the ultra-idealists. Not only had the word Commune been dropped from the official vocabulary in early 1967, but the establishment of early Soviets was nowhere in sight. By the end of 1967, the arming of the population was being looked on with great disfavor and even being punished by the PLA. The Cultural Revolution as an attempt to institute revolutionary social change had obviously not succeeded.

This attempt at social revolution, even at its height, was neither a national nor a total movement. It was predominantly urban and did not significantly affect workers or peasants in most parts of China. Except for a brief period from December 15, 1966, to February 5, 1967, when Red Guards and other revolutionary groups were allowed to enter factories and communes, the Cul-

5. *Peking Review*, No. 33, August 12, 1966, pp. 9–12.
6. *Ibid.*

tural Revolution remained primarily an urban phenomenon. In accordance with the effort to cultivate new leaders, most activities were aimed at continuous debate and struggle against the people in authority at all levels, and at remolding their attitudes. As usual, the problem of sincerity and distinguishing between sincere and tactical repentance became foremost. The Foreign Ministry of the Chinese People's Republic during 1967 and 1968 was not immune to this general trend.

This social revolution, if successful, would have created a truly revolutionary regime with a far-reaching impact on the international system. Time and again, international systems have been divided between ideological factions. This, however, must not be confused with the division between the haves and have-nots. A have-not regime must be distinguished from a revolutionary regime. A have-not regime generally deals in power politics and understands both the realities of power and the necessity for a balance between power and policy. A have-not regime is not necessarily a threat to the general principles of the international system. It may, however, be a threat to the predominant actors in the system.

A revolutionary regime, on the other hand, wants to change the rules of the system, and therefore may be perceived by all actors of the system, haves or have-nots, as a threat. It must and will support similar revolutions abroad. The threat perception of a revolutionary regime, therefore, is universal. China has not been a revolutionary regime in this respect since 1954 or 1955. Many have-nots identified with her because she was challenging the predominant actors while preserving the basic fundamentals of the international system, like national independence and national sovereignty.

The impact of the Cultural Revolution on Chinese foreign policy must be viewed in this light. When attempts to achieve social revolution in China became virulent, the perception of the Chinese regime as a threat increased. The basic rules of the international state system, which the Chinese had not violated since 1955, were openly attacked. The insistence of the Red Guards that national sovereignty must give way to the Thought of Mao Tsetung was universally perceived as a revolutionary threat. But like the domestic aberrations into civil violence of an essentially non-

violent social revolution, the Red Guards' attack on the fundamental principles of the international state system cannot be
looked upon except as a minor and insignificant deviation. The
radical-idealist groups were more characterized by nonpolicy than
by any coherent or alternate vision of an international order.
Most writers on the impact of the Cultural Revolution on foreign
policy have emphasized the impact of the Red Guards on the style
of foreign policy rather than the content.

If the social revolution had succeeded and China had become
a revolutionary regime, and if the younger idealists had come into
total control of foreign and domestic policy, then such stray events
would have assumed great weight. The universal perception of
Chinese foreign policy as a threat would have increased, and a
virulent cold war between China and the rest of the world would
have become inevitable. In addition, if the nonpolicy of the radical groups had continued, Chinese foreign policy would have be
come thoroughly confusing.

But the social revolution did not succeed, and even at the height
of its uneven success, it was unable significantly to affect the total
operation of Chinese foreign policy. Its impact on the style and
even on the working of the Foreign Ministry, together with its
symbolic insistence on elevating the Thought of Mao Tse-tung
above the concept of national sovereignty, should not blind us to
the fact that the important content, goals, and objectives of Chinese foreign policy remained virtually unchanged. Even in the
areas where foreign policy was most affected, analysts are now
recognizing that in the heat of the dramatic events, the impact of
the Red Guards was significantly overestimated.

Thus, Chinese foreign policy toward the Soviet Union or
Vietnam did not basically change throughout the period of the
Cultural Revolution. Similarly, by 1969, it was becoming obvious
that in spite of both the Vietnam war and the Cultural Revolution
Chinese foreign policy toward the United States had not under-
gone any significant change.

Conversely, it can be maintained that the significant inputs in
Chinese foreign policy with long-range consequences came from
events outside China. Thus, the invasion of Czechoslovakia by
the Soviet Union and the invasion of Cambodia by the United
States in 1968 and 1970 respectively, affected Chinese foreign

policy much more profoundly than all the headlines of Red Guard activities in Peking and Rangoon throughout the Cultural Revolution. Both of these invasions gave to the makers of Chinese foreign policy opportunities for initiatives which they have not missed.

This chapter does not intend to disregard the Cultural Revolution in the Foreign Ministry or to slight its impact on the style of foreign relations. It merely holds that the basic content of Chinese foreign policy remained unchanged. Another reason for this consistency is that from 1966 to 1968, foreign policy was a secondary consideration in the minds of the social revolutionaries of China. Throughout the history of the Communist Chinese government, the urgency of domestic developments has tended to push foreign policy to a lower priority, particularly during major mass movements. The period of 1966 to 1968 was no exception; elite attention reached its limits.

The Chinese Communist political system is probably the best example of what has been called a Communist "movement regime." It utilizes mass movements to effect significant social changes at home and to keep energizing myths alive.[7] The course of the movement concentrates on mobilizing the people in support of dynamic myths. The Chinese leadership therefore tolerated Red Guard excesses committed against the Foreign Ministry and embassies, just as it sanctioned the revolt of younger bureaucrats and diplomatic functionaries from within. Their symbolic importance to the general mass movement was far more important than the price in foreign policy.

In spite of these symbolic and stylistic inputs, and in spite of the civil strife and violence, the permanent impact of this attempt at social revolution on the Chinese economy, industry, and foreign trade was neither extensive nor significant. One of the aims of Chinese foreign policy has been and continues to be to expand and diversify trade with non-Communist countries. Such attempts lagged somewhat but nevertheless continued throughout the Cultural Revolution period.

7. Richard Lowenthal, "Development vs. Utopia in Communist Policy," in Chalmers Johnson, ed., *Change in Communist Systems* (Stanford: Stanford University Press, 1970), pp. 33–116.

1966 was a record year for Chinese foreign trade. Both imports and exports reached a total of $4.3 billion. 1967 and 1968 were generally lower, when the total figures reached $3.8 and $3.6 billion respectively. In 1968, Japan, West Germany, Hong Kong, and Singapore became China's largest trading partners. By 1969, there were sufficient indications that China was making a conscious effort to improve economic relations with other countries, both haves and have-nots, non-Communist as well as East European.

The drop since 1967 was due in part to the decline in China's trade with Hong Kong and Macao.[8] In 1968, the import of fertilizers, nonferrous metals, and wheat rose, while purchases of iron, steel products, and machinery dropped. China's export in certain foodstuffs, crude materials, and basic chemicals may have risen slightly. Although China's trade did jump from $3.7 billion in 1965 to $4.3 billion in 1966, the impact of the Cultural Revolution on the overall foreign trade picture was not as severe as could have been assumed from the domestic and foreign events of 1967. Except for the year 1960, when she suffered a very small trade deficit, China has consistently had a favorable balance of trade ever since 1955. This basic fact was not changed by the Cultural Revolution, nor by the supposedly growing bias against trade with China because of the change of style in foreign relations that erupted in 1967.

Chinese foreign trade does not follow the flag—ideological or otherwise. Not one of China's thirteen top trading partners is an ally or even a lukewarm friend of China. Ten of them are allies of or friendly with the United States, and are strongly opposed to Communism's ideology and social system. Five of them do not even recognize China.[9]

In spite of both her identification with the have-nots and her verbal bias in favor of revolution, China follows the basic principles of international economics. These principles do not favor underdeveloped countries trading with other underdeveloped coun-

8. Staff, "Macao's Imports Still Declining," *South China Morning Post*, September 20, 1967, p. 12; Staff, "Macao's August Trade," *South China Morning Post*, October 16, 1967, p. 10.

9. Japan, Australia, Malaysia, Singapore, and West Germany.

tries. Chinese trade, therefore, is substantially in favor of developed countries, and even there diplomatic relations often do not represent economic ties. For example, her trade with West Germany and Italy is higher than with France or the United Kingdom, with which she has diplomatic relations. If Malaya, Argentina, and Mexico were removed from the list of underdeveloped countries, Chinese trade with the entire underdeveloped world in 1964 was as low as 15 per cent of her total foreign trade. The situation in this respect has not appreciably changed since then. Therefore, the gap between verbal protestation and actual policy becomes clearer by the concrete statistics of China's foreign trade. Peking's trade does not follow Peking's principle that you cannot separate trade and politics. Peking can and Peking does.

A further example proving that the Chinese do not allow their express desire for international revolutionary change to become an obstacle to their foreign economic relations is China's trade with Japan. In 1969, Sino-Japanese trade reached its highest dollar mark of $625 million. This was $4 million higher than the previous record for Sino-Japanese trade set in 1966. Between 1963 and 1969, Sino-Japanese trade increased roughly 500 per cent, from $137 million to $625 million. The Japanese ministry of foreign trade estimates that in 1970 this trade may cross the $700 million mark. Furthermore, China insisted in 1967 that the Japanese Communist Party subordinate its domestic struggle against Japanese monopoly capitalism to the struggle against Soviet and United States imperialism. The CCP has often taken the position that if a Japanese company was willing to trade with China, then it must not be attacked, regardless of its economic policies and their effects on Japanese domestic politics.

Throughout 1969, agriculture and industry continued to recuperate. In 1970, while the central press has been silent, the provincial press has suggested that a leap forward in both agriculture and industry may be coming during the year. Estimates indicate that the total value of agricultural and industrial products in 1969 may equal the record year of 1966. Similarly, foreign trade in 1969 increased 10 per cent over 1968, and steel, machinery, and equipment imports rose substantially. Although the Chinese have not purchased any total plants since 1966, there were sufficient indications in 1970 that such purchases may soon resume. 1969 purchases included trucks and heavy construction equipment, which might lead one to conclude that industrial expansion is once again underway in China.

In 1969, exports from China to Hong Kong reached $445.5 million. Although still 13 per cent below 1966, this figure may not be solely due to continued tension in Hong Kong–China trade but to the rise of alternate outlets like Singapore to service Chinese foreign trade and partially replace Hong Kong. Since 1967, what Hong Kong lost, Singapore gained. In 1968–1969, Singapore had become China's fourth largest trading partner. This fact is particularly significant because China's trade with Singapore is mostly one-sided, with Singapore serving as a major outlet for Chinese exports.

A significant impact on Chinese foreign trade may be felt in the near future as a result of a partial lifting of travel and trade restrictions with China by the United States. American policy in July 1969 moved from containment with isolation to containment with partial isolation. On July 21, 1969, the State Department announced that U.S. citizens would be permitted to bring home up to $100 worth of goods produced in China, but that these items could be imported only for non-commercial use and could not be resold. Six categories of persons were henceforth to be automatically cleared by the U.S. for travel to the Chinese mainland. These included members of Congress, journalists, teachers, scholars with postgraduate degrees, undergraduates enrolled in colleges and universities, scientists and medical doctors, and American Red Cross representatives.[10]

On December 19, 1969, the Nixon Administration further eased the embargo on trade with China by allowing United States subsidiaries and affiliates to buy and sell nonstrategic goods from and to China in foreign markets. Throughout the second half of 1969, United States policy was easing toward China. In August, Secretary of State Rogers, speaking in Canberra, gave *de facto* recognition to the separate and permanent existence of Taiwan and Communist China. On September 9, Under-Secretary of State

10. *New York Times*, July 22, 1969, pp. 1 and 11.

Richardson emphasized that United States policy toward China should be independent of the Sino-Soviet dispute; [11] in other words, Washington would no longer worry about the impact of an improvement in Sino-American relations on the Soviet-American thaw.

The lifting of American restrictions came at a time when China had started the heavy buying of metals in the world market. Chinese buying was significantly affecting world prices—so much so that in 1969 antimony rose to $7800 a ton from its 1968 price of $860 a ton. Similarly, the shipments of nonferrous metals, copper, and rubber led to speculations by observers at the London Metal Exchange that China was preparing for industrial expansion.[12] Also in 1969, Chinese trade with Britain reached $45 million; this was roughly double the 1968 figure. By the end of 1969, China was considerably increasing her purchase of British machine tools.[13]

Commensurate expectations of trade with China were increasing in the United States. At the Thirty-third Mid-America World Trade Conference in Chicago, speakers stressed the need for swifter moves to develop economic ties with Communist China. Mr. Najeeb E. Halaby, president of Pan American World Airways, noted with approval the Administration's decision to ease trade restrictions by allowing American subsidiaries and affiliates to trade with Communist China, and forecasted the possibility of a direct Pan-American air route to Shanghai by 1972. He then added:

I see no sense in refusing the same privilege to their parent companies. And I'm sure that all of you here in the Midwest realize that Canada earned almost $700 million by selling grain to China over the recent past. I can't see how anything would have been drastically changed if some of these sales had been made from here except that I might have had a slightly wealthier audience.[14]

11. *New York Times*, December 20, 1969, pp. 1 and 4.
12. *Wall Street Journal*, January 26, 1970, pp. 1 and 25.
13. *South China Morning Post*, Hong Kong, December 16, 1969, reprinted from the *Financial Times*, London.
14. *New York Times*, February 18, 1970, p. 67.

According to Mr. John Wolf, President of the American Chamber of Commerce in Hong Kong, American-owned firms in Hong Kong could do as much as $6 billion worth of business with China a year. Considering that China's total foreign trade was only $3.9 billion in 1969, Sino-American trade could substantially aid China's economy.

The general impression that the Chinese are not reciprocating to these overtures by the United States is not correct. American subsidiaries of important corporations like Dow Chemical, based in Japan, may already have participated in trade with China. Generally, American affiliates and subsidiaries in Japan, Hong Kong, and Western Europe were quick to take advantage of the easing of trade restrictions on December 19, 1969. A more significant example came when General Motors was authorized by the Department of Commerce to sell engines and spare parts amounting to $400,000 to Communist China through the Robert Perlini Company of Italy. This company had made a deal to sell eighty Italian heavy dump trucks for construction, costing $4.2 million, to China. Although it had made similar sales to China before, the Perlini Company announced that this time the transaction had been made at the express request and initiative of Chinese officials, who had specifically asked that these trucks be supplied with General Motors engines and spare parts.[15] This case represented another major step in the lifting of restrictions on direct trade between American corporations and China.

Chinese interest in the expansion of foreign trade without regard to politics is not a new phenomenon. What the above analysis shows is that during and after the Cultural Revolution Chinese policy in this regard did not substantially change. Even more strikingly, the Chinese are willing to pay high and even exorbitant prices, whether for antimony or for cargo rates for tramp steamers. Communist China has paid higher prices for the movement of cargo on tramp steamers than any other nation in the world. One of the chief reasons for this willingness is that the Chinese do not want to get involved in the contract litigation which is normal in such transactions. For example, cargo rates from the Antwerp-Hamburg range to South China would normally be

15. *New York Times,* July 30, 1970, p. 7.

around $10.50 per ton, while the Chinese paid $15.84. Added to the fact that China is one of the largest users of tramp shipping in the world, this makes it impossible for owners of tramp steamers to refuse their services to China.[16]

China's growing utilization of Hong Kong and Singapore as trade outlets, as well as the increasing possibility of trade with United States subsidiaries and affiliates and even with U.S. corporations themselves, indicate not only the normalization of Chinese trade but also the health of the Chinese economy, increasing industrial expansion and sophistication, and a rapid growth in its foreign trade. A comparative picture of such growth with Hong Kong and Taiwan does not show that Communist China is lagging far behind these two rapidly expanding Asian trading centers. For example, from 1958 to 1965, Hong Kong's trade grew by 30 per cent per year, while China's trade grew by 25 per cent for the same period. China also compares well with Taiwan, whose foreign trade growth from 1963 to 1966 was 47 per cent, while China's during the same period increased by 40 per cent. These comparative figures become doubly significant if one takes into account the fact that Communist China during this period suffered from considerable trade restrictions and embargoes while Hong Kong, and particularly Taiwan, had protected markets in the United States.

By 1964, Sino-Soviet trade amounted to only $500 million a year, most of which went for the repayment of China's debts. 1964 was the last year when Sino-Soviet trade was tied to the repayments problem, as China paid off all her debts to the Soviet Union in that year. Total principal and interest owed to the Soviet Union amounted to 1,406 million new rubles, out of which China had already paid 1,389 million new rubles. The remaining 17 million new rubles came from the balance of trade with the Soviet Union in 1964.[17] Sino-Soviet trade continued to drop to $318 million in 1966 and to only $107 million in 1967.

Relations with Cuba underwent dramatic changes. During

16. *New York Times*, April 27, 1969, p. 94.

17. "Chou En-lai's Report on the Work of the Government at the First Session of the Third National People's Congress," NCNA-English, Peking, December 30, 1964, in *SCMP*, No. 3370, January 5, 1970.

1963 and 1964 *People's Daily* regularly reprinted speeches by Fidel Castro, Raúl Castro, Che Guevara, and other Cuban leaders. After January 1965, however, the Chinese stopped this practice. Meanwhile, *Pravda* and *Izvestia* increased their coverage. Between 1961 and 1964, China's trade with Cuba had amounted to about $200 million a year, a figure which represented an unfavorable balance of trade for China. Exporting rice and consumer goods, the Chinese considered their trade deficit a form of economic aid to Cuba.

By 1966, the mood had shifted. On January 2, 1966, Castro disclosed that the Chinese were cutting their purchases of Cuban sugar as well as their supply of Chinese rice. In 1965, China had exchanged 250,000 tons of rice for 370,000 tons of Cuban sugar. In 1966, however, Castro revealed that China would sell only 135,000 tons of rice instead of the 285,000 tons which Cuba had expected. According to Castro, there had been a long-term understanding that 250,000 tons of rice would continue to be supplied yearly. As a result of the Chinese cutback, Sino-Cuban trade fell lower than at any time during 1961–1965, and Cuba had to slash her rice rations in half. Meanwhile, the Chinese Ministry of Foreign Trade attacked Castro's interpretation of a long-term agreement as groundless.[18]

The same official also attacked Cuba for exploiting the opening of the Tri-Continental Conference in Havana by taking a public stand on trade difficulties with China. It was shortly after this that Sino-Cuban relations reached their all-time low. In a bitter exchange, Castro accused the Chinese of "hypocrisy, insolence, absolute contempt, betrayal of confidence, friendship, and brotherhood." The Cuban government further attacked the Chinese for continuing to distribute anti-Soviet material in Cuba in spite of its prohibition, and for doing so "with the insolence of the omnipotent."[19]

18. "Answers by Responsible Official of the Ministry of Foreign Trade of the People's Republic of China to Questions Put by an NCNA Correspondent on Trade Between China and Cuba," NCNA-English, Peking, January 9, 1966, *SCMP*, No. 3616, January 13, 1966, pp. 28–31.

19. For a detailed account of Sino–Latin American relations, as well as China's relations with Cuba, see Daniel Tretiak, "China and

On the other hand, the Chinese signed a trade and payments agreement with Yugoslavia on March 18, 1969, and even suggested that cultural exchanges be resumed. It seems that Tito's revisionism is less offensive to Peking than the Soviet counterpart. Mindful of national interest, the Chinese are not ready to antagonize everybody at once. Not only are they prepared to tolerate a large gap between ideology and foreign policy, but they are quick to grasp concrete opportunities as well. Specifically, they quickly recognized the opportunity provided by the Soviet invasion of Czechoslovakia to improve and widen their relations with Eastern Europe. Their initiative had a particular impact on Yugoslavia, which had strongly denounced the Brezhnev Doctrine of the limited sovereignty of Communist states.

The impact of the Cultural Revolution on the style and management of Chinese foreign policy became increasingly pronounced between the summer of 1966 and October 1967. In this period, Red Guards and younger bureaucrats continued to exert pressure against the top policy-makers, including Foreign Minister Ch'en Yi and his Vice-Ministers. In direct contrast to international trade, the diplomatic corps, Ministry of Foreign Affairs, and relations with selected countries like Burma were affected.

Throughout this period, it is difficult to assess with accuracy the impact of these disturbances on the actual decision-making processes. It is certain, however, that the ability of the decision-makers to focus attention on urgent foreign policy problems declined. Decision-makers were more concerned with crisis management than with initiatives and seizing of opportunities in the field of foreign relations.

We are still not clear as to what Mao's role in this crisis management was. There are stray indications that Mao did not favor the dismissal of Ch'en Yi. There is also ample evidence to show that Ch'en Yi was supported throughout this period by Chou En-lai and the Central Committee of the CCP. Chou's and the Central Committee's position seems to have been that Red Guards

---

Latin America: An Ebbing Tide in Trans-Pacific Maoism," *Current Scene*, Vol. IV, No. 5, March 1, 1966.

could indulge in criticism of Ch'en Yi and even act as overseers of the Foreign Ministry. But this permission would not entitle them to take over the Ministry or to demand the replacement of Ch'en Yi.

In mid-December of 1966, Red Guards were permitted to enter government organs. In addition, between December 1966 and the spring of 1967, ambassadors and senior diplomatic personnel were recalled to China. The only exception was the Chinese ambassador in Cairo.[20]

These two actions seriously undermined Ch'en Yi's position in early 1967. Ch'en Yi had been successfully fighting the radicals throughout the latter half of 1966. But the advancement of the Cultural Revolution through all areas of the Chinese polity by the end of 1966 started seriously to affect the implementation of foreign policy. The recall of the ambassadors provided an opportunity to the radicals to criticize their life style and demand further purges.

The Cultural Revolution in the Ministry of Foreign Affairs, leading to the first temporary seizure, came in January 1967. The Foreign Ministry was no exception to the serious effects of what has been described as the "January Storm," a period of intense resistance and counter-resistance. This attack was eventually successfully repulsed by Ch'en Yi and senior members of the Ministry. But Ch'en had to deliver a self-criticism on January 24, before a mass rally of 10,000, which, significantly, was presided over by Chou En-lai.[21] Ch'en was severely attacked for sending work teams before and after the Eleventh Plenum in August 1966. Ch'en admitted having bureaucratic work attitudes and agreed to emulate the Chairman and comrades of the Cultural Revolutionary Group. This seems to have been effective in his weathering of the January Storm.

It does not seem that Ch'en was really convinced of the correctness of the attack or the sincerity of his self-criticism. By February 12, Ch'en had apparently told Red Guards that his investigation was forced and had taken the offensive against his

20. JPRS, No. 45359, August 28, 1967, pp. 15–19.
21. JPRS, No. 42070, pp. 13–16.

critics. By April, it seems that Ch'en Yi's patience against the out-
rageous conduct of the Red Guards had reached its limits. Having
had forty years of faithful service to the revolution to his credit,
Ch'en was not to be easily cast aside.

Ch'en Yi's firmness and the inability of the Red Guards to force
a confrontation with him between February and April were certainly due to the fact that the People's Liberation Army, ordered
to halt chaos and juvenile-type behavior, came onto the scene on
January 23. The PLA already had been increasingly evident in con-
trolling the three-way alliances. It is also interesting to note that
among the conservatives who fought back and pushed out the
revolutionary rebels in January 1967 were such individuals as
Hsiao Chien, Section Head of the American and Australian Departments of the Foreign Ministry.

If the Red Guard wall posters are accurate, then the Foreign
Ministry suffered from intermittent turmoil between April and
September 1967. The height of this turmoil came on May 13,
when a group of Red Guards effected a forcible entry into the
Ministry building and opened safes containing classified materials.
These Red Guards belonged to the Red Flag Detachment of the
Foreign Language Institute and supposedly occupied the Foreign
Ministry for six hours. On May 17, Chou intervened and categorically asserted that senior members of the diplomatic personnel
could not be replaced. April and May witnessed a dual approach
by Chou and other members of the Cultural Revolutionary Group,
like Ch'en Po-ta. On the one hand, they wanted to placate rising
Red Guard radicalism; on the other hand, they wanted to protect
ranking members of the Foreign Ministry as well as their own
authority. This effort apparently was not successful and did not
pacify the radicals. This may have been the correct policy in terms
of crisis management, but it was not an effective policy for the
functioning of the Foreign Ministry.

The complete failure of the dual policy came with the explosion
of August 1967. Yao Teng-shan, China's ex-Chargé d'Affaires in
Djakarta, temporarily took over the Foreign Ministry. Having
been expelled by the Indonesian government in April, Yao was
highly critical of Ch'en Yi's handling of Chinese policy toward
Indonesia and held a strong grudge against him. In his takeover,
he was aided and abetted by a Red Guard faction from the Peking

Foreign Language Institute. For a period of time, the radicals controlled the Foreign Ministry and even sent telegraphic instructions directly to embassies.

This incident exhausted the limits of toleration and ended the dual approach of Chou and the Central Committee. On September 2, Chou categorically denounced the wrong seizure of power in the Foreign Ministry. Through the Central Committee, Chou ordered the Red Guards to withdraw. The crest of the Cultural Revolutionary wave in the Foreign Ministry had passed by September. From then on, the radicals steadily lost ground.[22]

Throughout the various stages of the Cultural Revolution in the Foreign Ministry, Ch'en Yi continued in power with the strong support of Chou En-lai and the Central Committee. Although he made a number of self-criticisms, he also fought back to preserve the policy-making prerogatives of senior personnel. But the Cultural Revolution finally did take its toll on Ch'en Yi and he had to be hospitalized in August.

The impact of the turmoil in the Foreign Ministry became increasingly evident between January and September 1967. It seriously affected normal international communication between China and foreign governments. Starting from January 1967, enormous demonstrations took place outside the Soviet, British, Indian, Outer-Mongolian, Nepalese, Indonesian, and Burmese embassies. Even Kenya came under attack during this period.

22. For a detailed account of the Cultural Revolution in the Foreign Ministry, see Melvin Gurtov, "The Foreign Ministry and Foreign Affairs during the Cultural Revolution," *The China Quarterly*, No. 40, October–December 1969, pp. 65–102. For a clear and analytical account, see Daniel Tretiak, "The Chinese Cultural Revolution and Foreign Policy," *Current Scene*, Vol. VIII, No. 7, April 1, 1970. Tretiak has divided the entire period of the Cultural Revolution in the Foreign Ministry into five stages, the last stage, from April to August 1967, being the most virulent. He further asserts that most of the charges against diplomatic personnel were not issue-oriented. The only major exception seems to have been in the case of the Chinese ambassador to Yugoslavia from 1955–58, Wu Hsiu-ch'uan. He had been long involved in international Communist liaison work for the CCP. This is interesting in the light of China's recent rapprochement with Yugoslavia since late 1968.

China increasingly turned toward enforced isolationism. To-gether with the ambassadors, Chinese students studying abroad were also recalled. China had few foreign visitors in 1967. With the exception of the visit of the President of Zambia in June 1967,[23] the arrival of foreign dignitaries was not even reported on the front pages of the Chinese press. A good example was the secret visit of the Prime Minister of Rumania in July 1967, which, even when finally revealed, barely attracted any attention in the Chinese press. The Cultural Revolution also affected travel by Overseas Chinese. According to information from Hong Kong, relations in China warned Overseas Chinese not to return to China in Western dress.[24]

The reaction of the international Communist movement to the Cultural Revolution was generally unfavorable. Adverse reactions of pro-Soviet and anti-Chinese Communists and of non-Commu-nists to the Cultural Revolution and to the excesses of the Red Guards poured in. Prominent among the contributors were the Communist parties of Austria, Bulgaria, Ceylon, Chile, Costa Rica, Cuba, Czechoslovakia, Ecuador, Finland, France, Great Britain, East Germany, Greece, Hungary, India, Iraq, Italy, Mon-golia, New Zealand, Poland, Uruguay, Yugoslavia, and Spain. According to *People's Daily* of September 7, 1966, the only pro-Chinese Communists supporting the Cultural Revolution were parties and groups in Albania, Australia, Belgium, Congo, India, Japan, Mali, North Vietnam, and scattered African groups.

Meanwhile a severe attack was launched against Burma. On June 26, 1967, the Burmese Ministry of Education asked students not to wear badges which did not belong to Burmese organiza-tions. A group of Chinese students violated this order not only by wearing their Mao badges, but also by seizing control of two schools. This led to anti-Chinese riots and the imposition of martial law in Rangoon. On July 3, 1967, Kuo Mo-jo justified the

23. *Jen-min Jih-pao*, June 22, 1967, p. 1.
24. *China News Analysis*, No. 662, June 2, 1966. For a detailed analysis of the impact of the Cultural Revolution on Overseas Chinese affairs, see Stephen Fitzgerald, "Overseas Chinese Affairs in the Cul-tural Revolution," *The China Quarterly*, No. 40, October–December 1969, pp. 103–126.

actions of the Chinese students in Burma and supported a Red Guard resolution emphasizing the doctrine that Burmese national sovereignty must give way to Maoism. Relations further deteriorated following the abrogation of the Sino-Burmese agreement on technical cooperation on October 6, 1967. This led to the recall of 412 Chinese experts and technicians.[25]

The change between 1961 and 1967 in Sino-Burmese relations becomes apparent by reading the following two quotes side by side:

The edifice of Sino-Burmese friendship is completed. Sino-Burmese friendship is in conformity with the fundamental interests of our two peoples. . . . Let our two governments and peoples continue to make common efforts so that the friendly relations between our two countries continue to serve as an example of peaceful co-existence between countries of different social systems. Chou En-lai—On a visit to Rangoon, January 1961.

The Chinese Communist Party and the Chinese people firmly support the people's revolutionary armed struggle led by the Communist Party of Burma. We regard such support as our bounden internationalist duty. It is our firm conviction that the Communist Party of Burma . . . which persists in the revolutionary line of "to win the war and seize political power," will assuredly . . . overthrow the reactionary Ne Win government and win complete victory in the revolutionary war in Burma.
Telegram from the Central Committee of the Chinese Communist Party to the Burmese Communist Party, August 14, 1967.

In the middle of May 1967, Associated Press reported from Singapore that the White Flag Communists in Burma had decided to start an armed struggle.[26] In June, the Burmese Communist Party sent a congratulatory message to China on the occasion of the explosion of a hydrogen bomb. In July, the Ne Win govern-

25. *New York Times*, November 2, 1967.
26. For detailed accounts of relations between Burmese Communists and China see *Jen-min Jih-pao*, March 27, p. 5; April 19, p. 5; May 8, p. 6; May 13, p. 5; and May 16, 1967, p. 6.

ment was strongly attacked in the Chinese press.[27] The matter of Nationalist Chinese in North Burma was once again brought up when the Chinese attacked Ne Win for supporting pro-Taiwan Chinese who were holding Burma-Chinese friendship meetings not far from the Chinese border.[28]

In early 1968, Asian capitals were becoming concerned about rumors that Chinese Communist advisors were coming into upper Burma to support White Flag insurrections.[29] Burma's Head of State, General Ne Win, who had remained silent throughout 1967, apparently warned in March 1968 that China was providing sanctuary to insurgent forces in North Burma. But at the same time, he also made it very clear that Burma would continue to follow her neutral policy and urged caution in provoking an open fight with China. By the end of 1968, Burmese rebels had apparently suffered serious setbacks, both because the Kachins and the Karens withdrew from their leaning toward White Flags and also because of the murder of Thakin Than Tun, Chairman of the Burmese Communist Party.[31] Throughout 1969, border skirmishes continued on the Sino-Burmese frontier.[32]

In spite of minor irritations, the degree of Chinese hostility toward Burma and Indonesia considerably declined after January 1968.[33] Since October 1967, Sino-Indonesian relations have been frozen. The Indonesians have been pursuing a policy of low-key tension since the mutual withdrawal of diplomatic personnel. They have left it to China to take the initiative. What must be emphasized, however, is that China's relations with Indonesia, like those with a number of other countries, deteriorated not be-

27. Editorial, "The Wild Anti-Chinese Attacks of Ne Win Government Will Destroy It," *Jen-min Jih-pao*, July 10, 1967, pp. 1 and 5.

28. *Jen-min Jih-pao*, July 30, 1967, p. 5.

29. *New York Times*, February 18, 1968, p. 1.

30. *New York Times*, March 30, 1968, p. 5.

31. *New York Times*, November 1, 1968, p. 5; and *New York Times*, March 22, 1969, p. 5.

32. *New York Times*, November 8, 1969, p. 7.

33. Daniel Tretiak, "Changes in China's Attention to Southeast Asia, 1967–1969. Their Relevance for the Future of the Area," *Current Scene*, Vol. VII, No. 21, November 1, 1969.

cause of the Cultural Revolution, but because of internal political dynamics in Indonesia.

In the same category would be placed the breaking of Chinese relations with Dahomey on January 3, 1966, and with the Central African Republic on January 6, 1966. Together with the overthrowing of Nkrumah and strains with Kenya in March 1966, these diplomatic disruptions were due to the changing political situations in the respective countries, rather than to the Cultural Revolution. In all of the above countries except Kenya, military regimes had come into being, bringing corresponding changes in foreign policy alignments. In the case of Indonesia and Ghana, national movement regimes were overthrown; military rule in both places was a reaction to the end of the energizing myths of Sukarno and Nkrumah. On the other hand, China's relations with Cambodia, which did suffer some setbacks in 1967, came back to an even keel during 1968. Sihanouk then was still in power.

Throughout this period, Chinese foreign policy was neither universally hostile nor inattentive. Peking's relations continued to be cordial with the Congo (Brazzaville), Mauritania, Mali, Nigeria, Sudan, the Arab countries (with the exception of Tunisia), Zambia, Tanzania, and Pakistan. The Chinese further agreed to build a railway line between Tanzania and Zambia on September 5, 1967, at the height of the continuing intervention in the affairs of the Foreign Ministry in Peking. By 1969, plans for this railway line were progressing on schedule [34] and construction work began in early 1970. China also supplied three radio transmitters to Zambia.[35]

During the Arab-Israeli War of June 1967, China did take some initiative by offering wheat and money to the United Arab Republic. Nevertheless, Peking could not effectively utilize the situation because of the pressing day-to-day problems of the Cultural Revolution at home. In this case, limits on available attention prevented Chinese leaders from taking advantage of an opening in a highly complex political web; basic changes were not immediately forthcoming. Accordingly, Chinese policy in this area has been re-

34. *New York Times*, September 28, 1969, p. 11.
35. *New York Times*, March 29, 1970, p. 4.

turning to normal ever since 1968. In that year, China established diplomatic relations with the newly independent republic of South Yemen. Meanwhile, China is paying increasing attention to military developments in the Middle East, particularly to the activities of the Palestinian guerrilla organizations.

An overall analysis leads one to the conclusion that except in selected areas like Burma, Chinese foreign policy during the period of the Cultural Revolution in the Foreign Ministry was only negatively affected. In other words, China's ability to pay attention to opportunities for initiatives declined. Even in the case of Burma, relations have started to improve since 1968.

By the middle of 1968, the radicals were successfully put under control in the Foreign Ministry and their ability to affect foreign policy continued to decline. Some of the positive indications were China's rapprochement with Yugoslavia in late 1968, a greater toleration of East European revisionism as compared to the Soviet variety, as well as her decision to reopen the Sino-American talks in early 1969. In this period the radicals still exerted some influence, however, making foreign policy follow a zigzag pattern, as evidenced by the postponement of the Warsaw talks.

Normalization of the style of foreign relations continued in 1969. Early in the year, the Chinese began to fill the vacancies left by the 1967 recall of diplomatic personnel. Between May and July 1969, seventeen appointments were made. Most of these appointments were made in capitals which are crucial to Chinese foreign policy, namely Albania, France (because of the Vietnam peace talks), Sweden (because of talks with Canada on the establishment of diplomatic relations), and Zambia (because of both the Chinese railway and good relations in general). Between May 1969 and June 1970, China appointed twenty-three ambassadors.[36] The new Chinese ambassador to Warsaw reached his post on August 31, 1970.

Fourteen of the first seventeen ambassadors appointed were established diplomats. Nine of them had already served as ambassadors before and the remaining five were members of the foreign service with considerable experience in overseas missions or at home in the Foreign Ministry. This is conclusive evidence that the

36. *New York Times*, August 18, 1970, p. 5.

impact on the ambassadorial services and the style of foreign relations, so dramatic and pronounced between January and August 1967, was not permanent. Actually, beginning in late 1968, Chinese foreign policy came increasingly into its own. It may now be said to be going into high gear with the announcement that Premier Chou En-lai will undertake an extensive foreign tour in 1970. This trip climaxes the end of a busy diplomatic year and the continued appointments of ambassadorial personnel.

The impact of the Soviet invasion of Czechoslovakia on Chinese foreign policy far exceeded the impact of the Cultural Revolution. More permanent in its effect, it provided opportunities for initiatives which makers of Chinese foreign policy were not slow to recognize. Within days of the Soviet invasion of Czechoslovakia, a Chinese commentator coined a new term, *she-hui ti-kuo chu-i*, "social imperialism." [37] This term was used in the Leninist sense and was taken from his "Tasks of the Third Internationale." Attacking social democrats, in this article Lenin defined social imperialists as people who are socialist in name, but imperialist in fact. A week later, this term was changed to *she-hui chu-i ti-kuo chu-i*, "socialist imperialism." [38] The Chinese were using this term against a socialist country, and the change in terminology was dictated by the need to clarify the difference between the Leninist usage and their own.

The Czechoslovakian invasion greatly increased Chinese insecurity. As early as August 24, the Chinese press started quoting Chou En-lai's fear that the Czech affair was not an isolated event.[39] The Chinese Chief of Staff, Huang Yung-sheng, on a visit to Albania, charged that the Soviets were already concentrating military forces on the Sino-Soviet and Sino-Mongolian borders and considered this as an intensification of armed provocation against China.[40]

Chinese opposition to the Soviet invasion of Czechoslovakia did not arise out of sympathy for the Dubcek regime. Actually, Chinese policy had the difficult task of condemning Dubcek's re-

37. *Jen-min Jih-pao*, August 23, 1968, p. 1.
38. *Jen-min Jih-pao*, August 30, 1968, p. 4.
39. *Jen-min Jih-pao*, August 24, 1968, p. 1; September 3, 1968, p. 1.
40. *Jen-min Jih-pao*, October 5, 1968, p. 3.

visionism simultaneously with the condemnation of the socialist imperialism of the Soviet Union. The Chinese therefore took steps to explain and clarify their position in Eastern Europe. A major effort in this direction was mounted only a few days after the invasion of Czechoslovakia when Chinese radio services started a new series of broadcasts in Czech, Slovak, Rumanian, Polish, and other East European languages.[41] In these broadcasts, the Chinese took pains to emphasize that the Soviet Union had committed socialist imperialism not against the Dubcek regime, but against the Czechoslovakian people.

The major impact of the Soviet action was a limited rapprochement on a state-to-state basis with the Yugoslavs. Not only did China sign a trade and payments agreement with Yugoslavia on March 18, 1969, but she also took great pain to project a new image of being a defender of the national sovereignty of Communist states against the Brezhnev Doctrine. China broke all precedent when Yugoslav officials in Prague were invited to attend the nineteenth anniversary reception of the Chinese People's Republic. This move was intended to show sympathy and solidarity with Tito's strong opposition to the Brezhnev Doctrine.

On her part, Yugoslavia welcomed and reciprocated Chinese support. Yugoslav papers and radio broadcasts stopped criticism of China and Albania, took a neutral line in the Sino-Soviet border dispute, and regularly reproduced Chinese and Albanian denunciations of Soviet imperialism and revisionism. They further started to emphasize, in contrast to the Soviet press, that Chinese foreign policy was no longer maverick. The Chinese reciprocated by praising Yugoslavia's independent policy and accused the Soviet Union of threatening Yugoslavia.[42]

China also started to take an active role in other parts of Eastern Europe. At a reception in honor of the Albanian government and party delegation in Peking, Chou En-lai accused the Soviet Union of posing a threat to the security and independence of Albania in particular, and the Balkan people in general, by massing troops in Bulgaria.[43] This led the Albanians to send a protest

41. *New York Times*, September 26, 1968, p. 6.
42. *New China News Agency*, June 15, 1969.
43. *New China News Agency*, September 29, 1968, and *Jen-min Jih-pao*, September 30, 1968.

note to Bulgaria in which they charged that the presence of Soviet troops in that country under the Warsaw Pact was in direct violation of the Albanian-Bulgarian treaty of 1947. The Albanians apparently also feared a naval attack by the Soviets.[44]

The Bulgarians naturally turned to the Soviet Union; the Soviets reciprocated by sending high-level delegations to Sofia in 1969, to demonstrate their support for and appreciation of Bulgarian loyalty. The Bulgarian Foreign Minister Ivan Bashev continued to support the Brezhnev Doctrine and even stated that such a joint action would be possible against China. This was a clear indication that the Brezhnev Doctrine might be applied to China and that Chinese fears of Soviet military invasion and intervention were not idle.[45]

Yugoslav-Chinese relations continued to improve in 1969 and 1970. Not only were ambassadors exchanged, but in April 1970 a Yugoslav shipping line carried its first cargo to China. It was also announced that regular cargo service between Rijeka and Tientsin would soon be established.[46]

Of course, Chinese ties with Yugoslavia were neither as good nor as cordial as relations with Rumania. At a reception celebrating the 24th Anniversary of the Rumanian liberation on August 23, 1968, Chou En-lai publicly condemned the Soviet invasion of Czechoslovakia and compared it to that of Hitler, thirty years before.[47] The Chinese had been continuing a policy of cultivating Rumanian opposition to the Soviet Union since 1963. The Rumanian Prime Minister, Ion Maurir, was one of the few dignitaries to visit China at the height of the Cultural Revolution in July 1967. This visit was secret, and the Chinese were supposed to have encouraged the Rumanians at this time to follow a policy of national independence.

Two days after the invasion of Czechoslovakia, China promised Rumania support in case of Soviet attack.[48] Rumania reciprocated the Chinese diplomatic support by taking a neutral attitude in the Sino-Soviet border conflict and by sending a warm message of

44. *New York Times,* October 7, 1968, p. 7.
45. *Times of India,* New Delhi, April 11, 1969.
46. *New York Times,* July 16, 1970, p. 11.
47. *New China News Agency,* August 23, 1968.
48. *New China News Agency,* August 23, 1968.

congratulations to the Ninth Party Congress in April 1969. The Rumanian Defense Minister even praised the People's Liberation Army and hoped that it would be strong enough to defend China against imperialism. This message was delivered on the forty-second anniversary of the PLA, on August 1, 1969.[49]

In May and June of 1970, Rumania was hit by severe floods. To prove that Chinese support was not just verbal, China shipped relief aid valued at some $23 million, twice as much as that sent by the United States. Significantly, the relief shipments included 50,000 tons of coke, which is vital to Rumania's steel industry and which in the past had generally been supplied by the Soviet Union.[50] In June of 1970, Vice-President Emile Bodnares visited Peking, an event highlighted by speakers from both sides strongly supporting Rumania's brave and independent policy against a strong and unnamed bully, obviously the Soviet Union.[51]

China's mounting effort to exploit the impact of the Brezhnev Doctrine on relations with Communist states also resulted in increased tensions with some of them. One such example is the Mongolian People's Republic (MPR). Well before the Czech invasion, the Chinese had already given up the idea of courting Mongolia. As early as 1965, the USSR, the MPR, and the PRC had met in Peking from September 2 to 9 to deal with the effects of a changeover from a Russian to a Chinese gauge on the trans-Mongolian railway track. This change confirmed that this railway link would now be utilized for China's domestic needs and for defense rather than as a transportation link to Ulan Bator. From now on Dzamyn Ude, the last station on the Mongolian side, and the city of Chining on the Chinese side became terminal points instead of midpoints for Sino-Mongolian and Sino-Soviet trade.[52]

Sino-Mongolian relations continued to deteriorate. By 1969, Mongolia was openly joining the Soviet Union in criticizing China.[53] Interestingly, Soviet President Nikolai Podgorny could

49. *New China News Agency*, August 1, 1969.
50. *New York Times*, July 16, 1970, p. 11.
51. *New York Times*, July 30, 1970, p. 18.
52. *China News Analysis*, No. 599, February 11, 1966.
53. *New York Times*, May 21, 1969, p. 8.

not get a similar condemnation from the North Koreans, who wanted to remain neutral in the Sino-Soviet dispute, while Mongolia started to perform the same role for the Soviet Union which Albania does for China.

In an interview in May 1969, Yumzhagiin Tsendenbal, Prime Minister of the Mongolian People's Republic, took the view that the Chinese were totally responsible for provoking the border clashes with the Soviet Union earlier in March. He also accused China of trying to destroy Soviet-Mongolian relationships and specifically supported the Vietcong position in the Paris negotiations.

Emphasizing Mongolia's desire to have better diplomatic, cultural, and economic relations with the West and especially with the United States, Tsendenbal stated that Mongolia had been trying to normalize diplomatic relations since 1961 and that it was now up to the United States to take the initiative. Such an initiative was not long in forthcoming. In June 1969, Secretary of State Rogers did propose that the United States recognize the Mongolian People's Republic. It was generally felt by the State Department that such recognition would provide the United States with a very valuable listening post to developments in North China and the Asiatic Soviet Union. President Nixon, however, was resisting this move because of strong pressure from the Nationalist Chinese government in Taiwan.

At this same interview, Tsendenbal even recalled with great fondness his visit to the United States in 1967, and particularly his meeting with President Johnson and his trip to Niagara Falls. This interview, given on the eve of Podgorny's visit, shows the extent of strain and hostility in Sino-Mongolian relations.[54]

During the same period, there have been flare-ups on the 2500-mile Sino-Mongolian border. The Mongolians accused China of subverting the Mongolian Communist Party through a Chinese faction. The Mongolians have also attacked China for her treatment of national minorities in Tibet, and particularly in Inner Mongolia.[55] On their side, the Chinese have responded to this

54. See Harrison E. Salisbury in *New York Times*, May 21, 1969, p. 8.
55. *New York Times*, May 26, 1969, p. 1.

tension with increasing awareness. Perhaps most important, they have started to dismember the Inner-Mongolian Autonomous Region. Districts from this area have been detached and added to the provinces of Heilungkiang, Liaoning, and Kirin. This move may or may not be connected to a Chinese fear that Mongolia may utilize the Mongolian national minority in China to her advantage.[56]

Direct Sino-Soviet tensions continued to increase correspondingly. As early as October 1966, trouble on the border started to mount. In December 1966, Soviet newspapers in Tadzkistan and Karghizia were reporting the institution of civil defense measures. Soviet students were ordered to leave China by October 10, 1966; the Soviets retaliated by expelling Chinese students.[57] The Chinese students protested their expulsion and clashed with the Soviet police.[58] In December, the Chinese Foreign Ministry expelled three of the six Soviet correspondents from China.[59]

Meanwhile, a series of stray incidents contributing to growing tensions coincided with the increasing tempo of the Cultural Revolution.[60] The Soviet Union has always regarded the Cultural Revolution in very negative terms, and incidents surrounding it only served to increase Soviet fears of a hostile China.

As early as November 1966, *Pravda* was already painting lurid pictures of civil disorders initiated by the Red Guards, including the beating up of Party members. The Chinese, while not directly contradicting these reports, retaliated by alleging that Soviet revisionists feared the Cultural Revolution because it would

56. Tillman Durdin in the *New York Times*, June 21, 1970, p. 7.
57. *Jen-min Jih-pao*, October 24, 1966, p. 1.
58. *Jen-min Jih-pao*, October 29, 1966, p. 5.
59. *Jen-min Jih-pao*, December 17, 1966, p. 2.
60. Some of these stray incidents came about when the Chinese staff of the Soviet embassy went on strike and demonstrated against the Soviet Union as part of the Cultural Revolutionary fervor. The Soviets fired all the embassy staff of Chinese citizenship, and the Chinese retaliated by expelling two members of the Soviet embassy. See *Jen-min Jih-pao*, March 12, 1967, pp. 1 and 4. It was also rumored that the Soviet Aeroflot was refused permission to fly over Sinkiang and had to reroute its Soviet-Indian flight over Afghanistan and West Pakistan. See *Sing-tao Jih-pao*, Hong Kong, January 6, 1967.

awaken the Soviet people.[61] Earlier in October, the Soviet press hinted at the possibility of war with China. The United Press reported from Moscow that Soviet President Podgorny, on a visit in late 1966 to the Soviet-Manchurian border, had declared that the Amur boundary was well protected by Soviet armed forces. During late 1966, the Chinese accused the Soviet Union of collaborating with the United States in hindering the development of independent Chinese nuclear deterrents.[62]

Throughout 1967 and 1968, the Soviets built up troop strength in the Far East. All this was apparently leading toward a Sino-Soviet border showdown. The first incident on Chenpao Island took place on March 2, 1969.[63] By March 11, the Chinese, quoting international law, were trying to prove that the central line of the main channel, which should form the international boundary, makes Chenpao Island indisputably Chinese territory.[64] By March 17, the Chinese had directly linked the Czechoslovakian invasion with the Sino-Soviet border dispute. *People's Daily* said:

Do the new Tsarist Soviet revisionists not say the same things about Czechoslovakia? . . . They are applying them to Asia too. The Mongolian People's Republic has been turned into a colony, and Soviet revisionists are planning to invade Chinese territory.[65]

The March 2 incident was followed by a less serious incident on March 14 and by a further major incident on March 15. These inevitably led to large-scale hostile demonstrations on each side. The Chinese intimated that during the border negotiations of 1964, the USSR had acknowledged that Chenpao Island was Chinese territory.[66] In spite of both these allegations and the

61. *Jen-min Jih-pao*, March 10, 1967, p. 4; March 30, p. 4; and April 14, 1967, p. 5.

62. *Chieh-fang Chun Pao*, August 25, 1966; *Kuang-ming Jih-pao*, Peking, August 26, 1966; *Jen-min Jih-pao*, November 15, 1966.

63. *New York Times*, March 3, 1969, pp. 1, 4, and 42.

64. *Jen-min Jih-pao*, March 11, p. 2; March 15, 1969, p. 3.

65. *Jen-min Jih-pao*, March 17, 1969, p. 2; and *New York Times*, March 5, 1969, p. 6.

66. *New York Times*, March 12, 1969, pp. 1 and 16.

seriousness of the two border incidents of March 2 and March 15, neither the Chinese nor the Soviets were prepared to enter into a large-scale military conflict. Instead, both sides tried to exploit the incidents diplomatically. This effort became quite clear within weeks of the incidents. On March 23, Soviet and pro-Soviet East European diplomats who were boycotting diplomatic receptions in Peking appeared at the Pakistani reception. In a speech at this reception, Deputy Prime Minister Hsieh Fu-chih did not refer once directly to the Soviet Union, and Soviet diplomats remained seated.[67]

These clashes came at a time when the Chinese had already made significant progress in reestablishing normalcy in foreign affairs and when the impact of the Cultural Revolution on Chinese foreign policy was in full retreat. As early as March 3, 1969, the Soviets had proposed the resumption of the Sino-Soviet talks on border problems which had been broken off in 1964. By the end of March, the Soviet press was continually hammering on the need for such talks and playing up the Soviet offer. Moscow also proposed a meeting of the Joint Sino-Soviet Border Navigation Commission to discuss navigation on the Amur and Ussuri rivers. On May 23, Moscow Radio reported that China had agreed to both proposals and announced that the fifteenth meeting of the Sino-Soviet Border Commission would begin on June 18. In short, both sides showed restraint and were not prepared to escalate the conflict into a major war.

Neither the limited nature of conflict on the border nor the resumption of talks can disguise the extent of hostility, suspicion, and tension between these two countries. Both sides apparently continued to make preparations for any eventuality. The Soviets have expanded their airfields in Siberia; the Chinese have continued to whip up popular support for a possible war with the Soviet Union.[68]

67. *New York Times*, March 25, 1969, p. 9. Colin McCullough interpreted this omission as an indication that a reassessment of Chinese foreign policy was already under consideration.

68. *New York Times*, May 24, 1969, p. 3; *Jen-min Jih-pao*, July 11, 1969, p. 1; *Kiangsi Public Broadcasting Service*, July 11, 1969; *New China News Agency*, November 27, 1969.

The border trouble in Sinkiang flared up in June 1969.[69] The Chinese were apparently very concerned about their inability to defend national minority areas, particularly Sinkiang. On August 28, 1969, the Central Committee of the Chinese Communist Party issued a directive to strengthen the security of China's border lands. This directive specifically asked for an end to armed struggle between Cultural Revolutionary Groups, the enforcement of military and civilian discipline, and the promotion of war-preparedness. China also showed explicit concern about continued unrest in the strategic areas of Inner Mongolia and Tibet as well.

In the middle of all these charges, countercharges, and precautionary measures, Kosygin met Chou En-lai at the Peking airport on his way back from Ho Chi Minh's funeral. This meeting came as a complete surprise even to diplomats in Peking for it was the first meeting between top Soviet and Chinese leaders in four and a half years. The impetus for this meeting must have come in Hanoi, because on his way there Kosygin had avoided even flying over Chinese territory. The Rumanians were apparently credited with the mediation effort resulting in this meeting.[70]

Shortly afterwards, the Soviet Union announced a ban on anti-Chinese polemics, which was not reciprocated by the Chinese.[71] The Soviets also announced that the Chinese had ceased all border incursions.[72] During September and October, the Soviet press continued to be optimistic about a possible rapprochement with China. On October 1, the Chinese finally reciprocated by emphasizing that border disputes must be settled through negotiations,[73] which accordingly began on October 7.[74] It was also announced that the border talks, broken off since 1964, would resume on October 20 and would be at the Deputy Foreign Minister level. The Chinese softened their position by saying that there was no reason for China and the Soviet Union to fight a war over the

69. *New York Times*, June 12, 1969, pp. 1 and 3.

70. *New York Times*, September 12, pp. 1 and 2; September 13, 1969, pp. 1 and 4.

71. *New York Times*, September 17, 1969, pp. 1 and 5.

72. *New York Times*, September 19, 1969, pp. 1 and 2.

73. Editorial in *Jen-min Jih-pao*, October 1, 1969.

74. *Jen-min Jih-pao*, October 8, 1969, p. 1; *New York Times*, October 8, 1969, pp. 1 and 10.

boundary question. They also reiterated that China did not demand that all the territories taken over by Tsarist Russia in the nineteenth century be returned, but only that such unequal treaties be renegotiated and that the Soviets should not indulge in further violation of Chinese territory. The Chinese statement also revealed that at the Chou-Kosygin meeting of September 11, the Chinese had proposed that both sides disentangle themselves from the disputed territories. Border talks did in fact open on October 20. These talks, however, halted neither cautious polemics nor a mutual military buildup.

By late 1968, China had also taken the initiative in another direction, this time toward the United States. The Chinese ambivalence toward the Sino-American talks throughout the year was probably due to pressure from the remnants of the radical groups in the Foreign Ministry, the central government, and the Party. In spite of this tension, Peking did propose new talks. On November 26, 1968, China proposed that the suspended Sino-American talks be resumed on February 20, 1969. These talks had been postponed earlier from May 29, 1968, to the middle or end of November. On September 12, the United States had proposed that the postponed one hundred thirty-fifth meeting take place on November 20, 1968, and the Chinese had rejected this as imperialist dictation. Six days after the suggested date, however, they proposed that the United States and China enter into a peaceful coexistence agreement.[75]

By January 1969, both internal pressures and corresponding ambivalence became more and more obvious as the Chinese press attacked Richard Nixon. This barrage coincided with the inauguration of Mr. Nixon as President.[76] The attacks on the Nixon Administration were kept up in the ensuing weeks. It therefore came as no surprise when on February 18, the Chinese canceled the one hundred thirty-fifth session of the Warsaw talks scheduled to begin on February 20. The immediate excuse was, of course, the January 24, 1969, defection of Liao Ho-shu, a Chinese diplomat stationed in the Netherlands; Liao was granted asylum in the United States on February 4. Nevertheless, Secretary of

75. *New York Times,* November 27 and November 28, 1969.
76. *Jen-min Jih-pao,* January 27, 1969; *Hung-ch'i,* January 27, 1969.

State Rogers, testifying before the Senate Foreign Relations Committee, stated that the defection and the asylum of the Chinese diplomat were not the real reasons for the cancellation of the talks. It is generally assumed that the real cause was internal difficulties in the Ministry of Foreign Affairs, where radical remnants were opposed to any rapprochement with the United States.

The United States government, correctly analyzing the sources of Chinese ambivalence and the rationale for the cancellation of the talks, continued to follow a path of partial erosion of the policy of containing China without total isolation. The United States had already planned to talk about the pact for peaceful coexistence proposed by the Chinese, the possibility of travel by certain categories of American citizens to China, and a solution to the payments problem for postal and telecommunications with China. In July and December 1969, therefore, the United States eased restrictions on trade and travel with China.

Meanwhile, pressure in the United States was increasing for a new China policy. In March 1969, a two-day conference on United States–China relations, attended by specialists on Chinese affairs, called for bold initiatives.[77] In April, the League of Women Voters asked for a new China policy, and in May, Senator Alan Cranston, with substantial bipartisan support, followed suit. The League of Women Voters asked for initiatives by the Nixon Administration leading to both diplomatic recognition and a seat in the United Nations for Communist China.[78] At the same time, American officials were already reevaluating the Chinese military threat to Asian countries. It was now believed that such a threat had been overestimated.[79]

By October 1969, new talks with the United States were again in the offing, and American officials were hinting that Chinese policy toward such talks was easing. On December 12, it was

77. For a complete documentation of this conference, see, Barnett and Reischauer (editors) with the assistance of Lois Duggan Tretiak, *The United States and China: The Next Decade* (New York: Praeger, 1970).
78. *New York Times*, April 27, p. 34; May 28, 1969, p. 6.
79. *New York Times*, August 17, 1969, p. 13.

announced that United States and Chinese Communist ambassadors had secretly met in Warsaw.[80] Other signs that the suspended Sino-American talks could begin soon came when Chinese and American diplomats stopped boycotting each other at diplomatic receptions in Warsaw.

It is interesting to note that within a week of these secret talks, on December 19, 1969, the United States further liberalized trade restrictions. It came as no surprise, therefore, that on January 8, 1970, the United States and China announced that the suspended one hundred thirty-fifth meeting would finally take place on January 20.[81] This was generally a period of growing optimism and increasing hope that finally both sides were in a mood to tackle seriously their outstanding differences. The seriousness on the American side can always be measured by the nervousness of the officially controlled Taiwan press. Taiwan was certainly worried. Partly to offset this worry, the United States had been providing large-scale surplus weapons to Taiwan in 1969.[82]

It is in the light of this background that the impact of the American invasion of Cambodia on Chinese foreign policy should be evaluated. The United States significantly underestimated Peking's capability to respond to events in Indochina in April 1970. Its immediate impact was not only the cancellation of the one hundred thirty-seventh meeting of the Sino-American talks scheduled to open on May 20, but also the general harm done to Sino-American relations. As usual, American policy in Cambodia sabotaged another chance for a major relaxation of Sino-American tension.

Makers of Chinese foreign policy effectively utilized the initiative offered by the Cambodian invasion. After a short period of hesitation, the Chinese made a decision to support Sihanouk. They also started to coordinate, on behalf of Sihanouk, a general united front of groups and parties in Laos, Cambodia, and Vietnam, which were already engaged in fighting America and her allies.

On March 26, the Chinese Foreign Ministry issued a statement

80. *New York Times*, December 13, pp. 1 and 21; December 15, 1969, p. 6.

81. *New York Times*, January 9, 1970, pp. 1 and 4.

82. *New York Times*, March 29, 1970, pp. 1 and 28.

supporting the Pathet Lao.[83] In rapid succession, Peking lined up the support of Hanoi, the NLF, and the Pathet Lao for Sihanouk's Cambodian National United Front (FUNK). By the end of March, attacks by the Chinese and their allies in Southeast Asia on the Lon Nol government, together with their unequivocal support for Sihanouk, meant at least *de facto* if not *de jure* recognition. It is quite possible that Sihanouk was not very eager to be allied with all of these groups. His foreign policy was aimed at keeping Cambodia independent of both Vietnam and Thailand. With this aim in mind, he had followed with relative success the policy of active neutrality for the past sixteen years. This policy, based on weakness, did not really represent a balance between power and policy. Sihanouk and Cambodia, therefore, were always at the mercy of great and not-so-great powers. After his removal from office, Sihanouk was left with no choice but to seek support wherever he could. This led him to the formation of an ideologically motley united front at home and a major accommodation with the Vietnamese abroad.

The impact of the United States intervention in Cambodia was as great as if not greater than that of the similar invasion by the Soviet Union of Czechoslovakia. This invasion vastly increased the insecurity of Asian Communists, led to the militarization of yet another government in Southeast Asia, and extended military conflict and civil violence to all of Indochina.

The Chinese moved rapidly to take advantage of this opportunity. Chou En-lai visited North Korea from April 5 to 7 and obtained Pyongyang's endorsement of Sihanouk's aspirations.[84] The Chinese also mobilized a Communist summit conference on April 24 and 25, probably in Nanning, within the Chinese border. This conference was hosted by China and was intended to coordinate the Cambodian FUNK with other Indochinese organizations. As witnessed by the conference, the Cambodian invasion encouraged the North Vietnamese, the North Koreans, the Pathet Lao, and the NLF to accept the Chinese lead. Mao, in a rare gesture, dramatically signified Chinese involvement by receiving Sihanouk and his wife on May Day.

83. *Peking Review*, No. 14, April 3, 1970.
84. *Peking Review*, No. 16, April 17, 1970.

Until United States policy is geared toward a complete and total withdrawal in both military and political terms, the Cambodian situation is not likely to improve. But neither the Nixon Doctrine nor the vision of American policy-makers is in favor of such a total withdrawal. In spite of all the debate over the vagueness of the Nixon Doctrine, it is a doctrine of maximum involvement without the direct use of United States ground forces. Even this limitation on American involvement cannot be guaranteed. A dramatic confirmation of this interpretation was the invasion of Cambodia itself. The United States did not invade Cambodia for the stated reason of destroying sanctuaries. It was not an operation for military benefits. It was, in reality, an operation to support the Lon Nol government; even if there had been no sanctuaries, such an operation would have occurred.[85]

Subsequent events in both Cambodia and Laos confirm that the Nixon Doctrine does not bar either military aid or operations. Furthermore, its definition of getting involved by "other than military means" is both curious and arbitrary. Presumably, the phrase "other than military means" includes not only the supply of military hardware, but also the direct involvement of the United States Air Force. The Lon Nol government is receiving as much air cover throughout Cambodia as the South Vietnamese. Furthermore, the United States continues to bomb, apparently without any geographical limits, Cambodian and Laotian territories. There is no perceived significant change in American policy, military or diplomatic, in Southeast Asia between the Johnson and Nixon Administrations. American military withdrawals confuse rather than clarify the policy. They are aimed at winning debate points and electoral victories over domestic opponents rather than at signifying a departure from a Cold War mentality which has characterized Mr. Nixon throughout his public life.

The American policy has not only followed a rigid strategy of denial to the other side, a fundamental principle of the Cold War,

85. For a detailed analysis of the real reasons for the Cambodian decision see Hedrick Smith, *New York Times*, June 30, 1970, pp. 1 and 14. For a further analysis of the impact of the Cambodian invasion on Chinese foreign policy, see Ishwer C. Ojha and Daniel Tretiak, "Washington Out in the Cold," *Far Eastern Economic Review*, June 18, 1970, pp. 29 ff.

but has further dangerously backtracked more than a decade. The Nixon Doctrine is a prime example of this regression. It is nothing more than the disguised resurrection of the Eisenhower belief that Asians must fight Asians. It is further motivated by the assumption that air power is decisive and least costly in terms of American lives. The first assumption has been proved erroneous so many times and for so long that it is not even worth debating. The second assumption is tied to the needs of domestic politics.

If air power is not decisive and if American military involvement continues, then the second assumption becomes illusory. It is impossible for American allies in Southeast Asia to fight successfully without American ground troops. If past experience in Vietnam is any guide, then success is highly doubtful. American air power can prolong the war, can even pulverize small nations, but cannot win the war. The Nixon Doctrine, therefore, is short-sighted and may continue to sow winds out of which future whirlwinds may be reaped.

Even in Cold War terms and assumptions, which unfortunately continue to be the touchstones of American foreign policy, the Cambodian venture was not worth the cost. This does not necessarily mean that the Chinese will get militarily involved in Indochina. For the last twenty years, they have remained cautious and have maintained a correct balance between their national power and policy. There is every indication that they will continue to do so.

The Cambodian venture also improved the Chinese position vis-à-vis the Soviet Union in Indochina. The American escalation has given the Chinese a diplomatic position superior to that of the Soviets in Southeast Asia. It has swung the balance of power, which had heretofore existed between Moscow and Peking, in favor of the Chinese. It has politically and diplomatically further exposed the weaknesses of Soviet policy and has put it on the defensive. The Russians can neither recognize Sihanouk nor denounce him. They cannot join China in a combined effort, but at the same time they cannot reduce their aid to Southeast Asia.

It would be unfair to assert that the entire range of problems faced by Soviet policy in Southeast Asia is concerned with the Chinese. One of the major assumptions held by American policymakers, namely, that Soviet influence can be utilized for the pres-

ervation and promotion of American interests to attain a negotiated settlement of the Southeast Asian war, is not accurate. The
Geneva settlements of 1954 and 1961 already exhausted the Soviets' diplomatic capital by forcing the Chinese, the Vietnamese,
the NLF, and the Pathet Lao to accept Soviet solutions.

Soviet assistance to North Vietnam is barely enough to maintain the level of Soviet influence, even at the 1962 level. The basic
problem is not with the amount of Soviet aid, but the dynamic
Communist nationalism of the North Vietnamese and the NLF.
The Russians cannot impose another Geneva conference and another Geneva-type settlement on Southeast Asia.

Both Peking and Hanoi fully realize that the Russians will not
get involved in a direct military conflict with the United States.
Turning pro-Soviet, therefore, could not significantly affect their
fighting ability and would certainly be detrimental to their diplomatic and political ends. Any negotiated settlement which negates
the enormous cost in men and material expended by North Vietnam and the NLF throughout the 1960's is unrealistic. The Chinese have always realized this, and their foreign policy has generally
supported Hanoi's diplomatic aims. Such support has been limited
and conditional, because the Chinese themselves do not want to
get involved in a direct confrontation with the United States.

The Cambodian invasion somewhat offset the Chinese fears
aroused by the Czechoslovakian invasion. The reason is that the
Chinese perception of Soviet capacity for military escalation on
the Sino-Soviet border has diminished. Such an escalation would
be politically and diplomatically harmful to the Soviet Union in
the light of China's gains in the Asian Communist movement
since April 1970. The gravity of the situation in Southeast Asia
did not escape Soviet attention. It was symbolically expressed by
Kosygin's press conference which closely followed the American
invasion of Cambodia. Meanwhile, Chinese foreign policy has
gained some respite, if not victory, in the Sino-Soviet competition.
The polemical attacks on each other, though not completely eliminated, have become less frequent and more subdued since April. In
July 1970, it was announced that the Soviets and Chinese would
exchange ambassadors for the first time since 1966.

Chinese gains over the Soviet Union in the area of Asian Communist diplomacy wore a price tag, however. This cost was paid

by both the United States and China. The growing Chinese rapprochement with the United States became a political liability for China. The Chinese very well understand the pitfalls of Soviet diplomacy and correctly learned the lesson that there is a limit beyond which they cannot support revolutionary aspirations in Southeast Asia and continue to have business as usual with the United States. It was therefore necessary that the one hundred thirty-seventh meeting of the Sino-American talks be postponed.

As yet there are no solid indications as to when the talks will be resumed. It is quite possible, however, that they may resume in the near future. According to reports in June 1970, Chou En-lai had hinted as much to East European diplomats.[86] Yet the Cambodian venture is obviously still a strong obstacle. On June 20, 1970, therefore, China informed the United States that she could not set a date for the next talks in Warsaw at this time.[87]

Chinese foreign policy, freed from the internal stresses of the Cultural Revolution and blessed by unexpected opportunities for initiatives from the Brezhnev and Nixon Doctrines, is rapidly moving into high gear. Chinese foreign diplomatic activity is now becoming both varied and far-ranging. In addition to aid to Rumania, China also provided earthquake relief to Peru and a message of sympathy for earthquake and flood victims in the Soviet Union.

Peking is once again on the diplomatic air routes of the world. Delegations of all kinds are converging on Peking. During the month of June 1970 alone, important visitors and delegations came to Peking from Pakistan, Rumania, Czechoslovakia, Albania, Somalia, Sudan, North Vietnam, North Korea, and the NLF. The top leadership in Peking, now free to devote more attention to foreign affairs, has come out of its semi-isolationist phase. This is evident from the growing number of meetings between visiting dignitaries and Chairman Mao and Vice-Chairman Lin Piao.

In July 1970, Chou En-lai attended a French embassy reception marking France's national day for the first time since 1964. This gesture coincided with the visit to China of a high-level French delegation. Incidentally, this was the first such delegation since the establishment of diplomatic relations between the two countries in

86. *New York Times*, June 18, 1970, p. 9.
87. *New York Times*, June 21, 1970, p. 1.

January 1964. Mr. Andre Bettencourt, Minister for Planning and Development, headed the French delegation. In a two-hour meeting with Chairman Mao, Bettencourt supposedly discussed not only the Indochina War, on which the views of France and China concur as far as Chinese participation is concerned, but also the prospects of enlarged trade with China.[88]

Bettencourt's visit was the first French ministerial visit since 1965. Such visits were not totally one-sided. In the same month, a Chinese military delegation was visiting the Congo (Brazzaville). China was also taking steps to repair her diplomatic relations with Britain. On another front, she had successfully detached North Korea from the Soviet Union; North Koreans were now echoing both the Chinese stand against Japanese militarism and aggression on the one hand and Chinese policy in Cambodia and Southeast Asia on the other. China also was both grateful and jubilant at the Asian rejection and coolness to the Soviet trial balloon regarding a regional security system.

As early as 1968, Canadian Prime Minister Trudeau had announced that Canada would soon initiate talks for the possible establishment of Sino-Canadian diplomatic relations. The Canadian External Affairs Minister, Mr. Mitchell Sharp, announced on February 10, 1969, that the Canadian embassy in Stockholm had been instructed to initiate talks leading to possible diplomatic recognition. The United States, informed of this intention, was afraid that such recognition would injure Taiwan's international status. These fears were exaggerated, because although Canada recognizes Nationalist China, she has not maintained an ambassador in Taipei since 1949.[89] For similar reasons, the Canadians were optimistic at the beginning of these talks, as the Chinese had maintained silence on Canada's ties with the Nationalist government.

The Chinese accepted the Canadian offer on April 10, and according to the Canadian announcement, no preconditions were set. The Canadian position toward China took a significant turn in May 1969, when Mitchell Sharp announced that Canada was

88. *New York Times,* July 15, 1970, p. 3.
89. *New York Times,* February 12, p. 18; February 13, p. 3; April 1, 1969, pp. 1, 11.

negotiating with Communist China on a strictly one-China basis.[90] By late 1969, although the talks had not led to diplomatic recognition, there were other indications signifying concrete improvement in Sino-Canadian relations. In October 1969, the New China News Agency was planning to reestablish its Ottawa bureau, and the Chinese were giving preferential treatment at the Canton trade fair to the Canadians. Finally, on October 13, 1970, Canada, after twenty months of negotiations, established diplomatic relations with Communist China, while breaking those with the Nationalists in Taiwan. This recognition of China by Canada had far-reaching implications, both for Sino-American trade and China's admission to the United Nations.

Canada was not the only NATO country to seek normal diplomatic relations with Peking. In January 1969, the Italian government announced its decision to begin talks on the possible recognition of the Chinese People's Republic. On November 6, 1970, Italy became the seventh NATO member to establish diplomatic relations with Peking, and there were indications that Belgium, Austria, Luxembourg, and Ethiopia would soon follow suit.[91] Important voices were raised even in Germany for the possible opening of talks leading to West German recognition of the Peking government. The Christian Social Union, the Bavarian wing of Chancellor Kiesinger's Christian Democratic Party, had asked for such recognition as early as April 1968. At that time, it was also rumored that Pakistan was prepared to serve as an intermediary between West Germany and China. The possibility of improved relations between West Germany and China, however, does not seem very bright at this time because of the nonaggression pact just signed with the Soviet Union. The Chinese are viewing this pact as releasing pressure on Soviet forces in Eastern Europe and therefore increasing the possibility of their future use in the Far East against China.

Chou En-lai at seventy-two seems to be in effective control of Chinese foreign policy operations. Most of the recent activity and successes in the field of foreign relations are directly attributable to him. By the middle of 1970, traces of the Cultural Revolution

90. *New York Times*, May 30, 1969, p. 27.
91. *New York Times*, November 7, 1970, p. 1.

in Chinese foreign policy are hard to find. There are major indications that Chinese foreign policy may be reverting back to the varied and flexible approaches of the mid-1950's, which made it so formidable then. The Chinese now seem determined to pursue dynamic and extensive initiatives. There is, as usual, a certain ambivalence in Chinese foreign policy, but this fact should not be used to characterize it as unique or abnormal.

It is normal for any dynamic foreign policy to take advantage of new opportunities, to cut its losses wherever adverse changes have taken place, and constantly and rapidly to shift its focus in both geographical and diplomatic terms. It was thus natural for China to shift her focus from Burma and Indonesia to Cambodia, Laos, and North Korea during the last two years. Not to have done so would have been dogmatic and would have led to a static policy. This shift does not mean that China has turned more revolutionary; it simply means that the period of the Cultural Revolution, with its attendant stresses with Burma, is over and that the American invasion of Cambodia has made it both necessary and possible for China to pursue an active policy in Cambodia, Laos, and North Korea. Similarly, the Czechoslovakian invasion shifted Chinese attention from Albania to Yugoslavia and Rumania. Chinese foreign policy, therefore, has shown considerable dynamism, flexibility, and ability to take advantages whenever and wherever they occur.

Another proof that China is not as interested in radical political activity as her verbal pronouncements sometimes would lead one to believe came during 1968–1969, when the Chinese showed unwillingness to back self-proclaimed Maoist radicals and revolutionaries on the campuses of Western countries. Firstly, the Chinese consider the New Left neither as an unmixed blessing nor as a great revolutionary potential. Although they did utilize the growing student unrest in Europe and North America for a short period in May 1968, their attention on this issue considerably declined by the end of the year.[92]

Peking was also very cool to some of the heroes of the New Left,

92. *Peking Review*, No. 21, May 24, 1968, pp. 18–19; *New China News Agency*, May 22, 1968 in *SCMP*, No. 4187, pp. 39–45; and *Peking Review*, No. 22, May 31, 1968, p. 10.

like Che Guevara and Regis Debray.[93] The basic reason, however, for China's distrust of the New Left seems to be its spontaneity, lack of organization, and anti-ideological stance. Mao believes in a revolution based on firm organization and clear leadership principles. Unlike the NLF and the Pathet Lao, the New Left lacks both of these and so could have attracted neither the enduring support nor the admiration of the Chinese.

What is more significant is that by a process of osmosis the Cultural Revolution may have contributed certain styles of behavior which some sections of the radical New Left increasingly followed in 1968–1969. This impact of the Cultural Revolution was not organized by the Chinese leadership, nor have they taken credit for it. It is a part of the internationalization of youth culture and political style rather than a conscious attempt on the part of China to export revolution.

Chinese foreign policy has avoided many pitfalls by not relying on unorganized and uncoordinated infantile revolutionaries. Their policy here was consistent both at home and abroad, even at the height of the Cultural Revolution. To the Chinese, revolution continues to be serious business which has to be performed by dedicated and organized people over a period of time. Historically, this view may be correct, but then, forms for the seizure of power and different patterns of social change do evolve. By ignoring the emerging revolutionary theory and leadership postdating the Chinese revolution, the Chinese may already have shown a certain amount of rigidity. Whatever the case, the New Left and its activities have not been and will not be of major concern to the makers of Chinese foreign policy.

As usual, Chinese foreign policy is concerned with China's vital interests. These include the creation and conservation of wealth and power, industrialization through international trade rather than aid, breaking through diplomatic and military containment, and above all, increasing China's ability to make her diplomatic influence felt on a global rather than regional level. The Cultural Revolution did not and could not slow down the race for atomic weapons. Nor did it seriously damage other aspects of China's

93. *Peking Review*, No. 30, July 26, 1968, pp. 11–12; *Peking Review*, No. 9, February 25, 1966, pp. 13–20; *Le Monde*, June 21, 1968.

weapons program; in April 1970, China orbited her first earth satellite, an achievement which has important consequences for China's capacity for long-range missile delivery.

Except for a period of ten months, from January to October 1967, the responsible leadership of China, led by Chou En-lai and possibly even Mao, has exerted all its energies in first minimizing and then obliterating the unforeseen and unintended foreign-policy consequences of what was a major attempt at social revolution. Their success by 1970 is self-evident, not only in the field of foreign policy, but also in the attempt to control the People's Liberation Army and to reestablish civilian supremacy over the armed forces of China.

China faces the 1970's with a great deal of renewed vigor and dynamism. Any underestimation of her renewed capacities would be both incorrect and tragic. She is no longer stymied, as in 1966–1967, by demands on her attention made by a major social movement at home. There are indications that her industrial and economic development, together with her foreign trade and diplomatic offensive, are rapidly gathering momentum.

The 1970's will also be marked by far-reaching changes in the leadership of China. The active role of the brilliant and nearly superhuman leaders who have guided China through the last twenty-one years cannot survive the decade. Chou and Mao are in their seventies. This does not necessarily mean that other nations should adopt a wait-and-see policy. China's vital interests cannot change; Chinese foreign policy, therefore, cannot change significantly in the decade to come. The impact of personality on policy should not be underestimated, but it should not be overestimated either. The question "After Mao, what?" can no longer be an excuse for Cold War attitudes.

Conclusions

The Cultural Revolution notwithstanding, the basic content of Chinese foreign policy continues to reflect the broad goals of a nation in transition. While it is true that every modern nation-state maintains a link between domestic politics and foreign policy, this bond is stronger than usual in the case of China. In part the parallel nature of internal and external events is bound by the tight web of Marxist-Leninist logic, in which an overall strategy or "general line" dictates similar policies in different fields. Mao's policy of maintaining the united front in the early 1950's, for example, found international expression in a friendly attitude toward many governments abroad. Similarly, domestic proclamations of class struggle dampened the prospects for cooperation elsewhere. In the USSR, Stalin's turn from the New Economic Plan to the policy of rapid collectivization and forced industrialization was the domestic counterpart to the drastic international shift announced by the sixth Comintern congress of 1928.

Yet the ideological link between domestic and foreign policy is by no means automatic. As the Cultural Revolution demonstrated, the most radical domestic experiments did not paralyze efforts to protect China's vital interests. Sometimes the apparent resemblance between domestic and foreign policy is merely a paper edifice. Deliberate calculations are naturally involved. No leader wants to be accused of inconsistency. Failure to coat internal and external actions evenly with the general line amounts to passing out doctrinal ammunition to domestic rivals. Even more important, harsh policies at home are well served by frigid isolationism abroad. During periods of coercion or upheaval, both Mao and Stalin preferred to block the vision of prying eyes from other countries. The long-range disadvantages of isolation do not negate its short-run benefits.

At this point, however, the Soviet and Chinese parallels part company. All in all, Soviet foreign policy is capable of many twists and turns that do not stem from a corresponding domestic snake dance. The Comintern's vacillations of the 1920's, the ring toss between the Zhdanov line, the collaborationist policy of World War II, the Maoist strategy from 1947 to 1951, and finally the rapid alternation of Khrushchev's smiles and frowns suggest fundamental differences from China. Soviet foreign policy, like other official spheres of action, is more manipulative than its Chinese counterpart, more divorced from the echoes of the grass-roots populism that characterizes Mao. Although Mao was quick to grasp Lenin's organizational insights, he did not share his utter contempt for the populist tradition.

The difference between the two major Communist capitals does not mean, of course, that Chinese foreign policy anxiously conforms to a weekly Nielsen rating. Here again, objective reality—if there is such a thing—is less important than what Chinese Communist leaders *think* such reality is. Knowing that he could not have won without a certain degree of popular support, Mao has projected prerevolutionary populism into postrevolutionary permanence. His frequent exhortations to "serve the people" do not merely serve a manipulative purpose. They ring with the strength of conviction.

Nevertheless, the representative character which Mao attributes to his leadership is sadly out of tune with the prevailing (but by no means the only) Western conception of representation. Mao does not stand for the Chinese people as they are but as he thinks they should be. As a populist he idealizes—and perhaps distorts—the human potential of the Chinese masses. Like Rousseau, he believes in restoring man to himself. What is at stake is a fundamental transformation of human nature.

As a nationalist, Mao urgently desires to unlock this potential as quickly as possible and to harness it to China's growing strength. More than anything else, he sees the people as the key to national strength. Mass campaigns directed at purifying the human character are not peripheral but central to the task of China's national resurgence. Unlike the self-strengthening movement of the T'ung-chih period, Mao's guidebook is not Confucianism but a new vision of human relations directed simultaneously at overcoming human selfishness and at projecting China into the status of a superpower. As a populist-cum-nationalist he thus wields double-strength dynamism.

This dual emotional character, while lacking in the Leninist tradition, is not unique to China. Preoccupation with the human factor is part and parcel of the introspective revolution. The rejection of the cultural past in favor of rapid modernization belongs to the age of transition from culturism through cultural nationalism to full-scale nationalism. Mao has eased some of the agony accompanying this transformation. While rejecting the past, he has not destroyed Chinese pride. By reconstructing Chinese history along revolutionary lines, he suggests that stamping on China's traditional culture with spiked shoes actually conforms to China's true spirit. Although not fully matured, similar efforts can be found elsewhere.

As contrasted with Moscow's manipulative approach, Chinese foreign policy thus possesses more genuine sparks of emotion. Reflecting continuity with the age of imperialism rather than with the era of Confucianism, it reflects a profound conviction that imperialism is not dead. Viewed from her borders, the ring of American bases adds fuel to this belief. Imperialism is more than a scapegoat for past humiliations. It is a towering wall that seems to block China's national aspirations in the present.

The United States has become a symbol of this frustration. Like right-wing fundamentalists in the United States, Mao refuses to compromise with a specter. It is true that the mid-1950's witnessed a conciliatory tone in Chinese commentaries on America. Whether this shift was sincere or whether it was made in the knowledge that Washington would not respond remains unclear. In any case, it did not reflect a belief that imperialism was no longer a world force. It merely gave Washington's policy-makers a chance to dissociate themselves from the alleged crimes perpetuated by a living phenomenon.

The central stumbling block to an improvement in Sino-American relations is Taiwan. This island symbolizes or incorporates almost all of the attitudes that motivate Chinese foreign policy. It has thwarted all efforts to make Peking renounce the use of force in international relations. It has dramatized Soviet unwillingness to support China's diplomatic aims, thus exacerbating the Sino-Soviet dispute. It is one of the few remaining obstacles to China's search for national boundaries. Like Tibet, both Nationalists and Communists insist that it is an integral part of China. Unlike Tibet, it poses the threat of an alternate government with its own claim to legitimacy. It is a symptom of China's weakness, a reminder that she is not yet strong enough to defy the United States. In short, it embodies all the major trends in contemporary Chinese foreign policy.

The problem of Taiwan, however, is merely the largest tree in the forest. Instead of responding to a crisis-to-crisis scenario, the United States must survey the entire scope of Sino-American interaction. Particularly pressing is a new definition of the so-called "national interest" of each side. What is China's legitimate national interest? How has America's national interest changed in the last twenty years? A starting point for both sides might be the recognition that to attempt the impossible is never in the national interest. If influence and prestige are components of power, then costly and drawn out mistakes must be ended as quickly as possible. International circumstances change, but errors tend to be self-perpetuating.

Domestic changes on each side have also been breathtakingly rapid. The emergence of new and articulate groups in America, and the absorption of young activists into a reconstituted Chinese Communist Party, in the context of technological growth, spell eventual shifts in international perspectives. Even the best institutions are slow to respond to social change. Both the State Department and the Chinese Foreign Ministry, being further removed from domestic politics than other governmental agencies, may be even slower.

Yet China is capable of shifting gears if faced with a genuinely fresh initiative from Washington. Promises will not suffice. Some actions must be taken to convince Peking that isolation and military encirclement have been discarded. Recent American moves are steps in the right direction. As a bare minimum, however, America must extricate herself from the Vietnam War in such a way as to rule out a repetition of large-scale fighting so close to China's borders.

These steps would require a painfully critical evaluation of such hitherto sacred tenets as the need for American bases on the Asian mainland. In a sense, the fundamental reorientation of America's Asian policy, combined with new and imaginative measures to cope with her domestic problems, calls for at least a minor introspective revolution. Such an agonizing process of maturation would eventually erode the already crumbling structure of America's present attitudes. In fact, the resulting improvement in Sino-American relations would have a spill-over effect on the interlocking chain of China's political attitudes.

Other areas of China's diplomatic activity reveal this same dynamic interrelationship between China's internal and external perspectives and between Peking's major foreign policy aims. First and foremost is the Soviet Union. In fact, hardly a single major diplomatic move is made without some ultimate reference to relations with the Kremlin.

In retrospect the brief period of Sino-Soviet friendship, however unsuccessfully it papered over the strains, was more surprising than the Sino-Soviet dispute. Here again, Mao's attitude toward the Kremlin reflects a combination of nationalism and populism. Considering himself to be the leading Communist ruler and theoretician after Stalin, Mao has strongly resented Moscow's condescending behavior. Both the strings attached to Soviet aid and the efforts to preserve tsarist privileges were further reminders that imperialism is not confined to the West. As with other neighbors, Chinese leaders are willing to make territorial and economic concessions provided that the spirit of the agreement is based on formal equality. Needless to say, the Soviets have discouraged this trend in the correct belief that it undermines their hegemony over the Bloc.

Sino-Soviet antagonisms also spring from totally different styles of domestic politics. Nowhere is this split more apparent than in the Cultural Revolution. The Soviets accuse Mao of bypassing the "people," that is, of jumping over the heads of the Party establishment and relying on non-Party groups. The charge is accurate, but Mao's rationalization adds up to the reverse. To him, the Party in China no longer represents the people as they should be or even as they are. For that reason he must push the Party aside and re-store the spirit of Chinese policy-making to his conception of the "people."

This phenomenon is anathema to Soviet leaders. By admitting that the Party can sometimes be wrong, it undermines the very basis of Communist rule in the Soviet Union. By contrast, Soviet leaders have been quick to blame the man rather than the Party. Khrushchev's speech at the Twentieth Congress directed all the guilt at Stalin in the same way that current Soviet pronouncements distinguish Mao as an individual from the Chinese Communist Party. Mao's major error, they charge, is isolating himself from the mainstream of the Party. As a petty bourgeois individualist he has stirred up troubles that only a return to Party rule can banish. Some revival of Party dominance, albeit on a reconstructed basis, is already evident.

The Sino-Soviet dispute is also bound up with the question of self-reliance. Both are major issues in the current factional dispute. On the one hand, self-reliance means a minimum of aid to national liberation movements or Communist revolutions abroad. It is a rationale for inaction. On the other, it justifies a refusal to heal the Sino-Soviet breach. By insisting that China does not need the Soviet Union, it perpetuates proud independence.

Opponents of this argument are similarly consistent in their link between relations with the Soviet Union and revolutionary move-ments abroad. Led initially by P'eng Teh-huai and later by Lo Jui-ch'ing, they argue that China needs Soviet assistance. Com-promising on doctrinal issues, or at least keeping silent, would be rewarded by material assistance to China's defense, industrial de-velopment, and nuclear weapons programs. By the same token, they favor more Chinese aid to revolutionary uprisings abroad. In the case of Vietnam, their case rested in part on a more serious estimation of the threat of a direct Sino-American confrontation. The risk of further American escalation would have strengthened their demand for a Sino-Soviet rapprochement and for more direct involvement in Vietnam. Ironically, Washington may have helped Mao to defeat his opponents by insisting that the war would not be extended to China.

The Soviet Union also overshadows all of China's efforts in the Third World. More important than the realities of Afro-Asian revolutions is the elimination of Soviet influence. As a developing country with her own taste of imperialism, China has an advantage which she pursues to the full. Her insistence that the Soviet Union is not an Asian country and is thus unqualified for Afro-Asian leadership stops just short of open racism. The Third World is an instrument to be used against Moscow. The hard-sell promotion of the doctrine of people's war adds up to a massive effort to undermine Soviet prestige.

If Sino-American relations are based on misperceptions, the Sino-Soviet dispute is founded on real antagonisms. In this sense the quarrel with Moscow is more serious, more all pervasive, and more meaningful than the rift with Washington. Once their hints of peaceful settlement were rebuffed, Chinese leaders no longer expected the United States to behave differently from any imperialist power. In spite of frequent disappointments and diplomatic slaps in the face, however, they still nourish faint hopes for Moscow. Suslov's warning that factionalism may be penetrating the Kremlin itself indicates that such hopes may not be totally unfounded. Just as several leaders in Peking apparently favored a Sino-Soviet compromise, so Moscow may have its own potential peacemakers.

By binding the perpetuation of the Sino-Soviet dispute so tightly to the doctrine of people's war, the Maoist leadership may be backing itself into a corner. Any future reconciliation between Moscow and Peking may endanger the entire scope of Mao's military contributions, including self-reliance. Since Mao himself interprets the significance of the Chinese revolution largely in military terms, the damage may be severe. Large doses of Soviet aid might appear to invalidate the entire Communist reconstruction of China's revolutionary heritage. China has staked everything on the very attitudes that keep the Sino-Soviet dispute alive.

As long as Mao is alive and remains in power, such a reconciliation is unlikely. In another form, however, this dilemma has already come to the surface in the debate over Vietnam. Mocked by Moscow for apparent paralysis, Chinese leaders must find a way to narrow the gap between words and deeds. One method is to build up China's military strength as rapidly as possible so that future threats will be backed by nuclear might. For the moment this achievement awaits further development.

Another attempt to bridge the gap is provided by the very notion of people's war. As interpreted by Mao and Lin, self-reliance is a basic part of this doctrine. The Chinese can shout about revolution without lifting a finger in its behalf. Yet even the notion of people's war does not rule out a modicum of Chinese aid. Although the basic thrust must come from below, sitting back with folded arms undermines China's credibility as a nation genuinely devoted to a change in the status quo. Pleasing only to Washington, this attitude supports the impression that China does not mean business. Joining hands with the Soviet Union and stepping up shipments of arms may restore China's prestige, but such actions would cast doubt on the viability of self-reliance in a modern technological world. The restoration of revolutionary respectability may tarnish the validity of the Maoist model.

China's actions with respect to the international legal order also mirror a host of interrelated priorities. Peking's leaders identify the present pattern of international relations with a world order designed to pepetuate the world domination of the status quo powers. International law serves only to frost a cake in which China has no share. Given China's exclusion from the United Nations, no international organization has any binding power, including that of making laws. To Peking the only valid commitments are those freely negotiated by sovereign nations.

This concern for the full trappings of sovereignty is nowhere better reflected than in China's treaty relations with her neighbors. The brief Red Guard effort to replace the doctrine of unlimited sovereignty with the Thought of Mao Tse-tung was abortive, at least in its practical consequences. China's concern for her own sovereignty is virulent. Even if the final result is the same, settlements imposed during the age of imperialism must be swept aside and renegotiated on a free and equal basis. The Sino-Burmese agreement, for example, repudiated a British arrangement only to repeat its terms in the settlement that followed. Similarly, the spirit of the negotiations is more important than the territory involved. China has signed away disputed areas in return for little else besides an atmosphere founded on equality and mutual benefit. China will simply not honor an imposed treaty.

Insistence on sovereign equality is shared by Chinese Communists and Nationalists alike. For all his quasi-traditionalist leanings,

Chiang Kai-shek heaped wrath on the unequal treaties. In fact, bristling at the possibility of unjust treatment is a characteristic of modern nationalism, not of a resurrected Middle Kingdom. Since the transition to modernization is partly a psychological process, involving the transformation of long-standing traditional attitudes, the priorities of nationalism naturally take certain psychological forms.

Both the West and the Soviet Union have long since moved away from this defensive stage of nationalism and this urge to assert their identity in terms of formal equality. Their nationalism, while still robust, has assumed a riper and more mellow form. To them, China's demand for formal equality looks like an immature charade. They may not remember that many other nations including themselves, passed through a period of self-definition and self-assertion and that still others have yet to begin.

Precisely the same perspective prevents both Peking and Taipei from accepting a two-Chinas solution to the problem of representation in the United Nations. To the Chinese Communists, waiting for admission on the basis of equality, legitimacy, and territorial sovereignty is far more important than participating in actual debates. As the talks in Warsaw testify, China's stance has not prevented the growth of a widespread network of international communication. Meanwhile, China will not abandon her quest for the symbols of sovereignty, including at least the pretense of control over Taiwan.

A Taiwanese Taiwan might point the way out of this deadlock, but that alone would not suffice. China wants freedom to enjoy the full privileges of sovereignty. Among these are domestic jurisdiction in such areas as Tibet, diplomatic accreditation from the world's major governments, and the renegotiation of all agreements to which Peking is expected to subscribe. In short, China wants a new international status that she feels is commensurate with her growing strength.

To expect at least minor adjustments is surely not unreasonable. International law and order, like their domestic counterparts, are always in danger of perpetuating the given establishment. Too often they overlook the fact that change is healthy. The ideal of peaceful change is seldom realized. When it is, small powers are usually the ones whose national ambitions have had to be curtailed. Great powers may make token concessions, but major losses have usually been extracted by war. In too many cases, a newly emergent world power has been forced to prove its credentials by force of arms. The way to recognition of Bismarck's Germany, for example, lay in a series of dazzling military victories.

China is not yet a superpower. She will be fairly soon. Meanwhile she has flexed every muscle to propel herself from backwardness to modernity. Neither her huge standing army nor the vast size of her population can be ignored. Building a ring of bases around her periphery is one way to pay tribute to her growing strength. A better way is to update the machinery of world diplomacy so that it reflects new power realities. As long as international law remains impotent with respect to the superpowers, China's membership in the United Nations may be irrelevant. What is more important is to adjust the levers of world politics to suit a changing constellation of world powers.

This perspective does not argue for submission to world government or even for a drastic reorientation of national interests. It calls merely for the realization that an international order which ignores new realities faces a serious threat of extinction. The world may not explode with World War III, but with a chain of firecrackers. Each of these small conflicts can be inconclusive, costly, and destructive, as the Sino-Indian border dispute illustrates. The time may soon come for voluntary concessions on the part of China's major antagonists. Losing a little now is better than trying to change when it's already too late. Even if American policymakers wish to enshrine the status quo under glass, the American economy may not be able to afford the luxury of repairing all the cracks.

If the foregoing analysis is correct, and if the major ingredients of Chinese foreign policy have been accurately analyzed, then the foreign policy implications of the Cultural Revolution fall into place. No description can be wholly conclusive, for the recent upheaval mirrors the profound complexity of Chinese politics. The Cultural Revolution has been a combination of pressures rolled into nationwide disruption.

To suggest a few, these pressures include the succession struggle, the post-revolutionary cleavage between the lull of normalcy and the urge to maintain revolutionary momentum, the cultivation of revolutionary youth, the rise of bureaucratic and professional classes, and the role of anti-bureaucratic mass organizations. One might also list the failure of radical economic measures, impetus toward ideological revival, the need for wider channels of mobility and for elite turnover, the conflict between the political style of Yenan and modern institutions, and the failure of revolutionary education.

The rollcall might further name the social dysfunctions of rapid modernization, the destabilizing effect of the Great Leap Forward, the emotional and ideological dynamism of the Sino-Soviet dispute, the structural implications of class struggle, and upheaval "from above" as well as "from below." These tensions supply some of the artillery behind the formulation of foreign policy. To measure the contributions of the Cultural Revolution to Peking's international behavior, and to test the major components of foreign policy against the touchstone of recent events, are thus enormously complex tasks.

From December 1966 to September 1967, the Cultural Revolution shook up the very mechanics of day-to-day foreign policy. Like all major institutions in China, the Ministry of Foreign Affairs received its share of Red Guard disruptions. During the most violent period of barnstorming, from April to August 1967, Chou En-lai and Ch'en Yi were only intermittently in charge. Although the reputations of both men were damaged, Ch'en Yi emerged the worse for wear. Even Mao was reportedly surprised at the treatment he received.

These disruptions were accompanied by changes in the composition shook up the very mechanics of day-to-day foreign policy. programs, Chinese visits abroad, and diplomatic relations were all curtailed. Meanwhile, radio broadcasts beamed at foreign countries increased, as did the international publication and distribution of Mao's works. Chinese chargés d'affaires would arrive for meetings with their host country only to read aloud from their little red books. Unable to cope, frustrated officials finally took to sending them diplomatic notes.

This disregard for diplomatic and public opinion on the part of Chinese personnel stationed abroad seems surprising, to say the least. Yet diplomats from Communist countries who are assigned to other nations fall under particular suspicion. Considered prone to foreign influences, they must be extremely reliable or even dogmatic before they are chosen in the first place. Once on assignment, they are usually supervised by one or more representatives of the secret police in the guise of minor aides. Any deviation may cost them their posts. In this specific sense, diplomatic personnel breathe freer air in their Communist homelands than they do abroad.

The surprising and sometimes ridiculous patterns of diplomatic behavior initiated by the Cultural Revolution brought with them a mixture of benefits and disadvantages. On the negative side, morale in the Foreign Ministry must have fallen to a low ebb. Carefully cultivated diplomatic paths were suddenly blocked off for political reasons. Chinese prestige, strengthened by cautious deeds abroad and by sensible economic programs at home, was severely cudgeled. During the time of greatest strife, Ch'en Yi and Chou En-lai were usually unavailable for consultation and reassurance.

On the positive side, the youthful fervor whipped up by the Cultural Revolution had an outlet in foreign affairs. Large-scale mobilization channeled latent discontent into mass proportions. Political energies, eager for new targets, could always be directed at some alleged violation of China's national dignity. Moreover, diplomatic isolation curtailed foreign intelligence and forced China's population to concentrate on internal politics without the distraction of foreign influence. While of dubious value in the long-term future, isolation had definite short-run advantages. As with other diplomatic tactics, it could always be dropped when no longer needed.

In fact, the recent vigor of Chinese foreign policy is apparent from Chinese responses to the opportunities provided by the Brezhnev and Nixon Doctrines. Since October 1968, China's Foreign Ministry, under the general supervision of Chou En-lai, has progressively regained its dynamism. Most of its recent activities and successes can be directly traced to Chou's moderating leadership. By the middle of 1970, the patterns of diplomatic behavior initiated by the Cultural Revolution had all but disappeared.

On a broader level, the Cultural Revolution does not invalidate the picture of a nation in transition. While day-to-day tactics shifted dramatically, the basic forces behind Chinese foreign policy remain. The international attitudes of the Maoist leadership continue to reflect anti-Western Westernism, motivated by the politics of cultural despair. Yet even these emotional forces do not prevent China from making clearheaded diplomatic moves.

Supporting this argument is the fact that disregarding the present postponement, almost the only country with whom China's relations have remained constant is the United States. In the talks at Warsaw the diplomatic barometer has remained at a fairly steady level until very recently. In other words, even during the most fanatic periods of self-righteous verbal bombardment, China has quietly maintained cautious contact with the alleged enemy of world progress. The realities of China's international position have not been overlooked.

The maintenance of Sino-American contact on this matter-of-fact level brings into question the apparent irrationality of China's leaders with respect to the Cultural Revolution. Mao's basic outlook is often assumed to be visionary and unrealistic in its goals. There can be little doubt that Mao idealizes and clings to the so-called "Yenan syndrome" of simple and wholesome life. His emphasis on self-sacrifice, revolutionary dedication, and the primacy of the human factor over technical expertise all smack of an age in which China's technological and institutional superstructure was still rudimentary. Yet rather than condemning technology, Mao simply wants to inject the Yenan spirit into an increasingly technological context.

The revival of the Yenan model is largely directed at China's youth. Even without the need to mobilize the Red Guards as a tool in the succession struggle, China's students would have been subjected to revolutionary pressures. Too young to remember the years of civil war, they saw the moderation of post-Leap policies as a permanent policy rather than as a passing phase. More important, they lacked the personal dedication and revolutionary enthusiasm which Mao wished to inculcate in his successors.

Intensive campaigns directed at the cultivation of these attitudes may not be irrational. From the perspective of domestic strength, the theory behind the Cultural Revolution may actually contribute to China's development. Specifically, Mao fears that the momentum for industrial development generated in past years may be halted by inertia, localism, and tradition. Significantly, the brunt of the Cultural Revolution has been aimed at China's elite.

Accordingly, the more drastic and sensational measures employed in recent years may be aimed at guaranteeing the effectiveness of the elite as an instrument of modernization. In fact, the values which Mao promotes may be eminently suited to a country faced with a continuation of consumer shortages and with the dysfunctions that modernization entails. If achieved, which is highly doubtful, self-sacrifice, enthusiasm, and revolutionary momentum might help all sectors of China's population to tolerate continuing shortages and frustrations.

What has been politely called the "revolution of rising expectations" appears to Mao like a dangerous and destabilizing form of mass greed. Judging from the coups and counter-coups in other developing countries, his efforts to resist this trend—however unlikely it is to succeed—may not be totally unrealistic. Even if only partly effective, the Cultural Revolution has prevented China from settling down into an overly bureaucratized rut of administrative routine.

On the other hand, the dangers of the Cultural Revolution are severe. Relying on mass organizations is always more risky than manipulating the secret police. Crowds can always get out of hand, as they certainly have done in China. Yet the real threat to China's future springs not so much from the Cultural Revolution itself as from its sudden decline. Having been elevated as future revolutionary leaders, the Red Guards have been abruptly and rudely demoted. Instead of being teachers they are now pupils. Lumped into the general category of bourgeois intellectuals, they now run a poor fourth behind the PLA, China's workers, and the peasants.

The shock of this letdown may lead to bitter disillusionment. The brusque change of pace may produce attitudes that are detrimental to any society, namely, cynicism and apathy. While stemming from different conditions, such symptoms on the part of Soviet youth already bother the Kremlin. Because of China's relative weakness in industry and technology, failure to mobilize youthful talent might damage the wisdom of domestic and foreign policies. The impact of this possibility on China's future diplomacy is still a matter for speculation.

Just as the Cultural Revolution has not belied Peking's international caution, so it has not effaced other features of Chinese foreign policy. Rivalry with the Soviet Union is more intense than ever. The fervent belief that the age of imperialism has not yet ended is enflamed by the conviction that Moscow is collaborating with imperialist powers at China's expense. The supposed link between revisionism and imperialism is now stronger than ever. Accordingly, the Chinese now equate international justice with revolution. Maoism, while also a developmental strategy, has been interpreted in increasingly revolutionary terms.

The occasional reminders of Chinese tradition which the Cultural Revolution has manifested do not deny the presence of anti-Western Westernism characteristic of an age of transition. The social reform programs adopted by modern nationalism always try to draw on national mainsprings to win domestic support. The similarity between the call to repudiate self-interest on the one hand and Mencius' pronouncements on the other is not accidental. Yet to brand this movement as a resurgence of traditionalism is to miss the essence of modern Chinese politics.

If the slogans of the Cultural Revolution seem to be non-Western, the goals are not. As the Anglo-Saxon model has spread, its adherents have often called for a revolution in social attitudes. Transforming traditional attitudes to fit the glove of modernization is not a new idea. From Jefferson to Mazzini, from Marx to Senghor, altering human behavior has been a basic component of the various spokesmen enunciating the path of modern life. If the West has overlooked this need, it is because tradition has long since ceased to be a potent force.

Nevertheless, tradition in all its many and complex forms remains strong in much of the developing world. As if that were not enough to hinder progress, corruption is often rampant. Whether mild and prolonged or severe and rapid, some form of revolutionary change seems necessary to spur on modernizing attitudes. This is the point at which the long-term, potential significance of Chinese foreign policy becomes clear.

Among all the leaders of transitional societies, Mao embraces populism to almost the greatest extent. Amid all the pressures for technological priorities, he still believes in redemptive revolution. Stalin did not, preferring external manipulation and terror to internal conviction and heartfelt allegiance. To the extent that the leaders and intellectuals of developing societies feel the need for a redemptive revolution, China may prove to be the more potent international force.

Several possibilities, of course, may banish this prospect. China may finally submit to the forces of bureaucratization and administrative routine. Even if Maoist policies continue to be pursued after Mao's death, however, underdeveloped countries may reject the path of redemptive revolution as costly and fruitless. This second prospect seems likely for the time being because of the revolutionary stages of Afro-Asian politics.

As illustrated by China and the Ottoman Empire, there are often three clear-cut generations of revolutionaries. The first wishes to reform along traditional lines and to purify leadership from within. The second sees the need to import foreign technological models but tries to preserve some form of traditional culture. Only the third goes beyond the importation of science and technology by calling for a social revolution. Only a generation disillusioned by the failure of its predecessors insists on an internal transformation of individual and societal values. Modern techniques cannot be mastered without corresponding modern attitudes.

The nations of the Western world have gone beyond these three stages. On the whole, modern attitudes are firmly planted in their societies. The nations of Africa and Asia, however, except for China, may only have reached the first and second stages. They still show a faith in machines which lacks the vision to see that modern attitudes are needed to run them successfully. The fate of technological development in India is a case in point. So long as Afro-Asian leaders cling to the belief that traditional cultural attitudes, disguised as the "African personality" or the "Arab soul," are compatible with modern technological development, they will suffer the fate of the Ch'ing Dynasty. Traditional values and modern techniques simply do not make good bedfellows.

The transformation from traditional to modern attitudes in the West was a long and largely subconscious process. It took at the very least a century. For this reason, Western analysts do not always understand China's preoccupation with the human factor. By relating it to traditional Chinese maxims dealing with the moral prerequisite of leadership, they are missing the point. They read the headlines of articles on the use of Mao's thought in spurring production but overlook the contents. They do not realize that China is in a hurry. Her leaders, unwilling to spend a century waiting for modernization, are trying to compress it into a few short and painful decades. In the process they may make ludicrous and even harmful mistakes. Yet in their insight into the human prerequisites of modernization they are ahead of their Afro-Asian contemporaries.

These priorities help to explain China's isolation. While both the West and the Soviet Union have moved beyond the third generation of revolution, Africa and Asia have not yet reached it. In this sense China is the most truly transitional society of all. She has translated her cultural despair into the transformation of social attitudes. She has harnessed her nationalism to rapid growth. By attributing Confucianism to the gentry class, she has discarded tradition without destroying her self-respect.

Whatever their factional differences, all Communist Chinese leaders believe in contributing to these general trends. Quarrels over specific policies relate more to the means than to the ends. As the Third World moves forward, the long-term significance of Chinese foreign policy may lie precisely in this direction. Both Soviet and American models may be condemned to irrelevance. China has already come a long way toward modernization. If she continues in this direction, she may overshadow all previous prescriptions.

INDEX